Learning to Think

LEARNING
TO
THINK

A Memoir of Faith, Superstition,
and the Courage to Ask Questions

Tracy King

Liveright Publishing Corporation

A Division of W. W. Norton & Company
Independent Publishers Since 1923

Copyright © 2024 by Tracy King
First American Edition 2024

First published in Great Britain in 2024 by Doubleday, an imprint of Transworld Publishers.

For information about special discounts for bulk purchases, please contact W. W. Norton Special Sales at specialsales@wwnorton.com or 800-233-4830

Manufacturing by Lake Book Manufacturing

ISBN 978-1-63149-873-2

Liveright Publishing Corporation, 500 Fifth Avenue, New York, N.Y. 10110
www.wwnorton.com

W. W. Norton & Company Ltd., 15 Carlisle Street, London W1D 3BS

1 2 3 4 5 6 7 8 9 0

To my family and friends,
especially Dad,
and Daniel.

Prologue

I'M TINY. A CHILD. Twelve years old, skinny and short. My black hair is unwashed, lank and flat against my head. I'm standing in the living room of our house, a single radiator pumping out dry heat, a small floor space made bigger by pushing the coffee table to one side. It's not really a coffee table: it's a small round dining table with legs that my dad had shortened with a saw. Usually the table stood in front of the settee but tonight I'm standing there instead. I'm wearing blue jeans and a Garfield T-shirt, white gym shoes on my feet. I always wear shoes in the house because I'm afraid of spiders.

Someone is standing behind me, hands heavy on my shoulders. He's a church elder, an enormous man named Bob. He smells of incense and has a very tidy house. His daughter is my age. She once gave me a foil-wrapped champagne and strawberry marzipan from a box she'd got for Christmas. It was the most expensive thing I'd ever tasted. In the too-hot living room, Bob's deep voice murmurs reassuring words of scripture.

To my right, on the flowery settee (we called it a three-piece suite, bought on credit from DFS), sits my mom. In Birmingham we say 'mom' instead of 'mum'. No one knows why. My mom looks like me, except her black hair is very curly where mine is dead straight, and she's wearing a 1970s dress, left over from the previous decade. We both wear small silver crucifixes on chains. I like that we match. She's also thin, and also afraid of spiders.

My heart is beating so hard I can hear it through my cartoon T-shirt. My palms are sweating and my stomach is full of something dreadful and alive. It's like the school musical a year earlier, performed for an audience of earnest proud parents at the local town theatre. I had one of the first lines and remember walking past the stage lights towards the auditorium, knowing that somewhere out there my entire family was watching, expecting me to be brilliant, willing me not to fail.

I glance at my mom and she smiles from the settee but I can tell she's nervous too. She's been smoking more than usual. The air is heavy from her multiple cigarettes, extinguished thriftily in the glass ashtray she used to share with my dad.

In front of me is another man. Another beard too, but golden this time. The minister of our church, a handsome charismatic American named Adam. His shoulder-length hair and blond beard make him look like the Jesus depicted in my Bible, an illustrated children's edition I'd won at Christian Youth Club. That's part of Adam's charm – he's a convincing stand-in for Jesus, a man with a direct line to God. I think everyone fancies him a bit. He's from America, and he's in charge. He's also young, and fun, with a wife named Denise and two small children. They moved to Britain in the early eighties to preach the truth, or the version of the truth represented by our church, his employer. As we dropped fifty pence we couldn't afford into the collection plate every Sunday, I used to think, This money pays your wages. As a salaried representative of the church, it was his job not just to preach on Sundays and run prayer study groups from his own – much larger – living room, but to administer pastoral care to his small but dedicated congregation made up mostly of council-estate tenants like my mom and me. Poor people. We'll get to the poor people later. Right now, I'm a little girl, standing between two bearded men, about to be exorcized.

I'm possessed by demons and Adam and Bob are going to remove them, right here in my own home. Adam asks us to pray with him. It's beginning. My mouth is dry. I close my eyes and clasp my hands, fingers folded together. It's briefly comforting, to hold my own hand, but now we're asking God and Jesus to help us with the forthcoming ritual and the fear, and the demons are real. I can hear my mom's voice murmuring. I'm moving from nervous to terrified. The thing that's alive in my stomach reaches up into my throat. What if the demons don't want to come out of me? What if they hurt me? What if they leave my body and possess my mom instead? The demons are inside me, to blame for all of my problems. Perhaps they are also to blame for my fear. If I close my eyes tighter and squeeze my hands together harder then surely Jesus will notice me and come to the rescue.

Adam is performing the words of the rite, and Bob is behind me, a solid wall of prayer. He needs to be close because when the final dramatic words of exorcism are spoken, 'I cast thee out!', Adam is going to strike towards my forehead with his palm. Not hard, it's not an attack on me – more a sort of symbolic gesture of casting out, like he's slapping the air between him and the demon that lives in my brain. I know this is coming and I know that to be properly exorcized I should fall backwards as the demon is expelled. I hold my breath and open my eyes, waiting for my cue. The room is suddenly very bright. Adam shouts, and as he strikes the demon from my body, I choose to fall.

PART ONE

1

A s LIFE STORIES GO, mine feels unbelievable. I've had – and overcome – a great share of trouble and trauma, and I spent decades hiding a lot of it for fear of not being believed, or fear of being shunned. Underestimated. Avoided, because trauma can make you feel like a freak, and poverty is shameful. But it's as simple as this: without resources, trauma and poverty are a chaotic maze. Because a lot of terrible things happened to me and my family we were not well-equipped emotionally or financially to navigate.

Margaret Atwood observed that a rat in a maze is free to go anywhere, as long as it stays inside the maze. One interpretation is that the rat believes it has freedom, unaware of its limitations or status as experimental subject, and is motivated only by the reward of food. The basic drive to survive in conditions outside its control. I suspect the rat would prefer to take its chances elsewhere, but I've yet to hear of an experiment that asks. The chaotic maze of my early life is not entirely figurative, but also a real one of red bricks and grey mortar, an experimental labyrinth of houses and graffitied walls with something ultimately monstrous at the centre.

I've had to navigate mazes – physical and figurative – my whole life, overburdened but underequipped. Eventually

I found myself in a safe, secure and successful enough position to look back and examine the path I'd taken. Some of the route looked like it had been laid out for me, and if I didn't like where it was going (particularly the dead ends), I would climb over the wall, or even smash my way through. These weren't shortcuts – I damaged both maze and self – but it was my way of simplifying. Eventually I thought I'd draw a map (or, as I'm a writer, write a book), and that meant retracing my steps, exploring my past to fill in the gaps. I had forgotten how hard it had all been, and was shocked to discover that I knew considerably less about the layout of that maze and the identity of the experimenters than I believed. It's very difficult to see your own parents as individuals outside their role, or understand that they were trapped too. They had lives before children, and lives outside children, and I hadn't considered what that might mean. As I began to research my family and my life story, I found complexity that I could never have predicted.

But it starts simply enough. An ordinary family in an ordinary red-brick council house on a low-rise, leafy estate in the Midlands. For the first five or six years of my life, a formal family portrait (if one existed, which it doesn't) would have appeared to show a happy early 1980s household.

My mom, Jackie, short and skinny with an attractive, vaguely Barbra Streisand face. A housewife with ambitious hobbies. In her own words, 'My life consisted of cooking, looking after two children, and writing poems.'

My dad, Mike, or 'Kingy', also skinny, prematurely bald with an unconvincing comb-over and sometimes a bushy moustache. He looked a little like Sean Connery, owned a collection of Ian Fleming novels, and smoked a pipe or home-rolled cigarettes.

My sister, Emily, an artistic child with jet-black, dead-straight hair at either side of a pale face. She looks more serious in photos than she was, because a school photographer once told her not to smile for the camera, as her teeth were crooked. She was a bit of a daddy's girl but also often to be found hiding behind Jackie. In public she was shy; at home she was a fun and doting older sibling.

And me, Tracy King. No middle name. I was loud, confident and often annoying, a more button-nosed, slightly showbiz version of my sister. All-singing, acting, dancing and opinions. The usual words applied: precocious; head-strong; bookworm; know-it-all. My parents affectionately called me Rent-A-Gob (after the eighties TV show *Renta-ghost*). 'She'll be prime minister one day,' Jackie would say, then pause and joke, 'Or in prison.' I *was* a know-it-all, even if I hated being called one. I enjoyed knowing things and believed everything I read in books. I got haughty when someone knew better than me, and if I didn't know the answer to something, I would simply and confidently make one up.

Making things up is how children explain mysteries, perhaps the same impulse that compelled early civilizations to invent gods to explain the sun. I would construct elaborate mechanisms to account for the things I didn't understand. When I stayed with my maternal grand-parents in Birmingham, they would drive me to places and – having little experience or understanding of roads and cars – I couldn't figure out how the traffic lights 'knew' when to change. I noticed that this sometimes happened when I blinked slowly at them. Perhaps, I reasoned, it was my blinking that controlled the lights. I would sit in the car and close my eyes, opening them a crack to peek. If the traffic lights changed, I'd done it. If they didn't, I would close my eyes tight and try again. I had a 100 per cent success rate with this method.

Once, my older cousin disputed the meaning of a word I'd used, so I opened a dictionary to prove her wrong and, by brilliant coincidence, opened it at the exact right page. She looked at me like I'd performed a miracle, and I began to believe that perhaps I had. We (children and civilizations) are supposed to grow out of this type of fallacious thinking, but that's not a luxury I had. While the traffic lights and dictionary beliefs were trivial, and examples of the sort of daft things most kids believe at one point or another, it's also typical of the way I was raised.

Poverty is best friends with superstition. They grow up together, go everywhere together. Everything about poverty encourages belief in luck and mysterious forces. How else to explain why some people seem to have randomly awful lives? And superstition encourages poverty to risk what little it has. Spend your last pound coin on a lottery ticket: today feels lucky. Your lottery numbers are your loved ones' birthdays, of course. How could love and family be anything but lucky?

When you're really poor, superstition looks like a tiny bit of control. Fingers crossed, with any luck, knock on wood, God willing, God forbid, don't tempt Fate. Depending on how strongly superstitious you are, you may be compelled to act it out physically, like a magic spell. Crossing your fingers or knocking on the nearest wooden object projects the thought into the physical world, makes it real. Luck is a benevolent or cruel god, granting favour or misfortune depending on how hard you wish. That's how it was in my house. Because of poverty, there was superstition. Without the sort of autonomy and choices that come with financial security and control, wishing was all we had.

Poverty and superstition are both important to this story, and I struggle to separate the two. When I think about growing up poor, I think about my mother giving the last coin in her purse to a woman who was selling 'lucky' crêpe-paper flowers door to door, because otherwise we would be cursed. I think about my grandmother Bernice shouting at me, 'Don't put new shoes on the table, it's bad luck!' when I was excited to show her my shiny black patent leather school loafers. I remember the panicked tears I cried when I dropped and smashed a mirror, not just because I'd broken something of value but for the seven years of misfortune that would follow. It takes more understanding, will and resignation than I had to accept my family's fate as the symptom of a broken system and a lack of education. It was easier and better to believe that, however bad it got, there was some force in the universe that might grant us a little favour or a magic power now and again, like in my beloved C. S. Lewis or Diana Wynne Jones books.

We hadn't always lived in a council house. In 1973, after two years of renting and saving, Jackie and Mike bought a tiny house in a Birmingham suburb. It was falling apart, in desperate need of renovations they couldn't afford, but it was theirs, a rung on the precarious ladder of upward mobility. In December the same year, their first child – my sister Emily – was born. A year and a half later, when the little King family was struggling badly for money, Mike was offered a two-year contract as an engineer for aeronautical giant Lockheed, to begin in February 1976. It paid well because it was in Saudi Arabia. The job would solve all of their financial problems. My dad would work overseas while Jackie raised their daughter and managed the house. He would be able to fly back every six months to visit. It wouldn't be so bad – 'And,' he said, 'just think of the money.'

But Jackie was pregnant again. An accident, but not unwanted: 'A lovely surprise,' Jackie said. Mike offered to turn down the Lockheed contract but she wouldn't let him. She could manage, she said. Her twin sister Miriam was just down the road, and her parents could move in with her. And, besides, there were no other job offers. So, a month before I was due, he flew more than three thousand miles from Birmingham, UK, to Riyadh, Saudi Arabia, and planned our future.

But the money situation didn't change, perhaps because my parents didn't change. Hope is eventually trumped by reality. Mike's blue airmail letters (first addressed to Jackie and Emily, and then, once I was born, to all three of us) are full of love but mostly concerned with the minutiae of his salary instalments and strategies for paying various creditors. In February 1976 he wrote:

> *I feel very useless here as far as money goes. I am trying to live on as little as possible. I feel very guilty that you are having all the work and the worry but I'm doing my best to earn as much as I can and things here aren't exactly a picnic but I'm keeping cheerful.*

Some letters from the same period are more hopeful, with the potential for promotion and perhaps even earning a bonus. They're also full of colourful detail about his life:

Found a sweet little lime-green scorpion yesterday while I was changing a wheel on the recreation vehicle, but he got away. They are not dangerous out here but they can give a nasty sting which is very painful. I won't tell you what the spiders are like – it may spoil your breakfast.

Those letters subtly reveal a truth. There are some problems that money makes worse.

Mike's drinking had started young. Residing in south Birmingham, his wasn't a close family, and he and his sister were raised without the affection and heartfelt 'I love you' that later characterized my own home. His mother worked full time, so Mike was largely raised by his maternal grandmother, Harriet, whose husband, William, worked in the sweltering, polluting heat of the local waste incinerator (known as the destructor). William had a side hustle making and selling bootleg alcohol, and spent his days battling the furnace temperature by drinking. He taught Mike how to distil alcohol and turn fruit into wine. He also taught him how to drink.

Mike's father, my granddad Edward, was a survivor of Dunkirk, about which he never spoke. 'Shell shock,' Jackie would say, to explain Edward's brittle, authoritarian attitude. He was as unlike Mike as two dads could be. Where Edward had been uncaring, strict, even violent, Mike was loving, attentive and nurturing, and it's perhaps no wonder the boy preferred spending time with his grandfather.

I was always afraid of Edward, on the very rare occasions we met. He had none of the warmth and love of Jackie's parents, and he and my paternal grandmother, Dorothy, seemed to dislike children. Edward and Dorothy were old-fashioned, buttoned-up English Christians of the sort that was as much about tradition and reputation as religion. There were very few adults I was shy around, but the two or three times they visited us, I tried to avoid Edward, picking up on my parents' own wariness. Jackie said he was 'a megalomaniac'.

Some of his mood might have been down to pain. After the war he had gone to work in a factory where an explosion caused severe injuries to his legs from which he never fully recovered. After that, he and Dorothy became managers of a post office in Birmingham. His spare time was spent on butterflies. Edward's interest in the natural world was one of the only things he had in common with Mike. 'He's a lepidopterist,' Jackie would say, enjoying the grandeur of the word. I understood this to mean he studied butterflies and helped with conservation efforts, but I didn't understand why it also meant he enjoyed them dead. There were rows and rows of once-beautiful butterflies, including rare species, with tiny pins skewered through their fragile dusty bodies, in special drawers in his study or framed on the wall of their seaside retirement bungalow. I was attracted to the colours and patterns but repulsed by their deaths and the brutality of the displays.

Mike was popular at school, if mischievous, and was intelligent enough to pass the eleven-plus exam and attend a local grammar school. University was expensive and not something his family did. After a deeply unhappy period as an apprentice at a steel-tube manufacturer, he joined the air force, which became his life. He trained as a telecoms engineer, his sparse military records showing his entire service conduct as 'exemplary'. He was promoted five times, but the records are otherwise uninformative. Several years of his service history are missing, including 1963 when he was stationed in Cyprus during the 'Bloody Christmas' civil war in which hundreds of islanders died and thousands more were displaced. Like his father and Dunkirk, Mike simply never talked about it. Whatever happened in Cyprus exacerbated his drinking, and haunted his dreams. He left the RAF in 1970, became engaged to Jackie, and they married two years later. 'He never adapted to Civvy Street,' she says, to explain some of his problems.

By the time he was working in Saudi Arabia in 1976, the sharp claws of alcoholism had him in a grip with no easy means of escape. His environment was not conducive to saying, 'Help me, I have a problem,' and he likely didn't yet realize he had one.

His letters show a man trying very hard. He hit on a scheme to change from twice-annual leave to tri-annual. In a letter dated 12 April 1976 he writes:

> *I will be home on Thursday 3rd June for about 2½ weeks' leave (subject to confirmation of aircraft flights etc.). Does that cheer you up as much as it cheers me? I still get me bonus but instead of waiting until August I get it in June – I also get an airfare rebate which can go to the Bldg Society so this will drastically reduce all the problems you have to contend with, and I will be happier knowing that you aren't getting nasty letters.*

Most importantly, can you book a table for us for anywhere you like for our wedding anniversary, yet another good reason for coming home in June. I expect you would prefer Hillfield Hall but the choice is entirely yours. We also need a lot of babysitters for the time I am home so can you take care of that too. You had also better warn your parents that they will have to evacuate the place temporarily.

I have gone from being totally depressed a week ago to being on top of the world now – 36 days to go!

I have no doubt that you are wondering all sorts of things about my sudden decision to change over but there are no problems here and it was mostly based on missing all of you, our wedding anniversary and the possession of some new information about airfares, rebates and bonuses etc.

I shan't be going mad lugging many presents this time around as we can't afford a lot yet but there will be 3 times a year when I am coming home with goodies for all.

A few months later, all his careful planning was ruined. Along with his letters, I have Mike's pocket diary from 1976, bound in green leather and smaller than my palm. It has four entries of note.

15 March, TRACY BORN
9 August, INCIDENT
10 August, NO WORK – SACKED
11 August TICKET – FLY HOME

Incident. Something bad enough to end his well-paid engineering career and send him home. I don't know why he chose to write it down in an otherwise mostly empty diary, or why he kept the diary thereafter, but it is chilling and sad to see. For many years Jackie was evasive about what the 'incident' had been, but eventually admitted perhaps he was caught selling home-brewed alcohol. In Saudi Arabia. Certainly it's the case that at the time alcohol was tolerated within work compounds, but outside could mean severe punishment. Whatever Mike's 'incident' was, it was enough to get him sacked and rushed out of the country.

Once home, he struggled to find work. Already heavily in debt, he was unable to pay the mortgage. Jackie had once been a secretary, but with a toddler, a baby and a belly full of anxiety, she wasn't able to return to work.

With debts and no income, and my dad's alcoholism unchecked, my parents had to sell their house. There was no one left to borrow from. At the time, the government was looking for families to populate a brand-new 'overspill' council estate. While the new estate was not local, and would therefore leave my parents isolated from their families and support network, it had no waiting list. In 1977, when I was eighteen months old and Emily was almost four, we moved. A brand-new three-bedroom home was an incredible stroke of luck.

2

THE HOUSE WAS ON an estate far away from Birmingham. It might as well have been a thousand miles, because we often didn't have a car to go anywhere. There was no nearby rail station, although trains were prohibitively expensive anyway. It would have taken hours to get to Jackie's parents' home in Birmingham by public transport. To me, Birmingham City Centre seemed as far away, exotic and intimidating as London. The rural estate provided a new life for my family, and we rarely needed to leave it.

The image that 'council estate' summons to those who have never lived on one is of high-rise grey concrete tower blocks, graffiti, and nowhere to play. Ours was quite different, although graffiti and broken windows would appear and disappear with regularity. In the mid-1970s, the local council had built a huge, experimental cul-de-sac maze of red-brick houses known as a 'low-rise estate'. It was part of a flurry of British council-house developments, instigated by the outgoing Labour government, that peaked around that time. Impossible to navigate, full of dead ends and narrow paths, this brand-new twentieth-century council-housing estate was developed around green spaces and trees.

Beyond my back door was my very own enchanted

wood, with a bubbling stream snaking through the trees, and the promise of the kind of adventure I would read about in *The Hobbit*.

In hindsight it wasn't a wood, but a skinny copse at best, and the stream was more of a murky brook, but it was a wonderful playground for children with imagination and sticks for swords. The council estate was my whole world, or would have been if I hadn't had a library card and encouraging parents.

Our house was a small but sufficient red-brick three-bedroom mid-terrace, with a tiny front garden and a slightly bigger patch at the back overlooked by the kitchen. The rent was paid weekly at the post office, reduced during the times Mike was out of work but always a worry. My parents had already lost one property. It would kill them to lose another, even if they didn't own it.

When I was very small the back garden seemed huge, and I was a dot on the grass, picking daisies to make a bracelet or leaving acorn-cup saucepans among the stones as a present for the fairies I was sure lived there. As I got older and stopped wanting to play, the garden shrank and became a neglected chore.

Our front door had a blue wooden frame, but the bulk of it was reinforced glass, large dappled panes with diagonal mesh embedded in them. A council-house door. The mesh provided extra privacy but also made the glass shatterproof, should someone kick it in or slam the door too hard. It let in a lot of light but also showed silhouettes of residents within, so almost everyone covered theirs with a net curtain suspended across a door-width piece of plastic-covered wire. If I visited a neighbour's house and they hadn't covered their glass, their house felt naked. The glass was a vulnerability, and a curtain kept out the bad things – or people.

We didn't have a doorbell. A friendly visitor would rap the letterbox a few times, maybe even lift the flap and shout, 'Coo-ee, Jackie.' But an official, like a social worker or debt collector, would knock hard with their knuckles on the glass. All the council houses had these front doors, a sort of 'tell'. Tenants were not allowed to replace them. Those who eventually bought their properties from the local authority would immediately change the front door for a nicer one and the black plastic house numbers for a fancy metal plate.

But when we moved into the house in 1977, all the front doors were the same. Inside, however, the estate was unusual in that every house was different from the next. No two houses had the same floor plan or layout, which made everyone else's home somehow inferior to mine, the 'correct' one.

I was aware that technically it wasn't our house, but it was every inch our home, and I loved it. Between the living-room wall and the kitchen was an airing cupboard, and in the early eighties Mike took it upon himself to defy council rules about modifying the property and use that space for a fish tank. He knocked a hole six feet long by two feet tall into the living-room wall, encroaching on the cupboard space, and installed a huge fish tank that had been built for free by his brother-in-law. Jackie had always wanted to keep tropical fish.

The obvious question here (apart from 'Why would anyone do that?') is, how could we afford such a bizarre luxury? How could a family who frequently had no electricity or phone and lived on luck and benefits possibly afford to run a huge fish tank? It's hard to explain. When you're poor, it's either feast or famine. The times when you have a little bit of money, you feast. You spend it. In our case, it was usually because Mike had got a job, so my parents would assume our fortunes had changed and it seemed okay to start splashing out a little, investing in lifelong ambitions, like tropical fish. One weekend afternoon he produced several buckets of Artex, a thick plaster-like paint into which patterns could be scraped.

'We're going to Artex the fish-tank wall!' he said, gesturing at the empty space above and below the glass. This was tremendously exciting. 'What pattern should we make?' Jackie sacrificed her comb and we took it in turns to make lines in a test patch of wet Artex. Emily drew a diamond. I drew a wobbly flower. Jackie drew a basic fish, like the Christian symbol, and under it a wavy line to depict water. We agreed this was the best design. Mike applied a patch of Artex, Jackie quickly scraped in a fish before it dried, and Emily or I added the wavy water line underneath. A few hours later the entire wall was covered with Artex fish. Ultimately these would prove to be a dust trap, but for a while it was the best wall in the world.

These financially carefree times were rare, with disappointment not far behind because Mike lost jobs more easily than he found them. Unemployment was at a record high and the new government doubled the rent. But the dream of a better life was always there, and spending beyond our means sometimes was a way to solidify that dream. The fish tank was proof that we could, like other people, have nice things. I loved that fish tank. It was accessed via the airing-cupboard door in the kitchen. Inside, the space was cool and dark and filled with the humming of the tank's electric filter. I would open the top of the tank and sprinkle a few flakes of fish food from the tub into the water, and a few onto my tongue, where they dissolved quickly. They tasted like Marmite.

Years later, when the tank had been standing empty for a long time, just before Jackie and I – the only Kings left – moved out, she sold it to a neighbour, who turned up with a mate strong enough to help him extract it from the wall and carry it away. They chipped the glass on the way out and it felt like a terrible omen.

Lack of money marked my childhood deeply, although I never resented my parents for it. It was what it was. There was no heating upstairs, so we'd gather, shivering, in front of the single white radiator in the living room on cold mornings to get dressed. Jackie would also dry our clothes on that radiator when it was too cold or rainy to use the washing-line in the back garden. Breakfast in the winter was hot Ready Brek, a type of porridge marketed as 'central heating for kids', with a thick topping of white sugar. I'd wait for the sugar to turn brown and eat it in layers, adding more sugar as I went.

There wasn't usually an abundance of food, and certainly not the regular supply of snacks, crisps and chocolate to which other children seemed to have access, but a bag of sugar and a tub of margarine go a long way. For my eighth birthday, Jackie promised me a party. We made invitations together and I distributed them among my friends and favoured classmates. The party was to be at our house after school on my birthday, but that morning Jackie – in tears – told me the bad news.

'I'm so sorry, love. We're going to have to cancel your party. I can't afford it.'

I was used to 'I can't afford it', and always adjusted my expectations without much complaint, but this was hard. There was no money for even basic party food. But I understood, and I didn't want Jackie to be upset any more, so I fought back my own tears.

'You'll have to tell your friends it's off. I'll make it up to you.' So I went to school on my birthday and broke the news to my friends. My party was cancelled.

At lunchtime, Jackie showed up at the playground gate with her best friend, Rose, who lived on a different part of the estate. I ran over.

'The party's back on!' she said, beaming. 'Rose has had a whip-round.' This didn't mean money. The mothers of the estate had gone through their cupboards and fridges and donated whatever food they could spare. Jackie and Rose spent that afternoon making sandwiches, jelly, blancmange and fairy cakes with 'buttercream', a crunchy mixture of raw sugar and margarine. Everyone on the estate was in the same leaky boat, so we pulled together.

The council-owned part of the housing development was to the south, mirrored by nicer, larger, privately owned houses to the north. Children from both areas met in the middle and attended the same schools. This was a deliberate social experiment on the part of the development planners, alongside the maze-like innovative layout of the streets. In the centre, serving social housing and private homes alike, was a small shopping and amenities centre, which everyone called 'the shops'.

First, a pub. Built from the same red brick as the houses and the shops, it was a low building with a tiled roof, surrounded by a small brick wall on which drinkers would sit in the summer. Inside there was a bar area with fruit machines, a dartboard and a sticky floor, generally inhabited by the men of the estate, and a more sophisticated carpeted lounge area where couples would drink. To the rear was a large function room with a dance floor for weekend discos, eighteenth-birthday or engagement parties, or charity fundraisers.

Past the pub were the shops themselves, tiny outlets in a single long row. A hairdresser, a fish-and-chip shop that also sold Chinese takeaway, a newsagent, and a small supermarket, which had a separate bakery and cake counter where Jackie would buy me an apple turnover or mini cottage loaf when she had a spare ten pence.

Next to the supermarket was a community centre with a café inside, and next to that a chemist. In front of the community centre there was another low red-brick wall, where teenagers would congregate at night.

Opposite the community centre were two phone boxes that were often vandalized or broken. These details seem mundane: a pub in the middle of a housing estate; the red-brick wall that attracted bored teens; the phone boxes. But remember them, because the banality of experimental estate planning soon becomes crucial to my life story.

3

WHILE MIKE SPENT A lot of time in the pub, Jackie – a teetotaller – rarely joined him. She was generally to be found at home, keeping an eye on us. There were no roads near by. The houses faced each other, encircling a grass-and-concrete area where children played, mothers sat and chatted, and later, when the first children of the estate grew older, teenagers hung out. But in the early days, when I was five or six, Emily and I would play with other children 'out the front', where our mothers could supervise from the window. There were no girls my age on our street, so I was friends with James, one of five brothers from the big house on the corner. One day, someone teased me that he was my boyfriend, so when he came to call for me to play out, I asked Jackie to tell him I didn't want to, which she did through the letterbox. After that he never spoke to me.

Estate boys were giggled about as future boyfriends while they were still just playmates. Five doors down from us there was a boy of Emily's age, a quiet, solitary lad named Reece Webster. He would join the neighbourhood games of hide-and-seek or Army but I was a little wary of him as he was older than us. Emily liked him, though. One sunny day in the early eighties, they were sitting with a group of other children when an older girl, the local bully, threw a blanket over both of their heads. Emily was momentarily trapped in hot darkness with him, and she felt panicked and ashamed enough for the event to leave a mark on her memory. She was shy around Reece Webster specifically and most children after that. He, too, would become crucial to my life story.

I was as happy with my own company as other kids'. When I wasn't at home reading, I spent a lot of time on outdoor solo games.

'Can I play out?' I would ask, skipping rope or ball in hand.

'Stay where I can see you,' would be the reply – and I did. If Jackie twitched the net curtains of the living-room window to peer out, she would immediately be able to locate me. If a strange or older child (usually a boy) from another part of the estate turned up, she would open the window, call me inside, and yell at them, 'Go and play round your own end!' Once, she marched to the home of an older boy who had been hanging around and lectured his mother. I felt righteous and protected.

Despite Jackie's fears and the strong message that boys weren't to be trusted, to me the early years felt fairly safe. But in a neighbourhood defined by poverty, there are always cracks for chaos to creep in. I was not yet aware how much crime, violence and neglect the estate was hiding.

Our neighbour Linda would sometimes be beaten up; on one occasion her entire house was trashed by a boy-friend, the bathroom sink torn from the wall and thrown through a window into her back garden, where it lay for a few days, until Mike and a plumber friend put it back. It wasn't until I was an adult that I realized Linda was the sort of woman portrayed in soap operas, whispered about by other women for her loud parties and the steady stream of men turning up at all hours. For the purposes of my childhood she was an 'aunty next door' who 'fell off a bike' – one of the many excuses Jackie invented to explain Linda's bruises and keep the truth from me.

Many of our neighbours were what others might call rough. Some would routinely leave their children home alone, while another, I later learned, was convicted of armed robbery. Domestic violence was common, as was child neglect. Single dads were not uncommon. A neighbour to our right was raising his two young children, his wife having run off with the husband of the household opposite. Reece Webster, the quiet, intense boy on our street, had a very young mother who treated him badly until one day she simply left, taking the entire contents of the house with her, including all the food.

Compared to this violence and neglect, my family felt normal, because we were happy and our house was full of love and fun. Mike's alcoholism never descended into violence against us, so it was almost a background problem, or at least one he and Jackie were good at hiding.

Until things started to fall apart, I thought our only real problem was money. I understood that living in a council house meant we were poor, and that other people's houses belonged to them. Not our neighbours, but schoolfriends whose houses were in the private area to the north. Their houses were made of different, smoother bricks. They had driveways with new cars on them, and entire shelves of Barbie dolls. Their bedrooms had radiators, their furniture matched, and their kitchen cupboards were full of crisps and fun-size Mars bars. Both parents worked, usually, in stark contrast to my own home where sometimes neither parent worked, and when one did, it was temporary and sometimes 'cash in hand', code for getting paid off the books while also claiming benefits. Many families did that to survive during the eighties period of extreme unemployment, even while the government erected billboards encouraging the poorest to report each other for 'fiddling the dole'.

I thought my friends with working parents and heated bedrooms were rich; they were merely upwardly mobile working class to our underclass. Their dads were bus drivers, the mothers worked admin jobs for the local council or in a supermarket. But they had enough income and stability to buy a small house and have annual holidays. I don't recall being particularly envious, though. I didn't have loads of Barbies but I did have a big fish tank and a mother who was home all the time. It was a point of pride for her that she was at home to raise her children herself, that we weren't 'latchkey kids' who had to get their own dinner. I didn't want my own front-door key. I knew Jackie would be home.

I didn't understand till I was six or seven that she was home all the time for reasons other than anachronistic housewifely pride. Jackie was paranoid about many things, including my being kidnapped, and always had to know where I was. Her paranoia was a symptom of something much more present and disruptive.

'Will you put your foot under the door?' Jackie was

caught short and wanted to use the public toilet in the shopping centre, and for this she needed my help. I hated it, because it pushed such a huge responsibility onto me, and because no one, let alone a child, wants to stand with their foot under a toilet door while someone else pees, long after the age where it's a matter of child safety. But I never said no. I stood patiently with my foot under the gap in the stall door so she could see me. If I didn't speak, she would say, 'You still there?' despite the toe of my shoe. She'd keep up a stream of chat to go with the pee, or she'd hum tunelessly. So I'd chat back, and sometimes I'd sing, reassuring her that, yes, I'm still here. Public toilets were the smallest of her fears. She couldn't get a bus on her own, go anywhere new, get into a lift or onto an escalator. In public places she would have panic attacks, so Emily and I got used to accompanying her everywhere, and she wouldn't take her eyes off us. To be out of her sight for even a second would result in a frantic shout and immediate descent into hysteria. After I passed the age of wanting to hold her hand in public, she still requested to hold mine, for reassurance and safety. Even after I refused to put my foot under the public-toilet stall I still had to go with her. I got used to hanging out by the sink, checking my hair in the mirror for something to do.

Most of us have a degree of fear – often irrational – of something bad happening, but when it turns into a serious anxiety disorder, like Jackie's, it's no longer a fear but a life-style. In one way or another, her phobias dictated our routine and our actions. If she was anxious or beginning to have a panic attack, I had to turn into the parent, reassuring her. The foot under the door developed into a precocious wisdom I could use to try to negotiate her out of extreme emotions.

Psychological disorders, like OCD and phobias, often manifest as superstitions. Jackie thought that bad things would happen if she didn't touch wood or say, 'Fingers crossed,' but she was also distressed by the belief that a corridor or path she was walking along might never end, or that, once she was in an enclosed space, the entire world and everyone in it would simply disappear. It got so bad that she couldn't leave the house alone unless she was going somewhere familiar and safe. I once asked her if her fear was that she would leave the toilet cubicle and I'd be gone, or that *she* would be gone. Transported elsewhere. 'Both,' she said immediately.

The word is 'agoraphobia', and I knew it young. I never knew her any other way so I just accepted what I called 'agra-phobia' as part of her and part of our lives. It expressed itself in many ways. Fear of crowds, fear of enclosed spaces, fear of something bad happening. Her phobias were the reason she couldn't go anywhere new or stressful by herself, the reason she didn't get on a bus alone or the train to visit her parents in Birmingham, the reason she couldn't get into a lift or onto an escalator. She was so afraid of something – anything – happening, she would have panic attacks, and then become afraid of having a panic attack. Easier, safer, better not to risk it. Her panic attacks were physical, overwhelming and debilitating, and she was failed by not being given proper help, despite asking for it many times.

Before she had a diagnosis of agoraphobia, it was called 'my nerves'. She'd had anxiety her whole life. The story of her birth was family legend. The Second World War was over but rationing was still in full force when Bernice, my good-time flame-haired grandmother (who had left home at sixteen to join the Auxiliary Territorial Service and shoot at Nazi planes along Britain's coast), found herself pregnant. Her husband, my granddad Symon, was the son of Ukrainian refugees, Jewish immigrants fleeing persecution. On arriving in Birmingham in 1900, his parents changed their surname to a more English one, perhaps to try to avoid the same discrimination they were escaping from. After serving in the Second World War, Symon became a barber, and the newlyweds planned for their baby.

In 1947 there were no ultrasound scans. Doctors would check the heartbeat of the baby by pressing a stethoscope to the mother's bump. Bernice's baby sounded perfectly healthy for her entire pregnancy. She went into labour and was admitted to a maternity hospital in Birmingham, where she gave birth to a baby girl. Ten minutes later, her contractions started again.

'We all thought it was the afterbirth!' she loved to say, oblivious to the effect such a statement might have. The 'afterbirth' turned out to be a surprise second baby. Identical twins, so similar that even their heartbeats had been simultaneous for the entire pregnancy and so went undetected by the midwife's stethoscope. Bernice and Symon took their two babies home and had to 'beg, borrow and steal' a second cot, pram, extra baby clothes, all things they could barely afford for one baby, let alone two.

Jackie's anxieties began in earnest with a brief episode of cruelty when she was about six years old. She and her sister were playing in the street when the bread delivery van turned up. She doesn't remember what triggered the event other than perhaps she 'was cheeky to the bread man' but, whatever it was, he grabbed her, threw her into the back of his van, slammed the door and drove off down the road to teach her a lesson. The petrified, screaming child he let out of the van was not the same one he'd bundled in. From then on, she 'suffered with nerves'.

Apart from anxiety issues, hers wasn't a bad childhood. Bernice and Symon were post-war upwardly mobile. Once the twins had started school, Bernice went to work cleaning houses, and later as a receptionist at Birmingham airport. Between the two of them they were able to buy a house and afford a cheap holiday in the UK every year. They even managed the holy grail, a holiday abroad to Italy when the twins were nine. Symon had a cine-camera, and would film family holidays and parties. When I was a kid, now and again he would set up the cine equipment and screen in their living room so we could watch the films, as Bernice gleefully narrated the detail. Sometimes she would tell a funny anecdote from a holiday and be so helpless with laughter she would have to get Symon to deliver the punchline.

I loved this portal into the past, a glimpse of the strange world where your parent is still a child: the twins, identical in beautiful matching clothes made for them by a family friend, Bernice striding around Rome, turning heads, looking like Rita Hayworth, doing things that, years later, would make for family stories. The beautiful redhead and her twins attracted attention wherever they went. Bernice revelled in it. She was a romantic, a dreamer. She wanted a more glamorous life than the one she'd ended up with, reminisced often about her war days of active service (during which she was incredibly popular with men, youths who died in the war, whose love letters and photos she kept for the rest of her life), and never let go of the thought that riches and fame were somehow just around the corner. She liked to host parties at home, gin and tonic in hand and a cigarette never far from her red-painted lips or matching fingernails (the cigarette was largely for show – I never saw her take a drag).

My grandparents weren't particularly religious, but Bernice strongly believed in the Evil Eye, astrology and spiritualism, taking Jackie to a psychic healer for her 'nerves', which of course helped nobody except Bernice, who was certain the solution to mental-health problems was simply a shift of attitude.

Jackie otherwise had an ordinary life. She left school at sixteen to become a secretary and did normal working-class 1960s things. She wore winged eyeliner, styled her hair into a beehive, went on dates and out dancing. Then she was introduced to Mike on a blind date, fell in love, and became a housewife and mother. Their wedding was secular, at a register office. The bride wore a floor-length brown dress splashed all over with a pattern of leaves and swirls in wonderful autumnal colours, and the groom a simple suit with a carnation in his buttonhole. In photos they look so happy. In the early days, when she was living in the run-down house they had bought, her anxiety had not yet become a condition. She didn't have regular panic attacks, agoraphobia or restrictions on her life. She was doing well. In a reply to Mike when he was working in Saudi Arabia she says,

I have 2 lovely kids, a home I am getting nicely decorated, a hubby who is clever (at work that is), good parents and relatives, please God I have my health now, I certainly can't complain. Enough of that, I'll be crying into my coffee. I really felt a pang of missing you today.

Like Mike's, her letters are full of love, family joy and money worries. But Jackie's writing also reveals growing fears, an accidental foreshadowing.

'I realize it must be difficult for you out there but please, please write to me, or I shall start imagining all sorts of things have happened to you,' she wrote in April 1976, after several of Mike's letters had been delayed. This one line is indicative of her nature, that if she doesn't have knowledge she will supplement with imagination, either of unrealistic hope or histrionic despair.

And then Mike lost his job, they lost their house, and moved to a strange estate miles from anything they knew. 'We didn't always live in a council house,' she would say, not ungrateful (the council house had a second toilet downstairs that she thought was an incredible luxury), but mournful that their rung on the ladder had cracked and broken. Her paranoia about something bad happening slowly turned into a debilitating phobia, so by the time I was old enough to notice something was different about her, agoraphobia was just an everyday part of her life.

She depended on me for many things. I went along with it, despite the inconvenience and limitations of her phobias, because I loved her and she was otherwise wonderful. I was a mommy's girl. We were a brilliant team. We had the same taste in everything, and the same imagination that gave her a superstitious nature also gave her a sense of wonder that was intoxicating. She would constantly make up silly words or songs, and write short stories and poems or encourage us to read. She loved stories more than anything. Worlds that were better than the real one, or that offered explanations for things out of her understanding or control.

She threw herself into fantasy novels. Tolkien, Anne McCaffrey, Ursula Le Guin. She loved any story with dragons in it and would paint them on glass, using Mike's Humbrol enamel paints. The resulting pictures decorated our hall wall and gained her a reputation as an artist among our neighbours.

These fantasy worlds spilled over into real life. I had invented two imaginary friends named BeeMee and JaJa, elves on whom I would blame my naughtiness. I really believed in them (and they in me), until one day when I was six their stern elven uncle came and took them away and I never saw them again. I announced this matter-of-factly to Jackie, who commemorated the event by writing a poem. I showed it to my teacher, who invited her to the school to read it to the class.

> *BeeMee and JaJa were two little elves*
> *(But please keep that secret to yourselves)*
> *They came to stay one day in spring*
> *And met a girl named Tracy King*

And so on. Maybe it should have been embarrassing but I glowed with pride. It was proof of her love, to take so much interest in my internal life that she wrote a poem good enough for my teacher.

4

M Y SISTER AND I were very alike, except that she was two years older and without my confidence. 'You wrap your first child in cotton wool, but let the second play with knives,' Jackie would say. It showed. While in toddlerhood Emily was bold and loud, by the time she was five or six she was shy and socially anxious. When it was just the four of us at home there was no sign of shyness. But where I would stand on the living-room table and sing for a room full of adults, she would hide behind a door. While I would confidently state an opinion to the class, she would make herself as small as possible so as not to be noticed. She was no less able than me, just afraid to show it. Or perhaps I took up so much space she needed to recede.

We both loved to learn and our family dynamic was centred around informal teaching. She fared well at the primary school we both attended from ages five to nine, and at home Jackie told us stories, read to us or with us, and ensured we had a steady supply of library books or second-hand books from jumble sales as we consumed everything in print that came our way. There was no library near by but the council sent a mobile version once a month, a large grey truck kitted out with books and the same ribbed carpet as the library proper. We adored the mobile library and the promise within, the small but well-curated selection of children's books from which we could choose three and have the little cardboard ticket stamped with the return date, which was slid into a brown-paper envelope gummed to the inside front cover. More than anything, I longed to use that date stamp, with its satisfying thump as the ink transferred to the paper and the countdown started. Three weeks to read the books as many times as I liked.

Mike taught us everything else, including the Greek alphabet, sowing little seeds of curiosity for us to nurture and, later, harvest. None of our peers knew the Greek alphabet. We thought it meant we were clever, sophisticated, worldly. I showed off at school the next day, even while having no clear idea of where Greece was. Mike's informal lessons were so challenging and interesting and fun, we didn't even realize he was teaching.

One spring day, he produced a large clean glass jar of the sort chip-shop pickled onions come in, and the four of us went for a walk. Because the estate was quite green, there were plenty of caterpillars about. Mike carefully cut a large leafy branch, placed it inside the jar, and plucked a fat hairy brown caterpillar from a nearby bush to come home and live with us. The top of the jar was covered with the foot of an old pair of tights Jackie had sacrificed for the occasion, secured with an elastic band. Emily and I kept the caterpillar well fed with cabbage leaves and watched it turn itself into a hard, hanging chrysalis. Two weeks later, it hatched, and while his own father would have pinned it to a card, Mike helped us carefully release it outside. I'd now say that beautiful orange butterfly banging around inside the jar didn't deserve to start its life with such limitations on its freedom, but at the time it felt like we'd been granted access to the secrets of the entire universe.

I didn't know the name for it then, but Mike was a lateral thinker. He loved logic puzzles and games, and did a broadsheet cryptic crossword every day. This is pretty typical of engineers, whose job is basically figuring out puzzles. He became an engineer because of his love for working things out and thinking things through, and that love informed his parenting. Because we had no money, weekends and school holidays were filled instead with family games. He would randomly spring a fun logic puzzle on us: 'A man goes into a restaurant, sits down, and orders roast albatross. When the dish arrives, he takes one bite, then immediately runs outside and jumps in front of a bus. Why?' We had to ask yes-or-no questions until we arrived at the solution. As children, our questions were often logically skewed ('Was it a magic talking albatross?'), but Jackie would join in and between us, laughing the whole time, we'd work it out.*

Another favourite game of mine was his 'alien' role play.

'Pretend I'm an alien newly arrived on Earth,' he would say. 'I don't know what anything is, and you have to teach me.'

---

* The man had been stranded on a desert island with three friends. He was injured so couldn't walk. One of his friends died and the other two took him away to bury him. That night, they cooked and ate meat that they told the man was from an albatross they had killed. This continued for some weeks until they were rescued. Years later, fully healed, he sees a restaurant that has albatross on the menu. Upon tasting it, he realizes that it is not the meat he had been served on the desert island . . .

I loved this, and would climb into his lap. 'Hello, Mr Alien, would you like a cup of tea?'

'What's a cup?' he'd ask, puzzled. 'Remember, I don't know anything.'

'It's something to put a drink in.'

'But what *is* it? I don't know what a drink is either, but we can come back to that.'

'Erm . . . a cup is a thing . . . made out of clay.'

'Clay? What's clay?' He'd pick up on any noun I used, which in hindsight was an adjustment for my age. Metaphysical concepts were a bit beyond me at seven or eight, or perhaps he was just an engineer to his core.

'Clay is a thing . . . I think they dig it up.'

'What's this clay made of?'

'Oh . . . er . . . sand?' I was so used to making an uneducated guess, I rarely felt the need to flat-out deny knowing, but the game was over once I couldn't explain something to the alien. If I got something wrong, he never made me feel stupid for it. He would guide me to the right answer instead. I learned that clay is made of minerals, and red oxide gives it colour. I learned that heat makes it harden and glaze makes it shiny. I learned that the water in the tea boils at 100 degrees centigrade and this is achieved via the filament in a kettle, which converts energy into heat. The energy is from electricity, which is generated by power stations, which burn coal or gas. 'What's coal?' the alien wants to know, and we both learn that it's a type of rock formed from millions of years of heat pressure on huge piles of dead leaves . . .

'Millions of years? So how do we make more coal, then?'

*

One afternoon he raided the ashtray. Four matchsticks and a cigarette butt became the classic Out of Glass puzzle.* A box of matches was half a dozen magic tricks. (My favourite, in which the inside cardboard drawer magically turned itself over, required some pre-preparation, but we never caught him doing it. His magic tricks all seemed spontaneous, which is why I could easily have believed them paranormal had he not shown us how the trick was done.) He had enough coin, matchstick or card tricks up his sleeve to entertain an entire school, but most adults will recognize that what he was doing was bar bets: classic tricks-with-a-twist from which one could extract an easy win from an inexperienced pub-goer. But at home these were not bets and he was not trying to catch us out. Instead, he set up the games as thinking puzzles, which he would help us solve with gentle hints or nudges along the way if we were struggling. He exuded patience, kindness, and confidence that we could do it, and of course we believed him. Everything was a curiosity, a puzzle to be solved and shared, a wonder to be figured out. We learned to be confident that we would always be able to find the answer.

Primary school couldn't really compete, but I loved that too. I was confident, happy, academically ahead. I was also the teacher's pet: she once told Jackie, in front of me, 'Tracy will go to university one day.' I didn't know what university was, but from the way Jackie grew inches taller with pride and flattery, it was a very special thing.

* Also known as Cherry in a Glass or Fly in a Glass, four matchsticks are arranged in the shape of a wineglass with a stem. An item (a coin or a bit of paper) serves as the cherry or fly that is 'trapped' inside. The bet is to move only two matchsticks so that the glass retains its shape but the object is now outside it.

Emily was also a diligent pupil. We'd get up in the morning, get dressed, and Jackie would walk us the quarter-mile to primary school, walking back with her friend Rose. Sometimes one or the other of us would feel ill and have a day at home with Jackie ('Don't tell your dad'), but on the whole we were well-behaved, good students. Happy little girls. I loved that my sister was in the same building as me, and was bereft when she left to go to 'big school', the local middle school in the centre of the estate.

Our local education authority operated a 'three-tier' school system, in which nine-year-olds left primary school to attend middle school for four years. Middle school was serious business. For a start, it had a uniform, a navy-blue skirt with white shirt and blue tie, which told us that our education was now in a different, more formal league. It was also a place with a reputation. Older children who had already joined this new fraternity delighted in scaring those of us still at primary school with rumours – some true – of disciplinarian teachers who made you do PE with no top on if you forgot your leotard, or screamed in your face. I was wary of one day having to go there, but time passes slowly for children and for me it was forever away. For Emily, the time came quickly enough.

When they were both nine, Emily and our neighbour, Reece Webster, had to attend an open evening at the middle school, in anticipation of them both going there that September. Jackie went too, and I stayed with a neighbour as Mike was in the pub. The school was less than ten minutes' walk away but that night there was the most extraordinary thunderstorm, and Reece's dad gave Emily and Jackie a lift to spare them a soaking. Emily was petrified of thunderstorms, and her shyness of Reece made her sit in terrified silence next to him on the back seat as the car rattled and shook in the blinding rain.

When they arrived, Emily was so scared that it might as well have been a tour of a prison. The school was enormous compared to the soft-carpeted colourful safety of primary school. The waxed parquet flooring of the assembly hall was cold and smelt slightly of vomit. There were strange children there. The storm continued to rage outside. Suddenly, a girl ran into the hall screaming a warning: if you had anything metal on you, you would be hit by lightning. The children panicked and started checking the soles of their shoes to make sure they were rubber, as that would – according to the laws of children in thunderstorms – keep you safe. Emily already couldn't cope with the rumoured horrors of middle school, and now she was going to die because she had the wrong shoes. She did not get struck by lightning, but the night of the thunderstorm cemented her fear that middle school was a bad place where bad things might happen, her own version of Jackie's childhood claustrophobia.

'There's a hole in the wall of the PE changing rooms,' an older girl told Emily, who told me. 'The boys can see through and watch you showering.' Physical education – PE, sometimes called 'games' – was already Emily's and my least favourite lesson, and being forced to get naked in a communal shower seemed like a torture technique. Ours was not a sporting household, other than doing the football pools and watching the snooker. PE lessons were mostly to be dreaded. The only sport I enjoyed was gymnastics (because it was the only one I wasn't terrible at), but Emily, too self-conscious to jump around in a leotard, did not share my enthusiasm.

Everyone knew that middle school PE was even more serious. The sporty kids were the most popular, everyone else was irrelevant. And the rumour that boys could spy on us while we were taking naked communal showers in the changing rooms of a school she was already afraid of tipped Emily over a psychological edge. She was tall and precociously developed, which made her a target for bullying and other unwelcome attention.

So Emily started middle school full of fear and a target for goading. Because of her long dark hair and her introversion, she was called 'Witch'. That wasn't unusual for our family: some of the nastier kids in our street were fond of calling Jackie 'Witch Hazel' because she had curly black hair and a large, hooked nose. They saw an archetype from their storybooks and ran with it, sometimes chalking 'A witch lives here' outside our house or shouting at us as we walked by. It scared me a little. I didn't think Jackie was a witch, but I did very much believe in witchcraft and it was upsetting that anyone might believe we were evil. Emily thinks now that her low confidence made her look miserable, which kids interpreted as 'bad person'. She became mortally afraid of being laughed at if she got a question wrong or did badly at sports. Mortally afraid of school.

It started on Sunday evenings shortly after the beginning of term. She would develop a headache or a stomach ache, symptoms of anxiety. She was so scared of Monday mornings she wouldn't sleep a wink the night before. It is extremely difficult for a nine-year-old child to do much if she hasn't slept. Jackie would get her up for school, Emily would say she hadn't slept or didn't feel well, and Jackie would make her go anyway. It took only a few Monday mornings of this before Emily's protests turned into full panic attacks.

How to differentiate between a child's panic attack and a temper tantrum? For a start, Emily wasn't a child who had tantrums ordinarily. 'I could take you both any-where,' Jackie would proudly say, of our exemplary behaviour and manners. That's not to say we didn't have our moments of conflict, but we never 'acted out' in public when we didn't get what we wanted (and we rarely wanted anything in the first place). I was a bit more outspoken and pontifical than Emily, who was the natural peacemaker, but neither of us had attendance problems at primary school. So it really was a marked difference in behaviour that she was having hysterics about going to school. She would grip the bottom of the stair banister as hard as she could, screaming, while Jackie and sometimes Mike, if he wasn't at work, would try to peel her off to get her calmed down and out of the door. They thought if they could just get her there, she'd settle in and be fine.

But it got worse. Over time, the fear of going to school developed into a phobia. Of course, questions have to be raised about the influence of Jackie's own phobias on Emily, and there are no easy answers to that. It's extremely unlikely that Emily, at nine years old, wasn't susceptible to negative influence, even while Jackie was trying so hard not to exert any. Perhaps it was the perfect storm. Bullying is recognized as a major contributing factor to what's now called 'school refusal', but there's also a place to acknow-ledge that anxiety can be contagious or even genetic. It would be naive to think otherwise. Whatever the cause(s), Emily simply couldn't go to school. My parents tried to make her. They tried so hard. But when a child is screaming in genuine terror, it takes very cruel stuff to throw her to the wolves anyway. Parents of children experiencing school refusal will recognize this; everyone else will be thinking, Why didn't your parents just *make* her go? After a point, it became clear that forcing a shy, sensitive girl to go through daily trauma would do far more harm than good. So Emily stayed at home. She would catch up on the sleep she'd missed the night before, help Jackie with housework, accompany her to neighbours' houses for coffee, to the shops, or to the local community centre, where she'd sit quietly and read while Jackie chatted to friends. It was a sort of routine, making the best of an impossible situation. By the time she was eleven, she had missed enough school for Social Services to come knocking.

5

I think I am lost, said the Skinnygooflygog
As he peered with his five eyes into the fog
One eye was brown, one eye was green
Two didn't work, another was called Dean

WE ROLLED ABOUT WITH laughter as Jackie read out her latest poem, a comic tale about the antics of a none-too-bright alien and his long-suffering wife.

We were good at finding joy in the debris of problems beyond all of our control. Just because a life is complex, it doesn't mean it can't also be happy. Jackie's phobias, Mike's drinking, Emily's school refusal, debt, sporadic unemployment, no obvious way out and up: all of these things were in the background, each exacerbated by the others but none overwhelming enough to change our dynamic. The stress on my parents must have been extraordinary. In hindsight we were, as a family, incredibly vulnerable. And yet the everyday routine and laughter carried on. We sort of lived around and with our issues instead of properly solving them, because we had neither the resources nor the knowledge to do anything else. Feast or famine, remember.

In 1985 Mike was working at the local Skill Share, teaching the unemployed how to use computers, until it was closed down and he had to sign on the dole once again and look for another technology job. As an RAF electronics engineer, a place in the growing home-computer market was a natural career step for him, but he couldn't settle in a civilian workforce and the only work available was commission-based sales. In the early eighties he had got a sales job with Apple and was flown to Cupertino, California, for training, but that role didn't stick. Then he moved on to a British computing company, Apricot, and after that the nearest town's branch of Tandy Radio Shack. Our house filled up with Tandy merchandise – half a dozen torches, branded batteries, stickers. And, unusually for the era and our social class, we always had multiple computers, either borrowed from various employers, or broken machines Mike wanted to fix. Our furniture was second-hand, the TV was hired from Radio Rentals, and the microwave had been an otherwise unaffordable gift from Jackie's parents, but we had computers as early as 1979. Mike taught us to code and Jackie taught us to touch-type right there on the big round coffee table (which used to be a dining table), all gathered round the same screen, in the same house that didn't even have a shower. We were a contradiction. Computer rich but money poor. Very happy and very troubled. Unsustainably fragile, but a solid, unbreakable family unit, held together by love.

For my part, I was doing pretty well. At nine, I was coming up to middle school. I loved learning and was good at it. I loved most aspects of school, and was used to being rewarded. I processed Emily's school phobia as something wrong with her rather than the school, particularly as she didn't tell us about the bullying, but I could only watch helplessly each morning as she unravelled, petrified and hysterical. I was a silent witness to the events that would take us from 'troubled but happy' to 'incoming hell'.

The tensions did show now and again, as they do in any family. Jackie and Mike didn't argue often, but when they did their rows were blazing. They would both shout, Jackie would cry, and when it got too much one of them would storm off. The internal doors of our house were flimsy and hollow, and Mike, in frustration, punched or kicked a hole in a few, as so many dads on the estate did. One afternoon he patched the holes he'd made with pink filler, but he never got round to sanding them smooth.

Once, Emily and I sat on the bottom step of the stairs, upset, as our parents argued in the living room. 'Will they split up?' I asked.

'They might do.'

'Who would we live with?'

'I'd live with Dad, and you'd live with Mom,' said Emily, as though it was obvious. I didn't ever want to be separated from my sister so was surprised at her logic, but it made sense that they'd get a child each. Otherwise they'd be lonely. I was closer to Jackie; Emily was a daddy's girl. As she was two years older than me, she might have seen his vulnerabilities. The thought of any of us leaving home had an odd shape in my mind, an impossible thing.

I'm wary about sounding like I'm making excuses. Of course it's scary when your dad punches a hole in a door, but I was never scared of him, not once. He was a patient and kind father. I once accidentally shut the living-room door while he was leaning against it, his thumb resting in the jamb. I heard a sickening crunch and saw blood as he yelled in pain because his thumb was crushed, but he didn't shout *at* me. He rushed to console me as I immediately started to cry about the pain I'd caused, even as he nursed his injury. My parents were considered unusual in that they didn't smack their kids when we were naughty and never swore at us. Their discipline was centred on mutual respect, even allowing for the jokey phrases common to the era. 'Stop fighting, you two! I'll bang your heads together in a minute,' Jackie would say (we were rarely naughty but we did argue a lot), and we'd stop fighting even though the chances of physical punishment were precisely zero. Mike might say, 'I'll give you a clip round the ear'ole in a minute,' but he never did. The only times I really heard him shout at kids was when local youths would congregate outside the house and make noise or – heaven help them – accidentally kick a football against our window. Then he would open the front door and swear at them to sod off. Sometimes they swore back, but they always left.

Emily and I respected our parents but weren't afraid of them. Even outside the odd argument, Mike's alcoholism was sort of gentle. His eyes would glaze over, he'd become distant, then fall asleep on the settee in front of the TV: a quiet, introverted drunk, because he was drinking to forget his pain, his depression and his problems, which were about to get worse.

Rather than excuses, I'm looking for clues to why Social Services acted as they did, because it seems unbelievable, even allowing for the ignorance of the era. Maybe the social worker turned up, saw holes in doors, and made judgements about Mike's temperament, Jackie's phobias or their marriage. I have no way of knowing what the social worker thought, because the local authority has mislaid my family's historical records and it's an expensive legal battle that will take years just to make them look properly, if the records still exist. During my research into the tangled maze of my family's past I learned that this is not at all uncommon, and only those who can afford legal action – financially or mentally – generally get anywhere. Whatever the reasons, when she was nearly twelve and had missed the majority of the last two years of school, Social Services took Emily, against her will, and put her into a psychiatric hospital.

I would never say I was too young to understand why they were taking my sister away. I was perfectly capable of understanding, had it made any sense, but it did not. We were nurtured, polite, intelligent children, happy outside Emily's school problems. We loved our parents and they loved us. We had a good home. I knew what bad homes and bad parents looked like because there were plenty around. My dad had a drinking problem but he was still a good person. My mom had social phobias but she was still a good person. This is not the defensive tint of hindsight or the polishing smooth of a rough environment; it is a simple observation about how my sister's and my most important needs were met and exceeded in difficult circumstances. To be loved, listened to, taught, inspired, held close and kept healthy, those were our fundamental requirements and the rights of any child, and we had them. We were poor, but clothed and fed, happy and safe. That wasn't enough to find a solution for Emily that didn't involve institutionalizing her. If the child didn't want to go to school then something must be very wrong with her, or her family, or her home, and she should be taken into care. But 'care' was what she already had. Taking her away to a psychiatric institution didn't mean she would be better cared for. It didn't even mean she would now be properly educated.

Perhaps if we had been a nice middle-class family, other arrangements would have been made. All Emily wanted was to learn at home instead of at school. But we were a messy, complicated council-house family. Without the Social Services records, I can only speculate, and look for clues among patchy memories and family testimony. It sounds like there must have been some other secret, terrible reason, some abuse or neglect, but there wasn't. She wasn't self-harming or sexually active or using drugs. She wasn't unhappy at all within the safety of our four walls. In any case, if there were concerns about our home life, it wouldn't have made sense to institutionalize her – she'd have been placed in a foster home instead. It was, as far as any of us can tell, all about 'curing' her school phobia. My parents couldn't make her go to school, but it wasn't because of truancy or naughtiness. It was a mental-health problem, years before school refusal was given its name, so she was sent to a residential psychiatric hospital.

The Adolescent Unit was part of the now-demolished Hollymoor Hospital, built in 1905 as an overspill facility to Rubery Lunatic Asylum, where chronic patients from the notorious Winson Green Asylum were sent to breathe country air and work on the hospital farm. During the Second World War, Hollymoor became a military psychiatric hospital, after which it was renamed Birmingham Mental Hospital. In 1969 a twenty-bed in-patient mental-health facility for adolescents was opened, and this was where, in 1985, Emily was sent. A low brick building in the grounds of a secure facility for adults, the mixed-sex Adolescent Unit was populated by teenagers who had mental-health problems severe enough (by the standards of the day) to institutionalize them. Some of the boys had mood disorders, could be violent. The girls mostly had anorexia nervosa. I was intimidated and confused by the place, not really understanding its nature or purpose. I knew the stigmatizing pejoratives for such a place – nut house or loony bin, the hospital where 'crazy people' were sent – but my sister wasn't any sort of crazy or nuts or loony. She was just a little girl who was really scared of school, and now she was in a psychiatric hospital.

The Adolescent Unit smelt of school dinners, bleach and vomit, and looked like a mix of hospital, school and Borstal, where the children had freedoms within strict limits. On our first visit, as Jackie and Mike talked with the staff, Emily showed me the girls' dormitory, a clinical room with half a dozen metal beds each surrounded by a curtain, just like a hospital ward. She had a bedside table and a shelf on which she'd arranged her collection of miniature ceramic owls. Decades later, she told me, 'I cried myself to sleep the first night. I had been taken away from my home and family because going to school made me feel ill. It didn't seem right. I spent a lot of time thinking I was mentally disturbed in some way, or there was something wrong with me that they weren't telling me. Why else would I end up there?'

At the far end of the dorm was a private room with a door, which she soon found out was for force-feeding girls who refused to eat. The single-bed room was occupied by a teenage girl named Kathy, so thin she looked transparent, her organs on the cusp of failing. There were at least four other girls in the unit with anorexia. Emily witnessed staff restraining them after they refused to swallow food or tried to hide it in their napkins. 'The staff were harsh to them,' she says carefully, in the rare instances when she talks about it at all. She made friends with some of those girls, saying, 'Most of the time they were in bed due to weak limbs, so I would sit on their beds and chat. I was the youngest kid in the place, so I think they felt big-sisterly towards me.'

Some of the other kids could be violent, aggressive and loud. Bullying was inevitable. 'We were allowed to go out in groups to the local shops, et cetera. I had been there a little while and went along one day with a mixed group. One boy started to comment on my figure. He was egged on by some of the other kids and before I knew it he pushed me into a bush and was trying to lift my top up. I struggled and luckily one of the older girls told him to get off me and leave me alone, which he did. I ran back on my own, crying. I don't think I told anyone in case they either didn't believe me or they got him into trouble, which would come back to me. The girl said to me after it was just a bit of messing around and to forget about it.'

I remember those boys. During a family visit, one of them, who seemed like a giant, was walking past us in the corridor, accompanied by a member of staff. Suddenly he grabbed me and pinned me against the wall by my throat. Adults pulled him away, shouting. That was just a split-second in time for me. Emily had to live there, and was overwhelmed with dread for much of the time. Homesick, scared, lonely, and increasingly convinced there was something wrong with her, she was horrified when one weekend our parents arranged for a friend to visit her as a surprise. 'No one from my old school knew where I was. They just knew I had been taken away. When I saw her I was mortified. She now knew I was in a psychiatric institution. I imagined her going back and telling everyone.'

Emily's routine was part clinical, part educational. Psychiatric evaluations; group-therapy sessions, which were recorded on tape (she hated these); art therapy; the occasional game of basketball in which she was a target for bullying (she stopped playing). She also had cooking lessons, for which the children had to be escorted through the main hospital down long, cold corridors, where the adult inpatients would run out of rooms, wailing or jeering at them. One woman would walk up and down the hall carrying a doll, which she told anyone who would listen was her baby. Emily was as afraid of the place as she was of school.

Now and again, we were invited for a family-therapy session in one of the grey offices. Sitting on hard plastic chairs, illuminated by pallid strip lighting, the four Kings were encouraged to discuss Emily's school problems, our family life, our feelings. I desperately wanted to say things that would help her, but the three of us didn't understand what was 'wrong' with her any more than she did. At home, we had to make a new normal without her. I didn't tell anyone where my sister was, or that Social Services were involved, realizing even at that age that stigma was destructive. Besides, this was not a relatable problem. Even the most chaotic of families on the estate didn't have a child in a psychiatric hospital.

6

I N 1984, WHEN I was eight and Emily ten – a year before she was institutionalized – I got home from school one day and Jackie told me something interesting had happened. Her wedding ring had slipped off her finger as she was walking back from the shops. It had once been held in place by a small diamond engagement ring but she had had to pawn that to pay the bills a few years before. The wedding ring, a plain white-gold band, now had a habit of falling off. She had stopped to look for it in the grass and been approached by Margaret.

Families like mine were susceptible to sales pitches because we were under-educated and often desperate. The Provident credit or 'tally' man who went from door to door lending money and selling goods at inflated rates of interest helped pay urgent debts by creating even greater debts. He was an old-school salesman, persuading Jackie she deserved the new iron and ironing board that he would let her have at a 'special rate', just an extra fifty pence a week on top of what she already owed. Sometimes Jackie didn't have the money to pay him, so we would hide under the table until the knocking stopped. When a photographer from the local paper came round to take a picture for a story about her poetry, he offered money if she would pose for pornography (she declined).

Multi-level marketing schemes were common – most women on the estate hosted a Tupperware party at some point, trying to help a neighbour earn a little commission on plastic tubs they were promised would transform their domestic lives for a bargain price. Every street had an Avon lady – even Bernice sold bubble bath and lipstick to her friends from the small colourful catalogue. Jackie fell for one of the more obscure offerings, a company selling tubes of paint and fabrics with printed designs. This suited her artistic nature, and she invested in kits she couldn't afford to make art she didn't keep. The same materials were available cheaper elsewhere, but the selling point was the ambition, the glossy brochures that showed grand artworks created from a rainbow of glittery paints.

Unfulfilled ambition is a vulnerability, just like lack of education, but my mother's greatest weak spot was her mental health. Decades of fear and phobias, poverty and family issues had chipped away at her, yet she never gave up looking for joy and hope.

For Jackie, the whole God question was one of belief, not rules. Mike wasn't Jewish, but neither was he particularly Christian or particularly atheist, and their marriage was secular. Religion just wasn't a part of our lives.

Even the mandatory Christian prayers in British schools were background noise, something to rebel against. Eyes closed, hands clasped together, peeping out of one eye to see who else was cheating. We didn't take it seriously although everyone loved the songs, belting out harvest festival or Christmas numbers with gusto and no insight into the lyrics. 'Round yon virgin, mother and child,' I'd sing in soprano, unclear what a virgin was but imagining a very large sphere of a woman and baby rolling bodily into a stable. The Nativity occupied the same space as Santa, stuff kids are told with a wink and no real conviction. 'Jingle Bells' and 'Silent Night' had equal weight. It was all about tradition and tunes.

Jackie had never pretended Santa was real, but everything else was up for belief. Dragons, fairies, aliens, the paranormal, superstition and luck; anything that brought joy, meaning or explanation to a difficult, unfair life was potentially real, including Jesus.

Margaret, the woman who approached Jackie to help look for the lost jewellery, was a born-again Christian. I knew her slightly, the mother of one of my schoolfriends from a different part of the estate. I had witnessed her being very strict with her daughter, who in response was rebelliously naughty way past the age when she should have been. Jackie told me that as they searched for the wedding ring they got talking about Jesus, who Jackie admitted she had always believed in. Margaret, originally a Jehovah's Witness, described her new church, which met at the local community centre. Then they found the ring, and the chance meeting began to look like Fate.

Jackie and Margaret became friends, and chats over cups of tea in the kitchen turned into invites to a chat at the minister's house, then church services and Bible study. It wasn't a British denomination of Christianity, but one imported from America by trendy missionaries who had come to save the estates from sin. Over the next few months Jackie was presented with new ideas, options she'd never considered before. The teachings centred on the New Testament, taking its doctrines literally while relegating the Old Testament, including the first five books that comprise the Torah, to the lower leagues. The old religions were wrong, this one was right, and learning this would change her life. Born-again Christianity would take what she already had – an innate belief in Jesus – and add structure, context and community. She could talk about her problems and get advice that sounded meaningful alongside reassurances that she and her family would be prayed for. The church was young and fun, nothing like the stuffy vicar-and-cardigans types she'd always associated with Christianity. All she needed to do was take the next step and convert.

Her formal acceptance of Jesus into her life was not a spur-of-the-moment decision, but something she thought about and talked about over a few months, with the nervous apprehensive excitement of someone deliberating on their first tattoo. She needed a catalyst to push her from consideration to final decision. Her new friends in the church invited her to see the preacher Billy Graham, who was touring sports stadiums across Britain and was world-famous, charismatic, and a personal friend of the Queen.

I don't know what it was about Jesus and his handsome American employees that attracted young British wives and mothers in the 1980s, but between our church's minister, Adam, and Billy Graham, Jackie was smitten. That's not to suggest any sexual interest (I really couldn't say), although it was the case that most new converts to the church were women; husbands and kids followed later, if at all. I wonder if that particular generation of women was stuck in an in-between place, no useful war effort like their mothers had had (Bernice's war stories were epic and impressive), and too early yet for the mainstreaming of feminism that would give women more professional and domestic options. As Jackie said, it was either become a wife and mother, or become a secretary. But here was a third option. Become a born-again Christian and then all other considerations are secondary. The unfulfilled life becomes fulfilled in an instant. What struggling housewife wouldn't want to be filled with the Holy Spirit?

Billy Graham had a policy of never being alone with any woman to whom he was not married (this 'rule' is now named after him but is sometimes called the Modesto Manifesto and says more about men who can't trust themselves around women than it means to). Jackie didn't need any alone time to fall for Billy Graham's charms. The church invited her to hear him preach at the Aston Villa football ground in Birmingham. The 1984 'Mission England' tour filled six football stadiums across the country, attracting a million people in total. Jackie would be one of thirty thousand that night, her first time at a football stadium.

Unlike most of the estate, the Kings weren't a particularly football-oriented family. Mike would watch the Cup Final and sometimes played the football pools, but the game and culture were not major features in our lives. Perhaps if he'd had sons they would have been, but he preferred the quietness of a game of snooker. By contrast, the rest of Jackie's family, including her twin, Miriam, were staunch Birmingham City fans, so it was an oddity that she should find herself – physically and spiritually – at the rival ground Villa Park.

She joined Adam, Bob, Margaret and a small, caring but deeply fundamentalist woman named Eileen, who was quickly becoming one of Jackie's closest friends. Eileen's speciality was the sort of listening that involves asking a lot of personal questions, then offering advice, both practical and spiritual. By coincidence she lived next door to my friend with the shelf of Barbies, in a big house on the private part of the housing development, and took a great interest in the Kings.

On the minibus from our estate, the group listened to Christian rock, laughed and joked as any group of friends would. But there was potential to their trip that was unique to religion. At the end of his half-hour sermon, as anticipated by all who attended, Billy Graham invited anyone who would like to convert to born-again Christianity to leave their seat and head down to the pitch to receive his (and therefore God's) blessing. This moment of agreeing to become a born-again Christian was called 'conversion', and Jackie was already on the brink.

There's footage of that 1984 sermon at Villa Park on YouTube. Billy Graham could certainly captivate an audience. With a strong, square-jawed face, a bright yellow jumper and tie under his suit jacket, he was a dynamic evangelist. He had the confidence of a man who believed he had been chosen specially by God to preach the good word and save millions of souls from Hell. If you want to convince people you're qualified to save their souls from eternal damnation, you have to project the sort of strength that could face up to the Devil himself on their behalf.

In the film footage, Graham stands at a wooden lectern on the pitch – a temporary pulpit – and begins to speak. His opening remarks are a string of anecdotes and musings about Jews, Hitler and sex. It makes sense to start with such provocative subjects. Fire your biggest guns first. His style of preaching is sensationalist, and sex and Nazis are a guaranteed way to get people on the hook. His sermon is about resisting temptation, 'lasciviousness and lust', but also excesses of alcohol, stealing, watching too much television. It was a sermon of hope, tailored to people like Jackie whose lives were affected by those very things. Would she have taken his many mentions of Jews as a personal sign? When he talked about alcohol, or the struggle of poverty, did she feel like he was speaking directly to her? 'And even in suffering,' he booms, 'when you come to Christ, God doesn't take away the suffering and he doesn't take away the problems and the difficulties of your life. Not at all. He doesn't promise if you're unemployed that he's going to get you a job tomorrow morning if you accept Christ tonight, he promises that he'll give you grace and strength and joy through it all.'

Grace and strength and joy through it all. In archive footage of a *Midlands Today* television interview of people arriving for the event, one woman says she's attending specifically to 'see people being saved'. Graham's showmanship riles up the crowd in advance of the spectacle: souls will be redeemed *en masse*. A temptation difficult to resist, despite the anti-temptation message of the sermon. Buy a ticket and go to watch the circus.

Once a few go, the floodgates open. They stream down from the stands at Villa Park, onto the pitch, moved by the

Holy Spirit and the electric atmosphere to commit their souls to the Lord. It's impossible to know how many of the thousands who descended onto the hallowed ground each night of the rally were already confirmed Christians, as opposed to those, like Jackie, who had already prepared themselves to answer yes in the moment, as though responding to an eagerly anticipated marriage proposal. In that environment, there's nothing spontaneous about it other than the courage to accept. Jackie, her fear of crowds and noise momentarily suspended, gripped a friend's arm as she made her way down.

She soaked up the manic atmosphere, the gaps in her life and psyche filled by what the church told her was the light of the Holy Spirit. When she came home from Villa Park she had changed. She was full of pride that she'd gone down to the pitch, excited, happy and focused in a way I hadn't seen before, exactly like when someone embarks on a new, intense relationship. She had a new identity: she was now officially a born-again Christian. With a new perspective and infectious joy, she embraced her mandate to live a Christian life and spread the good word.

The first order of business was her baptism, an even bigger deal than most because, as well as indelibly committing her soul to Jesus, she would have to overcome her fear of water. Baptisms were conducted at a private swimming pool that belonged to a wealthy Christian family who let our church use it now and again. A date was set, and we made our way there in our Sunday best, Jackie's new swimsuit on under her clothes. The pool was out in the countryside, in a light wooden-beamed building attached to the biggest house I'd ever been in (it's now a wedding venue). I loved to play 'posh ladies', and when Bernice took me with her to her domestic cleaning jobs, I would swan around the fancy detached houses holding a crystal wine-glass, pretending I was a hostess entertaining VIPs.

While I knew I'd never live in a property like that, I had a rich imagination and could easily pretend I did, but the baptism house gave me insight into a whole other world. There was free food, a private library, and leather armchairs I could sink into and get lost. The curtains were heavy, embroidered, held back by golden tassels that tick-led my hand. The pool was indoors, heated, and with an adjacent sauna that made other families ooh and aah and talk about foreign holidays they'd been on. (The Kings hadn't been on any foreign holidays, so I assumed saunas were a standard part of them and decided I wasn't missing out on much, it just being a hot sweaty room with no clear purpose.) At baptisms, the official dunking business would conclude and then we were free to use the facilities as we liked, a major perk for those from the estate. 'How the other half live,' we'd say, awed.

Mike, who was in general a sceptical man, had come too. We all sat on benches around the pool and watched as Adam guided Jackie, visibly afraid in a navy-blue swim-ming costume, into the water. Her hands clasped in prayer, she was tipped backwards by Adam. I held my breath as she was fully submerged, feeling her fear and my own – what if she opened her mouth to scream, and drowned? She wouldn't even let me lie down in the bath, hovering outside the bathroom door and every so often calling out, 'You okay?' for fear I had fallen asleep and died – but it was a split second until she was lifted back up again, her black curls clinging wetly to her head. And that was it, she was reborn. That moment underwater washed away her sins and her Jewishness and transformed her, substantially, into a Christian.

Afterwards, everyone got changed and played in the pool. Like Jackie, I was scared of water and unable to swim, so I sat on the edge of the shallow end and dangled my legs in. It hadn't really occurred to me that Mike could swim because we hadn't been to a swimming pool before, but I saw him emerge in light-blue swimming trunks I hadn't known he owned and, without pausing, dive head-first into the deep end.

7

J ACKIE'S NEW FAITH DID not go down well with her family, mainly because, from their perspective, she changed for the worse. Later, a family member told me, 'Your mom went completely weird during that phase, completely weird. I can't even describe what weird she went, but it completely changed her as a person and that's all she could ever focus on. It's like the church completely ruled her life and she couldn't do anything without the church knowing, or being involved, or saying she could, or she couldn't. She just wasn't her own person. And she went quite within her shell. I mean, your mom's not like an outlandish person anyway, but she went very, very withdrawn in the church, but would always say that she was very happy.'

The family's concern can only have grown as they saw first me, aged nine, and then Emily – whose school problems showed no signs of slowing – begin to join her. Always a mommy's girl, I observed two sides but supported only one. Jackie and Bernice having stand-up arguments in the kitchen, accusations of brainwashing. My uncle calling the church 'a cult', whispered conversations that ended when we entered the room. Criticisms that felt like blasphemy, a concept I learned from Jackie. I could see it made her unhappy, so I was unhappy with it too.

Blasphemy is a hell of an invention. Offence is a useless weapon because it's available to anyone to use. You're offended by me, I'll be offended right back: no one wins, no progress is made. But blasphemy is being offended on behalf of God, and that's the ultimate trump card. We had a new lens through which to view, judge and police everything, including things we used to like. Things that used to be funny were now horrifying, and our moral indignation could only be soothed by praying for the ignorant blasphemer and their lost soul. Because we were looking for it, we began to see blasphemy in the most benign things. I discovered that Jackie was completely open to all suggestions, and this gave me power. As we were writing Christmas cards (now the religious sort rather than the previously secular robin-or-Santa type we'd always bought), I suddenly piped up, 'I don't think it's right to put "happy Xmas" instead of "happy Christmas". It's like with the X we're erasing Christ's name.'

'That's a very good point,' said Jackie, impressed by my thinking. Neither of us knew that 'Xmas' was an established point of offence for Christians, for much the same reasons I'd come up with independently. We were also not aware that the X dates back to the sixteenth century, and represents the Greek letter *chi* – literally the *Ch* in Christ. My memorization of the Greek alphabet from Mike's book had been for show, without any context or further learning. A party trick that passed for knowledge. But even if I'd had a point about *chi*, it didn't occur to either of us that Christ would be equally (or no more) offended by an X than the anglicizing of his name in the first place. Instead, I was offended *for* him, and felt good about an adult agreeing with me and taking corrective action by writing 'Christmas' in full. Solving problems you've invented is a good facsimile of empowerment when you've never had the real thing.

Jackie and I took this new concept of blasphemy personally, and I felt for the first time a division: the Kings and the church on one side, and on the other, the rest of the world, including Jackie's family. This was exacerbated by her new Christianity being a big secret – Bernice and Symon made it clear that their friends and extended family weren't to know. It was a clash that felt like oppression. We were being judged for our new beliefs instead of being celebrated and listened to. Why wouldn't everyone be happy for us that we'd found out the truth about Jesus? Why wouldn't they believe us? Why wouldn't they join us? When you are saved, you have to save others. Imagine your loved ones burning in a fiery Hell because they hadn't been given the opportunity to accept Jesus. That was the reality of our belief, that we had found, by sheer luck or divine will, the one true religion and the facts about what happens when we die. We would all go to either Heaven or Hell, depending on how sorry we were for any sins we'd committed, and whether or not we'd accepted Jesus as our lord and saviour.

Jackie wrote a lengthy letter to Miriam explaining about Jesus, and why Christianity was the successor to Judaism. She persuaded Bernice to throw out an Evil Eye she had inherited from my great-grandmother, her distress at its presence persuasion enough for my superstitious nan. She proselytized constantly, conversations during family visits continuing late into the night long after I'd fallen asleep. We prayed for them to see the light.

It must have had a huge impact on them, seeing Jackie first lose her house and move away to a council estate, only to have her daughter removed, then have her vulnerabilities exploited by a recruiting religion. To them we were the 'problem' side of the family, rife with alcoholism, phobias and debt, and this perspective was alienating to me. They were the problem, not us. The more oppressed you feel, the more you turn to your community and away from everyone else. Once it's clear that others are just not as big Jesus fans as you are, uninterested in being convinced by the Gospel, you realize you can only be truly understood by the church. Born-again Christianity was our entire life, not only for Sunday morning.

Tuesday Bible study, Saturday picnics in the park, Friday-night dinner and board games, days out and sleepovers. School-holiday 'Bible school', and a Christ-themed youth club at which Jackie volunteered. She needed someone to go with her to all of these new places, at least until she got used to the routes and destinations, but we started to enjoy it as a family activity, and the church quickly became the centre of our socializing. We no longer had private problems. Everything was shared with our new friends, for spiritual guidance and the regular domestic sort. Emily's school difficulties were discussed, dissected, prayed about. Church elders tried to intervene, even lecture her. Mike was counselled privately by a church member, confiding details of his drinking and depression. Even Emily's social worker, Louise, was a Christian, and seemed pleased we'd found the guidance of God. It's no wonder we other three Kings followed Jackie's conversion with our own.

Nothing was off-limits for discussion. When Emily got her first period aged eleven, the minister Adam and his wife happened to be at ours for dinner. To Emily's burning shame, Jackie immediately announced the news to them. It was this spontaneity and naive exuberance that suited her to born-again Christianity. Her anxiety disorder forced her to live on instinct, rarely relaxing fully, her emotions often heightened. Panic was as close as peals of joy. The emotionally charged environment of the church – praying, up-tempo singing, tambourines and jokes, the laying-on of healing hands, miracles and speaking in tongues, fighting Satan's influence, the histrionics of baptism – suited her perfectly. Her superstitions and neuroses were justified: magic was real. Good and evil forces were real. Anything was possible.

Like my mother, I enjoyed attention, so we paid it to each other. I wanted to know everything, my curiosity awake to the potential of this strange new world she was in. We talked about Christianity constantly. It featured in everything. One evening as we watched the news, Jackie confidently announced she believed Gorbachev was the Antichrist. I believed her, and had trouble sleeping for weeks, petrified at the impending Armageddon. Jackie talked to her children as if we were adults (or perhaps as if she was also a child), and this made us feel included and mature enough to know our own minds.

The church had supplied plenty of new reading material. Pastel-coloured pamphlets imported from the American headquarters, an illustration of the classic young white Jesus, sometimes with a dove or a lamb or assorted children. There were booklets of guidance and Bible verses, printed sermons and, of course, a brand-new thick blue faux-leather book, the front embossed with THE HOLY BIBLE in gold.

The more time I spent with the church, the more Jackie talked about religion. As she listened to my questions and we learned the answers together, the more I began to feel something growing inside. The spark of eternal joy. The promise that my family would be okay. But I also loved all the new books that were appearing, the attention and free food, and the new enthusiasm of Jackie, who, as far as I could tell in my short life so far, couldn't possibly be wrong.

Becoming a born-again Christian is a lot like falling in love. The desire for God and Jesus's attention and approval grew in my heart in much the same way as a crush. The language of love was a big part of the sales pitch, and it was made very clear to me that the affection of the Lord was a sure thing.

But at nine years old I was too young to know about romantic love. It didn't occur to me that if I could fall into belief I could fall out of it. Just like Jackie, I was falling for the promises and potential of born-again Christianity. The idea of a benevolent, caring God who would sacrifice his son for my personal wellbeing was psychologically seductive. He would look after me and I could tell him anything in return for guidance, company and infallible nurturing. God was the ultimate Father, the perfect parent. Jesus was a big brother, a best friend, a role model. I was already Jackie's shadow, but belief brought us even closer together, and gave me a new community in which everyone had the happiness of religion and mutual love for God and Jesus in common, instead of the misery of poverty.

At that age, converting to a religion is not a choice in any meaningful sense. As a friend recently said, incredulous, 'At nine you're barely born, how can you be born again?' Choice is supposed to be informed, at least, but when my brain wasn't developed enough to process it, and the information was deeply biased in the first place, how can I claim it was fully my choice? I wasn't presented with a range of gods and religions to choose the one that best made sense, and how would I be qualified to judge anyway? I wasn't told that to have no religion at all is an equally valid choice, or that there is no evidence for the claims being made other than anecdotal. Indeed those claims, such as miracles or the existence of an afterlife, were presented as factual simply because they had been repeated in print and in pulpits for so many years. That was all the evidence a child needed, especially one like me, who assumed that if something was in a book it must be true. The world was suddenly binary, goodies and baddies, like a children's novel – and that was my language. I was a child, so I didn't have the critical faculties or the education to query whether or not these adults were simply wrong. Even if I had, there was nothing I could have done. One little girl is not going to turn David and bring down the Goliath of organized religion.

I'd been given my own Bible, a children's edition just as hefty as Jackie's sombre blue pleather tome but full of colourful illustrations to attract kids. The cover depicts Noah and his ark of animals, a rainbow glowing happily in the sky. I still have it, my name and address written inside in wobbly handwriting. I recognize the handwriting, but not the child who wrote it. I also wrote the date, 29/2/86, a few weeks before my tenth birthday. I'd added a colourful sticker that says, 'OUR GOD IS MERCIFUL', the shouty uppercase contradicting the peaceful message. Under it I'd written in pencil,

God is love, who ever lives in love lives in God and God in He.
I John 4:16

Love was a currency the King family understood, because for much of our lives it was the only thing we had. Suddenly we were rich.

Rich people get to have parties in big houses. My baptism took place in April 1987, a month after my eleventh birthday, at the same location as Jackie's. I had told her that I, too, wanted to convert, and she was elated. Nothing was more inevitable, and nothing could have stopped me short of Jackie changing her own mind about the church. But if she was in, I was in. I don't really see how our family could have functioned otherwise. Whatever path she took, I was going with her. I believed all of it, every word. More than that, I could feel it. The warmth and safety of the very thought of Jesus and his endless attention: a circle of beliefs with me at the centre.

It was like getting to choose my own birthday. Jackie made the announcement to the church that I was going to convert, a date was set for my baptism, and I'd get presents and attention. A silver-plated crucifix on a chain, to keep Jesus close to my heart but also so that everyone would know I was a Christian. I wore a brand-new swimsuit, a shiny black one-piece. My first. Mine wasn't the only baptism that day, although I don't remember the others. I was too nervous, not about the rebirth but the water. It would be my first time fully submerged and I truly believed I might drown. That was part of it, I was told. Overcoming fear and trusting God.

Really it was the minister Adam I had to trust, as we waded into the shallow end up to his hips and my waist. I clasped my hands together as Jackie had done, and Adam placed one hand on my back. With the other he held my wrists. Someone in the church had told me about a woman who had become an occultist and was told to walk through a bonfire to meet Satan. She did, but it was Jesus who met her in the middle and guided her out, unharmed. Thereafter she belonged to him and not the Devil. I thought I might meet or at least feel the presence of Jesus under the water. I screwed my eyes tight shut, and as Adam spoke the words of baptism he deftly tipped me backwards. The memory is of sudden deafness. I felt nothing but fear and the shock of cold. A second later I was tipped upright again, and the golden-bearded man in white guided me out of the pool, officially born again.

8

I N OCTOBER 1987, ONE of the worst storms in British history ravaged the island. Twenty-two people died, insurance companies paid out £2 billion, fifteen million trees were lost in England alone and the field of meteorology changed for ever. I remember the night of that storm and the media one that followed, as a population unable to prepare for the worst, because of a lack of information, lost trust in the authorities.

Emily's few months in the psychiatric institution two years before had done nothing except exacerbate her fears. On her release, she had been enrolled in a different middle school a short bus ride from our house in the hope that she had been cured. A fresh start at a new school, press the reset button. It didn't work, of course. She had all the same panic attacks, shyness and anxiety issues as before, but this time she was the new girl, the one who had been sent away, surrounded by rumours and reputation, even more of a target for bullying. She tried anyway, as did my parents. But the reasons she was petrified of school did not go away just because the school was different. This new place was even stricter, the uniform more restrictive, and she had missed too much schooling to slot back easily into the curriculum.

She lasted a matter of weeks, then was back to long

stretches at home with Jackie. Social Services intervened again and, not knowing what else to do with her, temporarily enrolled her at a pupil referral unit a slightly longer bus ride away. This school was for children who had been excluded (expelled, as we said then) or had serious behavioural disorders. Everyone knew it by reputation, it was where the Bad Children had to go when they were too disruptive or violent for regular school, an educational bogeyman with which to threaten truants. It was as loud, undisciplined and – to Emily – as full of frightening boys as the Adolescent Unit had been, but at least it was just for a few hours a day. Louise, the social worker, drove her there and back for the first few weeks, knowing it was an unsuitable placement but having no other options in the meantime.

This was Emily's dilemma: she wanted to learn, and was perfectly capable of doing so, but she was too afraid of regular school. The pupil referral unit, while in some ways comfortingly casual (no uniform, no scary disciplinarian teachers), was chaotic and she couldn't learn anything.

There didn't seem to be a middle ground, a quiet, unthreatening environment for her to learn in. I've read a lot about school refusal, most of it chillingly familiar. It tends to kick in when the child moves up from primary school to a bigger school; it doesn't usually correlate with any other behavioural issues or aggression (indeed, the child is often well-behaved and of above-average intelligence), and there are often complaints of physical symptoms such as stomach ache or headache. It's different from truancy, particularly in that the child is not remotely duplicitous about it.

Most of the literature is from the early nineties onwards, and the recommended treatment is – with appropriate support from all parties – to get the child back to school as quickly as possible. Many parents do not agree. There is a parent support group called Not Fine in School, which advocates 'no forced attendance', in which many parents say physically forcing their child to attend school made things worse. In a 2018 survey, a quarter of families experiencing school refusal had been referred to Social Services. It's clear that there's a disconnect between how authorities handle absent pupils and what parents believe works for their child, and there is also evidence that forced attendance is causing trauma that simply exacerbates the problem.

So, Emily tried to attend the pupil referral unit, just as she had tried the other schools, because she had no choice. The threat of prison for our parents loomed large, a grotesque emotional blackmail by authorities on the shoulders of a too-sensitive child. At the age of thirteen she was going to class as much as she could, but it was clear that she wasn't having her educational needs met, let alone her mental-health needs. The teachers were kind, but the other kids were so disruptive it wasn't really possible for the teachers to teach or for Emily to learn. Instead, she got her education at home, reading books and helping me with my homework. Her spiritual education had paid off too, and she decided to convert to born-again Christianity and be baptized at the big house.

Around the time of the storms, we had a visit from Emily's social worker, Louise, who had huge news. The local authority had agreed to pay for Emily to attend a private boarding school. It was very expensive, thousands of pounds a term, the sort of sum nothing else in our lives ever cost. The school specialized in children who didn't thrive well in a normal school environment, and while they weren't experienced in 'school phobia' (she didn't say what exactly they were experienced in), the alternative educational setting might just be what Emily needed. Louise seemed very proud that she'd got Emily funding for a place there, and we understood we should be excited and grateful. There was no uniform, no formalities of any kind. Teachers were addressed by their first name, and the lessons were oriented towards the arts and individualized learning. There were downsides, of course. No television or other technology, no fizzy drinks, chocolate or 'processed' food, no makeup. She'd have to leave her family again, but was promised that a volunteer would be available to bring her home at weekends and school holidays. She would have a bedroom of her own, piano lessons, and an education. Louise presented it as a lifeline, a last chance before the terrible final legal consequences of not going to school.

It was raining the day we drove seventy miles down the motorway to check out the school, a strange journey to a south-western part of the English countryside I had only read about in books. The school was a converted limestone farmhouse in which the pupils lived, with classes held downstairs and in various outbuildings. It nestled miles from any main road, in bleak, rolling countryside a different shade of green from council-estate grass. In a paddock behind the school there was a pony, on the front drive a white minibus. I was scared of the remoteness, was used to living and sleeping in the middle of a tight terrace of modern houses with dozens of other families, their noise and lights. The school and its surroundings had a medieval creepiness and I was immediately unhappy. I imagined witches gathering in the woodland, spying on the school and kidnapping my sister.

When we arrived, Emily was whisked off by Louise and the school's head teacher, while Jackie, Mike and I were shown into a lounge and offered cups of tea. There was a glass of apple juice for me, but I was too nervous to swallow, so Jackie drank it. The house wasn't like any I'd been in before. Wooden floorboards with the sort of fancy rugs that Aladdin was always pictured on, heavy solid-oak furniture with decorative carved legs, beams on the low ceilings and a chill in the thick stone walls. To me, the staff were a new type of person, too. Colourful tights, home-knitted jumpers, velvet skirts and floaty scarves in prints I'd never seen before. I didn't know about 'middle class' or 'new age', but I did recognize 'posh'.

Jackie was handed a leaflet and I sat on the arm of her chair while we looked at it together. Mike went outside to smoke. The front page, emblazoned with a rainbow, proudly proclaimed 'Residential Special School'. My heart paused. Special school? Like . . . for special needs? Emily didn't have learning difficulties or a developmental disorder. She was just shy and scared of going to school. It didn't make sense.

We were asked to stay for dinner and, after holding hands and saying a blessing, were served organic wholemeal spaghetti, a world away from the tinned stuff in tomato sauce or (my favourite) Jackie's homemade 'spag bog'. The wholemeal pasta was gloopy and the smell made me feel sick, so I didn't eat it and felt embarrassed about wasting food. Half a dozen children had joined us for dinner, all older than me. Most were either neurodivergent or had developmental disorders, but I hadn't heard of any of those things, had no experience or understanding or empathy. No one said the word 'autism'. They dressed differently from any kids I had known, and asked questions that seemed weird to me. One was obsessed with tractors; another claimed he was a bus; a third asked me if I had ever seen a dead hedgehog. (She had taken up taxidermy as a hobby and, Emily told me later, was eventually allowed to stuff a squirrel corpse she had found. In the spirit of the school's green ethos, the girl didn't waste the flesh but cooked and ate it.)

When you're eleven and it's the 1980s, different is bad. Different is shame, embarrassment. This was a lot of different all at once and I didn't know how to process it. The environment, culture, sights, sounds and smells were so completely, utterly unlike anything we'd experienced before and I just didn't see how Emily could possibly fit in. Perhaps Jackie and Mike also had misgivings – but they didn't have any choice, so it didn't matter. Emily's feelings didn't figure at all.

I recently asked her about the day we went to view the school. 'Did you like it?' I typed. There was no delay before the reply: 'No.' But she had been told our parents would both go to prison if she objected, or that she would be taken somewhere way worse, like a Borstal, so she was going to have to live at this new school and that was that. We trooped home, pretending to be upbeat about the pony and the countryside and the piano, and prepared for Emily's big move.

In December 1987, shortly after Emily's fourteenth birthday, we did the trip down the motorway again, and this time returned home without her. We'd been in this situation before, our family of four reduced to three, and I recognized the dull ache of her absence in my chest.

Emily experienced a type of culture shock. In any other circumstances her new home would have been idyllic, the sort of place writers and artists dream about. Roses climbing around the door, a thatched roof, lavender growing in pots in the garden against a dry-stone wall built centuries before. Her bedroom was in a cottage on the school grounds, where she lived with half a dozen other pupils and almost as many staff, including a married couple who acted as legal guardians. She was to refer to them as her 'house parents'. To Emily it was more like a prison, miles from estate civilization and the comforts of home, every semblance of her normal life missing. In its place: chamber music and carob, an inedible, disgusting chocolate substitute (a 2018 *New Yorker* article entitled 'How Carob Traumatized a Generation' describes it as dietary suffering for children). She badly missed television, in particular *Neighbours* and its heartthrobs.

Popular culture is youth currency; knowledge and gossip gleaned from the latest *Smash Hits* or *Just Seventeen* were traded for popularity. In the playground and across the estate, last night's *Top of the Pops* or *EastEnders* was analysed, imitated and worshipped. Fear of missing out is strongest in kids, in part because knowledge is often the only power they have.

Emily was seventy miles from home but also seventy years back in time. She had put her Michael Jackson and Madonna posters on the wall, her Garfield comic books on the shelf, and her Forever Friends duvet cover on the bed, but it wasn't enough. A member of staff phoned Jackie to say Emily wouldn't stop crying, wouldn't eat, didn't want to leave her room and the familiarity of her scant belongings. She was confused and angry, once again deprived of her liberty and desperately missing her family and friends. Jackie asked to speak to her. Emily was in hysterics, begging and pleading to come home. 'I just want to come home, please let me come home.' She said she was on hunger strike.

After the phone call, the remaining Kings sat around the big coffee table in the living room. Whatever crime or neglect Emily's school phobia was supposed to represent did not justify the misery the authorities were putting her and us through. They had no right to take her away and even less right to put her into a residential special school so different from anything any of us knew. We had prayed about it, individually and together, but that did not bring back Emily. Jackie had gone to pieces. I was crying. Mike, drinking lager, started crying too. I'd never seen him cry before and it upset me even more.

'Don't cry,' I told him, through my own tears. 'Men don't cry.'

I'll never forget his response: 'No, that's not true. It takes a brave man to cry.'

I can still feel the pain around that table, but I can also feel the sharp injection of bravery and hope. I don't remember if Jackie or Mike said it out loud first. 'Let's go and get her. Right now.' We'd been in the power of Social Services and under the spell of authority for so many years, it would take an extraordinary feat of bravery to defy them now. But we had no other resources and bravery is free. We would drive down the motorway and rescue Emily, right there and then.

It was already dark, past 8 p.m., and the stormy weather that defined that winter had no intention of relaxing just because we were in a rush. We dashed to the car, ignoring the rain and thunder. Ill winds make poetic metaphors but brutal travel. It was precisely the sort of storm you'd order as the backdrop to a dangerous rescue if you were making a film. Our little old white car zooming at top speed along, first, motorways and then the tiny winding roads through the countryside.

Mike drove determinedly through the terrible weather. The winding roads turned into treacherous hillside tracks, illuminated only by the stars and the occasional crack of lightning. I was petrified, curled up in the back, watching the rain lash against the windows. There were no rear seatbelts, so I gripped the seat tightly. We drove up a road wide enough only for one car, a cliff face to our right and a sheer drop to the left. I expected another car to come the other way at any moment, and prayed and prayed for our safety. I assumed my prayers worked because Mike navigated the dangers without incident and eventually we arrived at the stone cottage where my sister was being held.

It took a while for anyone to answer the door. Presumably the staff were unaccustomed to late-night visitors and it must have been somewhere around 10 p.m. We probably alarmed them: the council-house family coming to claim their Social Services child. Most pupils at the school were there voluntarily, the fees paid by wealthy parents in return for an alternative approach to the child's special educational needs.

The man who answered the cottage door was tall, bearded and wearing a jumper, the sort of person you'd confidently call a hippy. We were shown into a tiny sitting room and offered tea. I sat on the stiff settee alone and picked at the antimacassar while my parents went into the kitchen to talk to the tall man, who had told us Emily was asleep upstairs. I kept expecting to hear footsteps on the stairs and her voice. She would ask what we were doing there and we'd say, 'We've come to take you home.'

Then she'd go and pack and get into the car with us, and we'd drive the hour and a half home, and the rain would stop. But she didn't wake up and come downstairs and home with us. Instead, my parents and the tall man came back into the room and he explained that if we took Emily it would be kidnapping because my parents didn't have legal custody of her any more. The tall man would have no choice but to call the police, and she would be forcibly removed from us. Again. But this time my parents would be arrested. I imagined a high-speed chase down the motorway in the storm, sirens and blue lights, all of us in handcuffs, Emily dragged away screaming.

I could have run upstairs to find her and wake her and tell her that I was sorry, we'd tried. I could have started yelling so she would hear me and make her way downstairs. I could have had a tantrum on the floor until they gave my sister back. But I was a good girl and I knew that wouldn't have worked. If Jackie and Mike had no power in that stone cottage then I certainly didn't. Instead I followed them meekly out to the car and we drove back down the lethal winding road and onto the motorway towards home in the dark and the storm. At some point the three of us must have agreed not to tell Emily about that night, perhaps because it was kinder that way. She was legally trapped there for the next two years.

The school had told us to give it time, to wait and see. But waiting and seeing can feel impossible when you've all been through so much with no good outcomes, only failed psychiatric hospitals and schools that either swallowed Emily or singled her out for bullying. There was nowhere at those places for Emily to feel safe.

Our main family activity, apart from the TV, had always been card and board games. Newmarket, canasta, pontoon (played for matchsticks or marbles rather than money), lengthy sessions of Scrabble and the classic Chinese tile game mah-jong. Jackie would clear the big table of everything but the ashtray while we'd bring in chairs from the kitchen, then the four of us would set up the game and spend entire evenings or afternoons playing together.

We played so often Mike made custom boards. He had started keeping all of the matches he and Jackie used to light their cigarettes. He painstakingly cut the heads off all of them and made an intricate parquet Scrabble board for our family games. It took him months, a work of art and patience. He let me and Emily help glue the matches together, and paint the squares with Humbrol enamels in shades of red and blue before varnishing the whole. For mah-jong, he made a wooden display board depicting the 'winds', points of the compass that dictate various aspects of the game, and Jackie had carefully painted the letters N, E, S, W above each, a demonstration of how much we valued our family gaming sessions.

Emily's house parents didn't play board games with her. Instead, they took her out. To local classical-music concerts, weekend trips to London to the Proms, the National Portrait Gallery and the Victoria and Albert Museum. They took her to the ballet, and visited the *Cutty Sark*. She was having swimming lessons, and there was already talk of her taking her first piano grade. Emily wanted to be an artist, so she was given lessons in watercolour, oil, pottery and woodworking. Just like at home, her curiosity was nurtured. But unlike at home, her resources seemed unlimited. At the psychiatric hospital and pupil referral unit she had been one of the youngest children, but now she was one of the oldest and fell into a big-sister role with the children who shared her new home. So she started to build a family.

9

THIS SPRING DAY IN 1988 is a jubilant one. My sister has completed her first term at the new school and is coming home for the holidays. Somehow, miraculously, she is happy. Her school phobia has gone. She is learning new skills. She still hates maths but no one makes her feel stupid for not knowing an answer. There are problems – some of the other kids are disruptive, sometimes aggressive, and she misses her old life and family. She had told me that one of the girls deliberately urinated on another girl's teddy bear and duvet in revenge after an argument. I cried when she told me, thinking of my own beloved orange bear that Emily had made for me out of an old dress. I couldn't conceive of such cruelty or spite, or that something similar might be done to Emily's favourite Garfield plush that our parents had saved up to buy. But there's an older boy in the village she likes, and her house parents treat her like an adult. There are still a few rainclouds in the sky but it's going to be okay.

I'm newly twelve, only a year away from being a teenager, although I'm in thrall to Emily's fourteen-year-old wisdom, desperate to be as grown-up as she seems. Every book she reads at school, I read too. *The Catcher in the Rye, The Chrysalids, Of Mice and Men, One Day in the Life of Ivan*

Denisovich. She is learning *The Rime of the Ancient Mariner* so I try to learn it too. 'It is an ancient mariner, and he stoppeth one of three.' I love how the words sound without really understanding them and want in on the secrets hidden behind unfamiliar language. One terrible act, the poem tries to say, can change the course of your life for ever. I take the Albatross too literally, even as Emily explains it to me on one of her weekends at home.

When she was away in hospital, we had relied on writing letters, and we have taken up the practice again to bridge the distance. In her letters she dispenses advice and adolescent gossip; in mine I draw stupid pictures, relay the plot of *Neighbours*, and write poems to make her laugh. I turn the shame of her situation into a boast, telling my friends that my sister is at boarding school. If they think we're rich, that's their problem. I never say otherwise, would never admit she was removed from our home or that my parents were threatened with arrest. Why would I say, 'My sister is in care,' when I could say, 'My sister is at boarding school'? One of those is aspirational and full of adventure, like the posh families in an Enid Blyton book.

Emily and I giggle in the back seat of Bernice's little car as rain speckles the windows and the traffic moves slowly. Our grandmother is driving us back from collecting Emily from school, a hundred-and-fifty-mile round trip. We are dropped off in the car park by early evening, tired but excited, happy to be home to Mike. My dad had, after years of living in a house of religion, recently agreed to become a born-again Christian too. He had been baptized in the same pool as the rest of us, and has taken to carrying a pocket version of the New Testament. He has a new job and has applied for a government grant to set up his own computing business. He has also just shaved off his moustache, which pleases Jackie immensely. She recently started working part-time at the community centre, easing some money worries.

My sister is home, her school problems solved. The holidays stretch out before us. We have found a community and answers from the church. God is finally smiling on us. Such an atmosphere calls for celebration.

All good celebrations involve food, and for us a real treat meant a takeaway, because we usually couldn't afford them. Jackie could feed us for a week for the same price as one fast-food family meal. McDonald's was a mystical paradise (I'd heard that if you had your birthday party there, the birthday girl was allowed to go into the kitchen and make her own cheeseburger). Meals at home were designed for value. Usually, Jackie cooked from scratch, but the most memorable meals were the most convenient. Instant mash (I loved the Smash aliens from the adverts, so begged her to buy it, much to her disgust) and tinned hot-dog sausages, sometimes a Fray Bentos pie and homemade chips (never oven chips: Jackie's pride wouldn't allow that, even after the chip pan and faulty cooker set the kitchen on fire). It isn't easy to be an adventurous cook on a budget. If you risk something new and no one likes it, there's nothing else to offer instead.

Mike's tastes were less domestic. He had a shelf full of fascinating spices with which, a few times a year, he would make a powerful beef curry from a recipe he'd learned overseas. I loved helping him prepare it. It was rare that he could afford the meat, so it became an event in itself. I'd stand by his side as he cut the beef into small cubes. We'd both eat one raw, then he'd brown the meat as he carefully measured a teaspoon of turmeric, a tablespoon of chilli, a pinch of this or that, like an arcane potion. He let me throw in the cardamom pods and press the special plastic and wire gadget to neatly slice a hardboiled egg, which he'd carefully arrange on top. The resulting curry was his special treat to himself, far too spicy for the rest of us. He'd sit in the living room over the steaming bowl, bread in one hand and a handkerchief in the other to mop the sweat from his bald head as he ate, a pint of iced cider on the table. I would hover by the arm of the settee, waiting to be invited to have a taste of vindaloo, then dance about in delicious pain until he let me have a sip of cold cider too.

But tonight, no one is cooking. We're celebrating with a chippy dinner. Mike is going to drive to the town centre: there's a chip shop there that Emily is particularly keen on, and it's her special day. Jackie gives him some money from her purse. Chips have always been the cheapest option for takeaway, plentiful and filling. I ask to go with him, some father-daughter time. A drive into town to the chippy with my dad would be awesome, but for some reason he doesn't want me to come. I plead, pout; he refuses. I'm overstimulated by the day's excitement so I get angry and upset at perceived injustice, the beginning of a tantrum I'm probably too old for. But I really want to go with him. He still says no, and as he walks down the hall, opens the front door and leaves, I follow him and shout, 'I hate you!' I kick the front door in temper, but the reinforced dimpled glass can take it. His figure is distorted, a blurry shadow in a blue jumper, as I watch him walk down the path and out of the gate.

Emily cheers me up with her attention. We have so much to tell each other. As she's letting me in on her teen-age secrets and sharing the in-jokes and drama of her new schoolmates, and Jackie is in the living room watching TV, the phone rings. It's Mike. He says the queue at the chip shop in town was too long so he's driven back to our estate and is calling from the public phone box at the local shops. He tells Jackie to get the plates and chopsticks ready because he's splashed out and ordered an expensive Chinese takeaway. He's popping to the pub for a quick drink before heading home. Of *course*. A quick drink with the change from the money Jackie gave him is likely why he didn't want me tagging along in the first place. Quick drinks had, with my dad and with many drinkers before him, a habit of turning into long ones. 'I got chatting to a mate,' and suddenly it's hours later and his eyes are glazed and his pores leak booze. But surely not tonight: there's a family toast to be made at home. To the Kings, glasses clink for good luck. A quick drink.

Too much time passes.

Emily and I are in my parents' bedroom because it's the only one in the house with a view of the back car park. The bed is neatly made and covered with a frilly counter-pane. The pillowcases don't match, and neither does the furniture, but that doesn't matter. Everything is clean and neat. There is a small bookcase containing my dad's Ian Fleming novels, his copy of *The Hitchhiker's Guide to the Galaxy*, *A Clockwork Orange*, and Jackie's Anne McCaffrey fantasy books. On top of the bookcase is a glass bowl of red artificial roses. He buys her a new one every year on their wedding anniversary and she trims the wire stem and adds it to the bowl. Next to the roses is a small teddy bear named Lost-and-Found, one of the only things Jackie has kept from my babyhood. I dropped him from my pushchair one day and he was missing for a long time, then turned up at the local supermarket, sitting on the till, waiting to be claimed. She thought this made him special, renamed him Lost-and-Found, and gave him pride of place long after I'd grown out of everything else.

Emily and I are looking out of the window. If Mike parks there on his return, rather than in the car park at the front, we'll see him arrive. Our estate is a labyrinth, full of alleys (in the Midlands we say 'gullies') and dead ends. It's difficult for visitors to find our house, but it's great for playing hide-and-seek. It's dark by now, and Mike is really late, but it's not the first time and I don't feel as uneasy as I should. I'm too happy that Emily is back, my earlier tantrum forgotten. Of course I hadn't meant it when I said, 'I hate you.' I hope he knows that. I'm looking forward to his return so I can say sorry. I'm on the left, leaning on the windowsill. Emily is on the right, close to me, sisters chatting and watching and waiting. Then, suddenly, something different.

'A panda car!' I say. I'd recently learned that phrase and was excited to have a reason to use it. Perhaps Emily would be impressed. Perhaps she hadn't heard it before and I'd get to explain that 'panda car' is another name for 'police car', because they're black and white (although in reality they were blue and orange and white). It feels cute and good to say. Panda car, like cellar door or 'stoppeth one of three'. The panda car pulls up in the communal car park below us and a uniformed officer gets out. I watch him look around. He's probably looking for one of the houses opposite, one of the problem families. Not our family – we have no problems today.

We watch the police officer walk down the narrow path behind our row of back gardens and disappear from view. It takes about three minutes to walk from the back of our houses, down the gully, and around to the front. Three minutes for the officer to disappear out of sight and memory. Emily and I carry on talking about our day, our lives, our futures. Three minutes of hope. Three minutes of being children. Three minutes pass by, the rest of my life. There's a loud knock at the front door.

We didn't always have a telephone. It was part of the feast-or-famine nature of our existence – when Mike had a job, the council-installed cream-coloured rotary phone would be reconnected, sitting neatly on a crocheted doily on a little table at the foot of the stairs. Jackie would ring round everyone to give them the new number. Once, when I was bored, I sat on the bottom stair and told Jackie, 'I want the phone to ring.' It rang. Jackie was shocked, delighted, then suspicious I had some sort of extra-sensory perception. I thought I did too, in the same way I could make the traffic lights change or intuit the contents of a Kinder Surprise. After that, I tried to make the phone ring at will but never quite had the right magic thoughts or connection. It remained a tantalizing possibility.

The home phone was an essential connection to Emily, to family, to my best friend Michelle, whom I would call after school every day, much to Jackie's annoyance. 'You've just spent the day together,' she would say, warning me about the bill. If we hadn't had a phone, Mike wouldn't have been able to call from a phone box to say he was running late and would be home soon. If we hadn't had a phone, Jackie wouldn't have been able to call the men in the church frantically to see if any of them could come and collect us and drive us to the hospital.

'There's been an accident, Mrs King. Your husband has collapsed.'

The police officer at the door is a hundred feet tall. Emily and I stand behind Jackie in the doorway as he explains that he can't fit us all in the panda car: was there anyone who could drive us to the hospital, perhaps a neighbour or friend? Jackie makes several calls and I don't understand how any of them can say no, but they do. I feel panic rising as she rings everyone she can think of. Perhaps those she calls don't want to leave the house on a dark rainy evening, perhaps they don't realize that Mike being in hospital is serious. Perhaps they don't want to get involved; maybe they assume he's collapsed in a drunken state and the whole thing is his own fault. We silently consider that too, even though he isn't the sort of alcoholic who collapses. Eventually she calls Margaret, whose husband says, yes, he'll come and collect us and drive us to the hospital.

We are given our own waiting room. It has half a dozen hard plastic orange chairs. I sit on one next to Emily. My feet don't reach the floor. Jackie paces. A doctor arrives and gently explains that Mike had collapsed and an ambulance had brought him in. He is on life support. I've seen that on TV shows like *Casualty*, tubes and machines and beeping. I imagine my dad in a hospital bed, a green line going up and down on a screen. The beeping means he's alive – it's the sound of his heart beating. If there's life support, there must be life.

There are five main reasons why someone might suddenly collapse in a life-endangering way, and most of them are to do with the heart. The most common is heart arrhythmia, which can have many causes, from disease to drug overdose. Sometimes the person has no prior symptoms; they simply collapse and, in the majority of cases, die. The next is acute myocardial infarction, or heart attack, where blockages in the arteries stop oxygen reaching the heart. Then there's pulmonary embolism, a massive blood clot travelling to an artery in the lung that stops the heart pumping blood. The final heart problem is aortic catastrophe, in which a growing aneurysm finally ruptures.

Aneurysm. Funny word to learn at twelve, or ever. It's a bulge in a blood vessel, and it can kill you. Such a little thing can stop your heart, and more. The fifth reason someone might collapse as Mike did is a problem with the brain.

'We believe he had a brain aneurysm,' or words to that effect. The doctor is trying to tell us that something in Mike's brain has gone randomly, badly wrong. It can happen, he says. People walk around with a little bomb in their head for years, unknowing, until suddenly it explodes and the person collapses. I imagine a cartoon bomb with a lit fuse slowly burning in my dad's head, until one day – today – it goes *boom*. Do I have one too?

'Is he going to wake up?' I say. I don't ask if he's going to die because my dad can't die. That isn't in my worldview.

The doctor speaks in a kind but sad tone, his words clear and frank. The chances of recovery are slim, he tells us. If Mike does wake up, he will likely have brain damage, may be in a vegetative state for ever. This is surely impossible. My brilliant, clever, funny, kind father. I imagine him in a wheelchair, drooling, being spoon-fed, not knowing who we are, in pain he can't articulate. My heart breaks as I pray and pray for him to wake up and be fine. I know God doesn't just grant life or death for the asking, but I also know that when miracles and good things happen, we give credit to God, so clearly he does intervene when it suits. I just need to pray hard enough, to ask in the right way.

The doctor hands me a clear plastic bag containing the black leather wallet Mike was carrying. A gesture for the little girl. Inside are an expired bus pass, a BT phone card, his driving licence, some bus tickets, a plastic ID card from an old employer, an Amstrad business card, and an organ donor card. His precious things, which he won't need during his stay in hospital. I should look after them for when he gets home. He'll be proud of me for taking good care of them. It'll make up for the argument we had.

There's a payphone in the hospital. Jackie calls Bernice and Symon, who set out immediately. Then Mike's sister Sarah, who lives in the next town. She isn't at home. By coincidence she's staying with Mike's parents on the coast, so Jackie calls them and they begin the long journey through the night to join us. At some point Bernice and Symon arrive, and Jackie is taken to see Mike. She won't let us see him, says it would be too upsetting, because of the tubes and the machines and the beeping. Life support is traumatic. There's nothing for Emily and me to do but wait. So we wait, and I pray, and at some point well past midnight Symon takes the two of us away. I don't want to leave Jackie but she's in another world now. An adults-only world, serious and whispered above our heads, where our usual family hugs and jokes won't make everything magically okay again.

10

T HE NEXT MORNING, EMILY and I were at our grand-parents', waiting for the phone to ring. Jackie was at the hospital with Adam the minister. We were hoping she would call and say Mike had woken up and was asking for us, he was okay, we could go and see him. When the phone eventually rang, Bernice answered. She talked to Jackie for a while, then put the phone down and faced us, shaken and crying.

'The doctors have asked your mom for permission to turn off life support. They said your dad is brain dead. He isn't going to wake up.'

Brain dead. I was numb with shock. Then I heard a strange, unrecognizable noise. My granddad was crying, a choking hiccup, until Bernice, also in shock, shouted, 'Stop it, Symon,' in a desperate attempt to arrest the grief and potential hysteria in the room.

I wish I had been with Jackie when she had to make that decision, to support her and to say goodbye to Mike. I wanted to deliver that overdue apology and take back my last words to him, even though he wouldn't have heard me. But she could barely handle the trauma of the tubes and machines, couldn't even bring herself to describe them. She wanted to protect her children from what she had seen, and felt strongly that we would be better off if our last memories of him were as he was in life.

But my last memories of him were arguing, shouting, resenting him for a split second. I did not say a nice goodbye, I said I hated him. But I understand why Jackie didn't want us to see him in the hospital bed, and I didn't resist when she said no. I can't claim it would have helped to see him, regardless of what I wish in hindsight. I simply do not know.

Instead I imagined what the life-support room looked like, what they did to the machine when they switched it off. The beeping green line on a screen, then one long final *beeeeeep* and the line goes flat. I knew Jackie sat with him, held his hand, kissed his cheek and said goodbye. He would have been kept on life support while some of his organs were removed for donation. His body needed to be 'alive' for that, but once those organs were gone, there was no coming back, no miraculous waking up.

At the time, I didn't know enough to visualize in what way the machines had been keeping his heart going, his blood flowing. There wasn't anyone to ask. I know now that life support isn't a single machine but a system. There would have been a ventilator, a tube through his nose or mouth that pushes air into the lungs. Inflate, deflate. The body is breathing but the oxygen that usually keeps the brain functioning isn't needed, because his brain is already dead.

At twelve years old, I understood brain death as a simple concept. His body was working mechanically but his brain had stopped, and the brain is where thought resides. The power had been cut off, like when our electricity meter ran out, but there was no way back, no way of putting more fifty-pence coins in the slot. I accepted this, though I was often troubled about whether they – the medics – might have been wrong. What if we'd waited, and some signs of brain function had returned? What if he was conscious the whole time, internally shouting to be heard? What if he might have simply woken up again, as if from one of his migraines, and been absolutely fine? I didn't want to ask.

But brain death is not a simple concept. It's an old idea, but has a relatively recent (and evolving) definition in medicine, politics and law. It became a necessary diagnosis once organ transplant became viable in the mid-1960s. Doctors needed a legal threshold, a way of saying that the patient cannot breathe without ventilation, and the organs are artificially receiving oxygen and blood flow. If there is also no measurable brain activity, and patients with this history do not recover, then death could be called while blood still flows.

In her 2021 book *Mr Humble & Dr Butcher*, the author Brandy Schillace wrote:

> You are your brain, while yet it lives. A dead brain, floating in solution, is an inanimate thing, bloodless and no more alive than the scalpel that cuts it into pieces. A brain suffused with blood and oxygen and sending signals to the EEG – that is a living and thinking brain. We can tell the living from the dead. But where is the fine and subtle line between one state and the other?

In 1988 that line was broader, but Mike had to be on one side of it or the other. It wasn't a coin toss, the diagnostic tests aren't guesswork, but it was a troubling thought, that in-between state where the body breathes via a machine while the brain has simply stopped. When, I wondered, did he ascend to Heaven? When the ticking time bomb went off, or when the life support was stopped? Did the soul reside in the brain or the heart? Or in every aspect of the body?

We consoled ourselves that he would live on through organ transplants. Jackie said signing the form was one of the hardest moments of her life because it was so final, so gruesome, but she wasn't conflicted. 'It would change other people's lives,' she said. 'I was sitting by your dad's bed holding his hand, still in shock, numb. He was warm, so still felt alive, but I knew it was the machine keeping him that way.'

Mike had always carried the small red and blue card emblazoned with 'I would like to help someone to live after my death', although the hospital still needed family consent. His corneas and kidneys were removed for donation, along with some skin for burns patients. A few days later a local paper ran a front-page story of a teenager's last-minute kidney transplant, which Jackie called a miracle.

In the back of Bernice's car, I leaned against the window and watched drops of rain chase each other down the glass. Emily was next to me, but we were silent as the car sped down the motorway. I was alone inside my head in a new, permanent way. I could feel myself looking out of my own eyes, as if my body, which had changed too, was no longer my business. My chest and throat were a solid mass and tension had entered every muscle. My stomach was a thunderstorm. I wanted to cry but shock doesn't always cry. Sometimes it waits.

We got home to Jackie. People came and went; none of them was my dad. It got dark. That night, Emily and I moved into our parents' room, me on a camping bed and Emily on a single mattress on the floor. There was just enough room for us all.

And then it was morning.

It was a sunny day, no sign of rain. People continued to come and go. Church, neighbours, family. Adults wanting details. I heard the same words over and over. Brain aneurysm, ticking time bomb, life-support machine, the end. The front door stayed open because it was too stressful to keep getting up to answer it. Everyone's movements were slow, their tones hushed, like I'd noticed at funerals. The smoke from their cigarettes stayed still in the air. Then suddenly the atmosphere shifted as Shannon, a friend of Emily's, ran breathlessly into the house with urgent news. At the shops where Mike had collapsed there was now a police crime scene. We looked at each other. Jackie agreed we could go but told us to come straight back.

Emily, Shannon and I approached the shopping centre, past the pub, to the open courtyard with shops alongside. I had seen this view my entire life. The red-brick pavement, people coming and going, the telephone boxes where Mike had made his call. These were now cordoned off in a wide area by blue-and-white police tape, like yet another scene from TV. A single uniformed police officer stood guard, and I suddenly realized that Mike's death was public. People could see the police cordon and would be gossiping, maybe even enjoying the drama, as I might have if it was someone else's problem.

Shannon and Emily hung back, nervous and unsure, but I wanted to get answers. The police cordon was clearly my personal business and I had a right to ask questions. The police officer was intimidating, but I confidently approached him and tried to summon an assertive voice. 'Excuse me, can you tell me what's going on here?'

'What have you heard?' he asked carefully.

'All I know is my dad collapsed here the other night and now there's this.'

'Ah,' he said, crouching to my height, his tone shifting into kindness. 'Well, we're just trying to find out what happened, see if anyone saw anything.' Or something like that. He didn't tell me much and I was new at being in charge so didn't know what else to ask.

The three of us headed home. When we arrived, there were two strangers in the house.

PART TWO

11

THE DETECTIVE CHIEF INSPECTOR had a moustache, a Welsh accent, and the largest beer belly I had ever seen. He sat imposingly on the faded brown settee next to Jackie, while his younger colleague stood near the door as though guarding it, although in reality it was because our living room was small and there wasn't really anywhere else to stand. DCI Burns explained that things were not as straightforward as the hospital had first thought. While we had been coming to terms with a random 'ticking time bomb' – a brain aneurysm in Mike's head that chose that particular moment to explode – the police had learned that it wasn't so random, after all. My dad's death was being investigated as a murder.

All police leave had been cancelled, and there seemed to be some sort of manhunt under way. I'd had a day of processing a random, natural but cruel death from a brain aneurysm, just one of those things that happen. No one had been to blame; nothing could have been done to stop it. His brain, the brain I loved so much, had simply failed. But now there was a detective chief inspector on the side of the settee where Mike usually sat, telling us that the police believed someone *was* to blame. That it wasn't an unavoidable natural death at all, but that someone had had enough malice and hate to hurt him deliberately.

Who would want to kill my dad? Why would anyone want to kill my dad?

The answer was as unexpected as a brain aneurysm.

FIVE QUIZZED ON BODY

Five youths were being questioned today by detectives investigating the death of a father-of-two, Mr Michael King, aged 45, whose body was found outside a telephone box.

He was taken to the nearby hospital and died 24 hours later.

Around 15 CID officers have been investigating the death and police have appealed for the public to come forward with information.

Yesterday four youths aged 14 to 16 were helping with inquiries into Mr King's death and today a fifth youth of the same age was also being questioned.

Chief Inspector Burns said: 'We would ask anyone who might have seen an incident outside a kiosk in the shopping centre to contact us.'

He said that there were not expected to be any developments in the inquiry until the results of a post-mortem examination were known, possibly later today.

Neighbour Mrs Linda Brown, aged 48, said Mr King was 'a man who would not harm anyone'.

His wife Jackie and their two children, Emilia, aged 14, and Tracey, 11, were being comforted by relatives.

Local newspapers were essential for communities like ours. We tutted over nearby crime or gossip, felt impressed when someone we knew was 'in the paper' and desperately hoped to be in it ourselves for some merit or other. Jackie had been once, the story about the housewife poet with agoraphobia, and Emily and I had had a moment of shining glory as little girls when a photo of us was used to illustrate a story. Bernice and Jackie had taken us to a summer fête in Birmingham and the local paper had asked if the two cute little girls could pose for a photo. The clipping had been pasted into the family album, an adorable black-and-white picture of the two of us, aged six and four, in matching chunky knitted cardigans, concentrating on pouring tea from a children's tea set into tiny toy cups. Being in the paper was a marvel, something rare to be proud of, as though that aspect of our lives – the poetry, the fête – were special enough to be cemented not just in our memories but in everyone's. Newsworthy, history-worthy, the local paper was the whole world. Now here we all were in solid black print again, in archives for ever, indelible. *Mr Michael King, aged 45, whose body was found outside a telephone box.* It must be true because it was in the newspaper. But he wasn't forty-five, he was forty-four. They had spelled Emily's and my names wrong. I wasn't eleven, I was twelve, and those small things meant a lot. The newspaper article wasn't about my family at all, but was some error-ridden copy, a flawed impression of us told by a neighbour.

But other words were true. Mike would not have harmed anyone, as the neighbour said, and we were indeed being 'comforted' by relatives, a polite euphemism for the oddly toned practical support that only appears in a crisis. Endless offers of cups of tea represent caring, sandwiches 'you must eat' but no one is offended when you do not, the circusful of elephants that fill every silence in every room Mike was ever in. Relatives putting aside their own grief to manage ours. No comfort is to be had, but it's all they can offer, and it gives them something to do when there's nothing to be done. The church told us Mike had been called to be with God, that it was his time. Thank goodness he had finally seen the light of Christianity, the last of us to be converted. His baptism would have secured the forgiveness of his sins and his place in Heaven. This was more comforting than the sandwiches and cups of tea.

Another article headlined 'YOUTHS QUIZZED ON DEATH' claimed Mike was 'found slumped outside a telephone box', a police spokesperson saying, 'We are treating this as a very suspicious incident. Four boys, aged 14 to 16, are helping us with our inquiries.'

'Helping with our inquiries' is another polite euphemism. Police had arrested a gang, first four then a fifth young man, on suspicion of murder. DCI Burns read the list of their names to see if we recognized them.

Andrew Reynolds, the oldest, was completely unknown to us.

Chris Hendon, also a name none of us knew.

Ian Barrows, whose name Emily knew from her time at middle school.

Anthony Mears, a former classmate of Emily whom we knew by sight, and . . . the final name on the list, Reece Webster, the boy who lived a few doors down. The boy Emily and I had played childhood games of Tig and Empty

Dustbin with. The boy she had accompanied to middle school the night of the terrible thunderstorm, and whose mum had been friends with Jackie. The boy who had shown me his *Star Wars* toys when Jackie popped in to borrow something. The quiet, serious, under-nourished, isolated boy with intense eyes, whom Jackie shouted at when his football accidentally hit our window. We'd had the same babysitters, had the same childhood memories. We knew him, and he knew us. And now he and his friends had been arrested for the murder of my dad.

The 'random brain aneurysm' version of Mike's death is something I might perhaps have had a chance of getting . . . if not over, then past – something tragic but just about conceivable, relatable to those who had also lost a parent to illness, eventually to be contextualized against all other death. Jackie, as vulnerable as she already was, might eventually be okay and even marry again. I would be indescribably sad but able to get my life somewhere back on the track it had been on before. But a murder is not that, not at twelve, and not without a stable environment and resources. Twelve is the perfect age to feel the full, adult force of a crime but without the emotional maturity to handle it. I was, to use an impolite euphemism, completely screwed.

DCI Burns had to take a statement from Jackie. She had been on the phone to Mike when the whole thing started, so she was considered a witness. Fragile yet certain, she insisted that Mike had sounded fine. He was happy and excited about the evening ahead, and she didn't suspect anything was wrong. She had to explain the circumstances by which he had come to be there, that she had collected her elder daughter for the holidays and the meal was to celebrate. No, he wasn't drunk when he left, she told them. She could always tell when he'd been drinking and, besides, four cans of beer in the fridge that had been there in the morning were still there on her return. Yes, he was going to pop to the pub before collecting the food: that was why he had phoned. His entire life potted into short paragraphs. What type of work he did and if he enjoyed it, whether he was a happy (sometimes), ill (often) or violent (never) type of person, what sort of swear words he used. *What*, the line of questioning seemed to imply, *did he do to deserve it?*

I got used to scouring the paper, at once desperate for and dreading any mention of Mike's name or the boys'. The following week, the local paper announced the 'youths' had been released on bail. Out on bail meant they had all gone home to our estate. The four youngest attended high school, a bus ride away, while I was in my penultimate year of middle school. But as Reece Webster lived a few doors down, and the rest not too far away, the chances of bumping into one of them were high. There was no avoiding the shops, the phone box, any more than we could avoid the whispering and gossip. This was a public crime, the victim and perpetrators known to everyone. Except us. Jackie and I had no idea what three of the five youths looked like. We could have passed them anytime. Every white teenage boy in a tracksuit jacket could have been one of them, every innocent group of lads the murderous gang. I memorized the list of five names, not out of any fantasy-fiction notion of revenge but because it was all I knew about them.

Andrew Reynolds
Reece Webster
Chris Hendon
Anthony Mears
Ian Barrows

They were now the main characters in my life story. DCI Burns returned and told us what he believed happened that night, a story pieced together from theory and witnesses:

It's a few steps to the garden gate, the one Mike built himself with wood salvaged from pallets. He carefully closes the gate behind him and walks to the car park. His eldest daughter is home from school, and his small family is together for the first time in a long time. He is a family man. A good father. A loyal husband. As a neighbour would shortly remark to a journalist, he would not harm anyone.

He drives first to the town centre some miles away, but finding the queue to the chip shop too long, returns to the estate shops, a twenty-pound note in his wallet. He is going to buy a pint of beer in the pub next to the Chinese takeaway. He is in the pub a great deal because, before everything else, before family, he is a drinker. It's not his fault. He's an addict. He has tried to quit, switched to alcohol-free lager, joined and failed to attend Alcoholics Anonymous. He is usually found sitting in the same seat in the pub's lounge, a comfortable padded bench by the window. Sometimes he drinks alone, sometimes he is joined by friends. He knows everyone, and everyone likes him.

Tonight, though, his drinking must be swift because he has a celebratory takeaway to buy and a family to get home to. The twenty-pound note was given to him by his wife from her purse, to buy the takeaway food from her housekeeping money. He has no money of his own because he tends to spend it on alcohol, so he gives what money he has to Jackie to look after. Mike had recently found work as a computer salesman after another long period of unemployment, and the family no longer has to live on benefits. The car is not new, but it's new to him, a perk of the job. He has also applied for a new government scheme, a small-business grant to set up his own computing business, and expects to hear any day now. He parks up, heads to the takeaway and places the order, telling the couple who run the place that he'll be back in half an hour. Enough time for a quick drink.

Because of the drink in the pub, it becomes necessary for Mike to call his wife and say he's running a little late but is on his way. The public phone box is a little further up than both the pub and the Chinese takeaway, and to get there he passes a low red-brick wall, which tonight is occupied by a gang of five teenage boys. This wall is often a congregating point for the local bored youths, who don't really have anywhere else to go, including their own homes. They're not welcome anywhere. There's nothing to do and no money to do it with, so they entertain themselves. They might even be drunk, or smoking weed.

Mike gets to the phone box and fishes around in his wallet for a prepaid phone card. He dials his home number, and after a few rings, his wife answers.

The five boys on the wall notice Mike using the phone. At thirteen, Reece Webster is the youngest and knows the King family. The other boys, although local, do not know Mike at all. Despite this, the five of them begin taunting the man using the phone, 'taking the mickey'. Mocking him, the things gangs of boys mock adults for because adults are the enemy. While he's on the phone, the boys continue their taunts, and this angers him, although he says nothing about that to his wife.

Mike is not a violent man, he is a kind and Christian man, and he has an opportunity to set these wayward boys right. He goes over to talk to them. He recognizes Reece as the neighbour's son. The oldest of the gang – the ringleader, Andrew – is seventeen and from the privately owned part of the housing development. The younger boys want to impress him. Andrew does martial arts, karate, and this is obviously very cool. He is keen to show off, but Mike also knows martial arts. At home Mike has what most people call nunchucks, a pair of rubber batons linked by a thick chain. His daughters like to play with them, and he has shown them defensive moves, making them promise never to touch the weapon if he's not at home. To make sure, he keeps it stashed out of reach in the top of the wardrobe.

But at seventeen Andrew isn't so much a child, he's the ringleader of a gang, and Mike isn't thinking of safety. As their banter about martial arts turns personal, the two exchange strong words. Mike is offended. The four younger boys goad their older friend to have the last word, the last move. To win. In an instant of bravado, Andrew stands on the low red-brick wall and jumps, landing an expert karate chop to the back of Mike's head.

The blow is severe enough to cause instant brain death. Mike falls to the cold brick pavement. A moment of shock and guilt passes through the five boys like electricity. Without pausing to see if the man needs help, they flee.

12

DCI BURNS VISITED A few more times. He told us that the boys were insisting they were innocent and were now at risk of local vigilante justice. Anthony Mears had been cornered outside the pub and threatened by 'friends of Mike'. I didn't want anyone to harm them; I wanted proper justice, through the court. How would more violence help anything? I was disgusted by the eye-for-an-eye mentality, which was too Old Testament for me, and felt even more unsafe.

The shopping centre became a malicious, malevolent place that held in the air the potential for more violence alongside the empty space where Mike's body had lain, but there was no way of avoiding it. Our church met at the local community centre a few steps from the phone box. The GP's surgery and my school were over the road, the pharmacy where Jackie would collect her brand-new prescription for tranquillizers was just behind the brick wall from where the gang, we were told, had launched their attack. We had nowhere else to shop, to get a haircut or a dental check-up. The estate had been designed around the small shopping centre, to provide all the everyday amenities families would need, with no alternative if one of you is killed in the middle of it all.

For my entire life up to that point, Jackie had been unable to leave the house alone unless it was for a safe and familiar route. Now, there was no such thing. She would not be going anywhere on her own, perhaps ever again. Her worst nightmare, the one that fuelled her agoraphobia and anxiety, had always been that something terrible would happen. Now it had. She'd been proved right. The world, even the most familiar neighbourhood, was capable of great evil. It felt like Satan's work, even while a church elder told us about the vision he'd had of Mike being led to a seat in Heaven, next to Jesus himself. 'You know Mike,' he'd said, 'he was being his usual humble self, saying not to make all that fuss for him, surprised he was important enough to sit next to the Lord.' This vision was beautiful, visual, had the ring of truth, and was deeply reassuring, as it was designed to be.

The first few weeks after Mike's death were mainly handled by the church and family, particularly my auntie Sarah, whom I hadn't seen much of over the years. For whatever complex reasons, Mike hadn't been close to his family, but now his sister was in our house constantly, bustling and rallying and taking care of Jackie, like she'd stepped into my dad's place. There was always someone in the house, bringing food or news. A bag of home-grown tomatoes, a cake, puzzle books or comics, kind little gestures. Our neighbours were as poor as us, so their contribution was mostly company. The church had a whip-round and one night posted an envelope through our door with eighty pounds in cash inside.

I spent my time reading or napping or playing on the Amstrad computer that belonged to my dad's employer.

Jackie wasn't yet as heavily sedated as she would be soon, and 'keeping busy' was the go-to remedy for managing mental health.

One afternoon, she was gripped suddenly with an urgent need to do something. She took me for a walk around the estate, knocking on the doors of everyone she could think of, the few mates of Mike whose names but not phone numbers she knew, to tell them he had died. Some had heard already via the papers or gossip, but others had not and she had to repeat, 'I'm sorry to tell you Mike died.' Each time, she recounted what we'd been told so far. The life-support machine, the gang, the arrests. She answered the same questions over and over. No, there was no date for the funeral yet, there was going to be an inquest first, it could be months. No, we didn't need anything, thank you, we had everything we needed, just wanted to let you know. Yes, the police were being very good. Thank you for the kind words. As she told and retold the story, a murder mystery pieced together from scraps, she moulded her words into satisfying phrases as I'd heard her do with other family anecdotes many times before. She was a natural storyteller, and while there was nothing enjoyable about this particular tale, she seemed to derive comfort or control from giving it narrative form.

For my part, I didn't know how to cope with any of my feelings, and neither did I know how to cope with the feelings of my remaining family and the effects of Mike's death on them.

Nobody is immune to death or the effects of death. There's no vaccine or cure. We are all going to die and we are all going to lose someone we care about. The human condition is fatal. But I would rather not have learned this lesson at twelve, and I fell into a serious and angry depression. It's not that I wanted to die, more that I just wanted to stop. I felt furious, rebellious and frustrated at not being heard or understood. More of an animalistic scream than a cry, and I wanted it to end.

I thought about death constantly, until it seemed like a place I could go too. I would lie awake replaying the dramatic scene of my dad's death, as vivid as if it was my own memory and not just a theatrical tableau conjured from a story heard via unreliable narrators. I thought about Andrew jumping off that wall, hand flat in the air in a karate-chop pose, body frozen in mid-air.

In the imagined death scene, Andrew is about to land the blow on the back of Mike's head. His four friends are frozen, each with a different pose but all cheering him on, or sometimes just sitting meekly, silent, still observers.

And Mike, where was he? If Andrew's blow had landed on the back of his head . . . was my dad walking away? I didn't know where to put him in the scene. He couldn't be cowering under the incoming rain of blows because, according to the hospital and Jackie, he appeared unharmed, which was why they thought it was an aneurysm. But if he was walking away . . . if he was done with those stupid boys, and was walking away from them and home to us . . . No, that was too much to imagine. Neither my heart nor my head could cope with that, so I would just imagine him standing there, arms by his sides. Neutral, emotionless, like a mannequin. Neither drunkenly happy nor sad at his impending death, the dad in my tableau was just a placeholder for the real thing. Andrew was real, though, and the frozen moment of the scene flashes into life as he lands his blow and my dad crumples to the ground. The four friends stand up quickly, and Andrew . . . does what? I didn't know, would never know.

I had heard a rumour that they fled the scene on bikes. That was the cruelty I struggled with most. Sometimes I tried to follow them as they left, but that meant leaving Mike behind on the cold brick pavement outside the phone box, alone. Better not to think about that so much. In my head, he wasn't dead yet: that didn't truly happen until the life support stopped. Children understand that you're alive until your heart stops beating. That is the moment the soul leaves the body. It makes sense to think that, as the heart is the most romanticized organ. Love resides there, as does the pain of losing a loved one. If his heart still beats, my dad must still be alive. But now that I knew there was such a thing as brain death, which were his final moments of life?

My sleepless imagination would switch to the hospital, where his heart was beating but his brain – and therefore he – was dead. But I didn't see him there either. The sights and sounds, colours and tone of his body on life support in intensive care were difficult to imagine, but I imagined them anyway. I knew they were not memories, but they were the next closest thing.

And then I couldn't supplement any more details of his death because I had nothing else to base a scene on, so I'd go back to the beginning, outside that phone box on the cold brick path. Maybe this time I'd change a detail, a pose, a facial expression. Maybe Andrew was more jokey this time, or more drunk, or his gang more taunting. Maybe Mike was angrier, maybe strong words were exchanged.

The one constant was that single karate-chop blow, landing on the back of my dad's head. I'd replay that moment over and over until, eventually, it became the back of *my* head, and I would clench my entire body in anticipation of the blow, prepared for instant blackness. Andrew landing his blow on the back of my neck would end the intrusive thought, until it started again.

I had told the doctor I couldn't sleep, although I didn't mention the obsessive repeating of violent images all night, and he had given me sleeping pills.

I didn't like taking them, not wanting to put anything mood-altering into my body. If you get drunk or do drugs, you lose control and someone will die, I reasoned. I believed the gang had been doing exactly that, so I needed to remain hyper-vigilant at all times, ready to run or help if needed. Pills had sedated Jackie, so one of us needed to stay mentally clear, on watch for the family. I didn't want to take anything that might dull my senses or make me anything like that gang of boys.

But that was calm me. Angry me had no control whatsoever and became hysterical over the tiniest things. Jackie and I would have a disagreement about something and suddenly I was screaming and desperately gasping for breath just to scream some more. It felt like the whole of my brain had turned to pitch-black liquid, boiling and steaming and spitting pure rage at whoever was in my way. During one such episode, I ran upstairs, grabbed my sleeping pills from the floor of Jackie's bedroom where I spent my nights, and sank down in the corner between her bed and the bookcase, sobbing desperately.

She came to find me immediately and prised the open

bottle of pills out of my hand, screaming, 'Did you take them?' I refused to tell her. Even in my rage and grief I realized I wanted her to think I had. She was in hysterics herself then, and our roles shifted. I had the power. I told her I hadn't taken any pills. They were still in the bottle and the extreme frustration that had driven the whole awful thing was gone. I was just left exhausted and over-whelmed by the guilt of my newly widowed mom thinking, however briefly, that her child had wanted to die too.

This was the beginning of my demonic possession.

13

OUR ESTATE LACKED A graveyard. A modern purpose-built church had sprung up at the same time as the shops, and our own church met at the community centre, but there was no place for a Christian burial. A few miles outside the estate, towards the countryside, a tiny village church had stood since the thirteenth century. I'd visited it on a school trip a few years before, had been petrified of the rumoured ghosts in the nave.

Sitting at Mike's funeral on the front pew of that church a month after his death, the hard wood uncomfortable and the air full of the same damp, musty smell found in old bookshops, I looked at the closed coffin and wondered why I wasn't crying. I hadn't seen my dad's body, either at the hospital or at the mortuary where it was kept until the funeral, so had no sense of what might be inside the box. After his death Jackie had been taken by DCI Burns to see the body, and she took me with her. I sat in the quiet plush waiting room of the coroner's office while she went into another room. I imagined Mike was in his coffin in that room, dressed nicely in his funeral suit, but most likely he would have been naked on a steel table under a sheet, scarred from the organ removal. Jackie told me after

122

that she had kissed his cheek as she had done when he was on life support, but this time he was cold.

She was sitting next to me at the funeral, her hand warm in mine. The coffin was in front of us, a beautiful wreath of red roses – chosen because of the rose he bought Jackie for their anniversary every year – on top of it. Adam conducted the service, and I found it strange seeing him in another church, a 'proper' church, one with a pulpit and engravings and stained glass rather than the modern hall in which he usually preached. He was wearing a black shirt and white clerical dog-collar for once, like the sort of vicars I'd seen on TV, and I didn't know he was allowed to do that. Before the ceremony, as we gathered outside, milling as mourners do, he made me smile by showing me that his clerical collar was actually a piece of the white part of a washing-up-liquid bottle.

The mourners sang hymns that had been chosen in advance by other people because Jackie couldn't face doing it. I don't remember if I sang, although singing was usually the only bit of church I truly enjoyed. I looked at the coffin and thought so loudly I'm sure everyone heard, *Why aren't I crying? That's my dad in there.* I tried to will myself to cry, but nothing came.

I wish someone had told me it's okay not to cry at funerals. I thought I was supposed to and was distressed by my own numbness. Something must be wrong with me. But by now I had stopped crying about my dad entirely. I cried all the time about anything and everything else, but acknowledging my grief and letting it flow was too exhausting. It wasn't solely my grief, it was Jackie and

Emily's too, and we tried to hide it from each other. There was no way of saying, 'I miss him,' that wouldn't set us all off and compound the trauma threefold.

I was the youngest person at the funeral, and felt in the way, lost, without realizing everyone feels that way at funerals. Emily gravitated towards our older cousin Dani, daughter of Jackie's twin, whenever she could, and although they were both very kind to me, I still felt like the unwelcome little kid intruding on their cool teenage bond. Jackie wasn't in charge of herself that day, moving from person to person thanking them for coming – that strange version of small-talk only done at funerals, where nothing trivial can be said but everyone manages to avoid 'He's dead.' I wanted to say, 'If you're wondering why I'm not crying, it's because he's dead.' If he had suddenly come back, walked into the church through the door as though merely late and said it was all a mistake, I would have cried and cried and cried.

After the service, I clung to Jackie as we trooped up the hill of the graveyard to the burial plot. The flowers, a great many of them, were arranged on top and around the mound of earth that now represented Mike's final resting place. The headstone was engraved with a crucifix and a short inscription, paid for per letter so kept simple.

Funerals are supposed to be a line in the sand, a formal farewell after which everyone can start building a new life. He's dead, he's buried, that's that. But when there is an ongoing police investigation, that is very much not that. Not only did we live in the limbo between police updates, we lived in the crime scene, among the accused.

Emily was given the choice of returning to boarding

school. It was a far more stable environment for her there and no one wanted to undo her progress, so she decided to go. Arrangements were made for her to return home every other weekend for the foreseeable future. The house parents she lived with on the school grounds gave her a middle-class environment and she had friends, a boyfriend, a piano, access to literature and learning, and tiny growing roots. She felt incredibly guilty for leaving us, she later told me, but I'm so glad she had somewhere to go, even though I hated that she went. Really, Jackie and I should have moved away too. But there was no way of doing that. We lived in a council house in an increasingly undesirable area. It wouldn't have been possible to be rehoused in Birmingham, where Jackie's family was: the waiting list was years long. It was the reason estates like ours had been built in the first place. All her friends and mine were here, my school, our church. I had never known anywhere else, and I had never known Mike anywhere else. Jackie's relationship with her family was strained because of our conversion to Christianity, while here we could be with our kindred spirits any time. So, Jackie and I stayed in the red-brick house, and Emily would join us every other weekend and during holidays.

Once Emily had gone, my own return to school had to be addressed. I loved my teacher, the immeasurably kind Miss T, who always let me and my best friend Michelle stay behind at break times instead of going out to the dreaded playground. But the last time I'd been in her classroom was the week my dad died. Symon had driven me to the school one lunchtime so I could find Michelle and tell her. She knew he was on life support, as did Miss T, who had been told why I wasn't in school. I passed the children in the playground, headed straight to the classroom where I knew Michelle would be spending her lunchtime, as she and I always did.

She was sitting at her desk in the middle of the room, while Miss T was sitting behind the large teacher's desk. They both stood up and looked at me expectantly when I opened the door. I burst into tears as I blurted out, 'He died.' It was the first time I had had to tell anyone, the first time I'd said it out loud. I saw Michelle's face crumple as she too started to cry.

I remember a sudden wave of guilt for upsetting her, and wanting to make her feel better, or maybe I wanted her to stop so I could stop too. She was still eleven, wouldn't be twelve till May, but our hug felt like the hug of adults. I think we both aged a lifetime in the duration, as though our grief would be the end of everything good. I did not know that letting go of the hug would also let go of the friendship.

In the four weeks between the death and the funeral, Emily and I had continued to camp on Jackie's bedroom floor, the three of us fitful and full of nightmares, Mike's absence challenging our sanity. We often slept late. There was no reason to set an alarm, nothing to get up for, so by the time the question of school came round and Emily had gone it seemed impossible to leave Jackie alone all day. I loved my mom more than school, and I needed her. I think she needed me too. I was carrying the weight of violent trauma and injustice, and the responsibility for us both. She was all I had left and, besides, something bad might happen to her while I was gone. If I knew anything, it was that bad things happened to people I loved.

I missed perhaps a couple of months of school. Eventually I did go back, but by then I was a stranger to my classmates and myself. The new Tracy took everything seriously, didn't seem to care about the things that had been important before, looked at everyone like they were from another world. I could catch up with lessons but I couldn't catch up with friendships. I had that new spark of bravery and rebellion I'd manifested when I marched up to the police officer outside the phone box. As the school tried to treat me as a normal child and get me back into a healthy routine, that spark of rebellion (whose real name is anger) grew. I wasn't a normal child any more and nothing could cure my pain and confusion, so those trying to force normality on me were – in my head – simply wrong and could, should, be resisted.

School quickly became part of my problem, and not just because to get there I had to walk over the spot where my dad had died. Not just because some of the boys involved in his death had gone to that school and still used the football field. Not just because I was whispered about or, worse, ignored as rumours spread and public trauma marked me as different even if I hadn't started acting differently. And not just because I had to leave Jackie alone all day with her grief and phobias. It was also because, at that time, school had nothing to help a young mind blown apart by trauma.

My growing spark of bravery and rebellion finally ignited into fury one afternoon as the home-time bell rang. Mr A, the deputy headmaster, and a few boys from the year above were distributing leaflets that had been photo-copied onto the standard school pale blue paper. As we poured out of the classroom to get our coats and bags from the pegs opposite, we were each handed a leaflet. The boys of my class immediately huddled together excitedly to discuss its contents. I was handed one. I looked at it and froze with confusion, my vision swimming as I tried to focus on the words.

Football Today Presents
CHARITY FOOTBALL MATCH
WITH STAR CELEBRITIES
In aid of the Mike King Fund

It was to be held one Sunday on the school playing field. Admission was a pound, which included a match programme and entry to the estate pub's function room for 'after-match activities'.

At the bottom it reiterated in a double-lined box

ALL PROCEEDS TO THE
MIKE KING FUND

I had absolutely no idea what the leaflet meant, or what the Mike King Fund was. If there was going to be a charity football match on school grounds for my dad, then surely somebody would have told me. It would be cruel and confusing just to hand me a leaflet about it as though I was any other child.

I walked up to Mr A, who was talking to another teacher. I felt like I was on fire, blinded with rage and confusion. I had previously always been petrified of the deputy headmaster. His reputation preceded him, and he was one of the reasons why I had been scared to start middle school, feeling a huge relief when I wasn't put into his class. He famously would throw chalk or the board eraser at unruly pupils, and once picked up a kid and wedged him into the bin, telling him he was trash. His booming voice echoed in the corridors at break time as he yelled at someone for whatever infraction.

'What's this about?' I said, trying not to shake. I held up the leaflet.

Mr A said, 'It's a charity match to raise money for a local family.' The other teacher, who knew me, said something in his ear.

'Oh. Didn't you know?' said Mr A to me, without concern. He did not seem to understand how awful it was that, no, I did not know. I was going to cry, so instead of answering I picked up my bag and ran home.

When I showed Jackie the leaflet, she said she couldn't remember if she'd already been told. Maybe a neighbour had mentioned it and she had forgotten to tell me, maybe not. By now she was heavily tranquillized. She had been told too many things – by the police, her neighbours, family, solicitors and social workers – and was struggling to hold everything in. She had recently let go of Mike's belongings. Jackie, guided by Bernice, bin-bags in hand, spent an afternoon clearing out his wardrobe, his drawers, his life, the banality of underpants and ties. I sneaked into the bedroom beforehand and took a few things without telling anyone, because I knew that otherwise they would be discarded and I didn't want Jackie to know I had them. It might upset her to see them, like seeing his ghost. I hid them under my bed:

His *Guinness World Records* trivia booklets
His pipe
His silver penknife, blunt
His copy of *The Hitchhiker's Guide to the Galaxy*,
    which he had picked up for himself the same
    day as he bought me the first *Chronicles of
    Prydain* book
A box of playing cards he used to show us magic
    tricks
His pocket diary for 1976, the year I was born
His practically unread pristine pocket New
    Testament, in which he'd written his initials.

I put everything into a box alongside the black leather wallet I had been given at the hospital. It was a small decision of my own in a world where everyone else chose for us. When I saw the leaflet about the football match, I could feel my ownership of Mike King slipping even further out of my grasp.

On the Sunday afternoon of the match, I had the penknife and New Testament in my handbag as I stood with my family on the school football field, dressed in my finest outfit, watching drinking buddies of Mike I'd never seen before compete against ex-professional footballers.

I stayed mainly by Jackie's side. Photos show me standing next to her, all in black except my white ankle socks. She is small and I am smaller. Emily, looking nineteen in a pale green suit and heels rather than her actual fourteen, is standing a distance away, with our aunt and uncle and our cousin Dani, who really was nineteen, as though she was more part of their family than mine, drawn to their normality as she was with her house parents. I stand out as the only one in black. Jackie is wearing a grey spotted dress, perhaps trying to make herself look less like a widow. A normal, nice dress, in which to stand on a school field on a hot afternoon as if for a fête or sports day. Local kids in tracksuits, on BMX bikes or with their parents, pepper the background. I remember scouring the field in terror that Reece Webster would show up, or that someone would point out a random boy and say, 'That's Andrew Reynolds,' but they did not appear, presumably knowing it would not be safe for them to come even if they had wanted to meet their football idols. Someone made a comment to that effect, that they 'wouldn't dare show their faces'.

At the start of the match there was two minutes' silence. It didn't seem right to pray with my eyes open so I stared ahead and tried to think about Mike. *He isn't here*, I wanted to scream. *He didn't even like football that much. He liked snooker. If you really knew him you'd know that.* Then the whistle blew and the game began. I'd never watched a live football match before. Neither had I heard of the ex-Aston Villa and Birmingham City players who turned up to play against the pub team, and felt even more of an outsider. I knew they had done a lovely, kind thing. I just didn't understand why. I felt suspicious of everyone. Those who had threatened the accused boys, those who had drunk with Mike in the pub every night, those who weren't family or church.

The celebrity team beat the pub team, and after, as

kids and their dads crowded the famous players to have their Mike King Fund programmes signed, a family member had one signed for me, various scribbles on the back of the folded blue paper that bore my dad's name on the front. It was valuable for reasons beyond the autographs, proof my dad had existed, so I put it away with the things I had salvaged of his life, in a special box under my bed.

14

'M OM,' I CRIED, CLUTCHING my stomach. She came running from the kitchen and was halfway up the stairs as I collapsed.

I was taken to the same hospital we'd gathered at earlier that year for Mike, where Jackie had agreed to end life support and said goodbye to my dad. But this time I was in the bright, cheerful children's ward, having been surgically relieved of my appendix shortly after arrival. I had tight, painful stitches, garish purple crosses holding together a six-centimetre wound across my stomach. The scar would eventually heal, but would remain ugly, like the scar a child would draw on a pirate's face. The sewn skin itched under its blanket of tape and gauze.

The bed to my left was occupied by Aaron, a beautiful blond teenage boy with both legs in plaster on a hoist: a motorbike accident. He was learning to play the drums and continually practised on his plaster casts and the metal frame of the hoist. Sometimes he would drop a drumstick and summon the nurse on a pretext so she would pick it up and give it back to him. The drumming punctuated the days. It sounded nice unless I had a headache.

Opposite me was Dean, thirteen but small for his age. I knew who he was, but not why he was in hospital. He had attended the same school for expelled kids as Emily, and had a reputation for dating older girls. Perhaps this gave him bravado. He took an interest in me, the only girl on the ward. He came over and asked what I was reading.

'*The Black Cauldron.*' I showed him the book, one of my favourites.

'That's for children.' He paused. '*I*'m writing a book.'

'So am I,' I countered, instantly competitive and thinking of my long-abandoned project, a novel called *The Chillside Sword*.

He challenged me to a competition. He sat on the chair next to my bed and we wrote to the backdrop of Aaron's drumming, then read our stories out loud.

Dean argued with me about my use of the word 'suburbs', which I had put in the opening line of my story without really knowing what it meant. I remember him because he was right about 'suburbs' and I was wrong, and because his notebook was black, and full. He was constantly writing, all day and night, the only person I'd met who had said they were going to be a writer, and who thought writing was an argument you had to win. I remember him because we talked to the backdrop of another boy drumming. As Dean was walking back to his bed, he casually said, 'By the way, I know who you are. I know the lads that killed your dad. They ran over his head with a BMX.'

The drumming stopped.

I knew it was a lie. Maybe Dean did know the boys, maybe they had been going around telling people that. Maybe they were boasting and laughing and exaggerating and celebrating, and making up stories to sound hard or untouchable. Maybe he'd heard it from some random kid who'd heard it at school. Or maybe Dean the Writer was the one making things up. Wherever it came from, I knew it was a lie, so I said so.

'No, that's not true.'

'It is,' he insisted, confidently knowing more about it than the dead man's own daughter. 'They told me. Everyone knows.'

I could see it, down to the colour of the bike, which in my imagination was red. It had muddy tyres, which added to the cruelty and indignity as the boys inflicted their parting injury on a helpless man. The picture was surely complete nonsense, but I saw it anyway, a new intrusive thought. Once you've been possessed by such a vivid scenario, it's hard to get rid of, particularly when you know strangers are using it as gossip. It opened up the possibility that adults were keeping things from me, and it hurt more than the scar on my stomach.

The boy in the hospital was part of a world of children I could no longer relate to. As I became more isolated, I became more Christian. I was much closer to Jesus than God, although I would sometimes pray directly to God for the big stuff. Jesus was more like the boyfriend of an older sister, who takes an amused or benevolent brotherly interest in you, despite knowing you probably have a bit of a crush.

God was there only when I wanted him, but Jesus was always with me. I took to carrying Mike's pocket-sized New Testament everywhere, along with the leather wallet he'd had with him when he died, and his penknife. I didn't carry it as a weapon – the blade was dull and it hurt my fingers to prise it open, so I rarely did – but it was a deep comfort to me. I felt safer with it, heavy in my pocket, as if my dad was with me. Between the New Testament and the knife, I was protected.

Some people lose their faith in the wake of a tragedy, reasoning that a God who allowed such cruelty wasn't worth worshipping, or didn't exist at all. I went the other way. There was no question of blaming God because I knew exactly who was to blame. Those five boys. I wondered if the gang had been sent by Satan as punishment, although one letter from Eileen passes on the suggestion from her friend that God took Mike precisely because Mike had doubts:

> *I was so pleased to hear about the vision of Mike being led to his chair by the angels. Brenda and her church have been praying so hard for you all. She said, 'Maybe it was God's way of saying, "You wouldn't listen to me; so come up here and I'll show you, Mike."'*

Our style of Christianity was about hope and joy, but it brought with it something else: fear. The paranormal forces Jackie previously believed in, like psychics, curses and ghosts, we now saw as satanic. I was petrified of evil. Fear inhabited me constantly, especially in the dark. Lying awake on the camping bed on the floor of Jackie's bedroom, listening to the rise and fall of her sleeping-pill breath, I would suddenly be gripped by an intense belief that she was in the process of being possessed by a demon. Frozen with terror, I could only hold my crucifix tight, keep my feet tucked well under the blanket, and pray.

Satan's hand was everywhere, from international politics to a missing necklace. Jackie was a great hypothesizer, creating a religious or paranormal theory, then immediately believing it. One afternoon, we had gone to forage for blackberries in the many generous bushes around the estate. But other kids, or hungry birds, had got there first and pickings were slim. Suddenly we were approached by a random nice old man we'd never seen before, who held out to us a bag of freshly plucked blackberries. 'I picked all these about a mile away,' he explained, gesturing down the path. 'I used to pick them with my wife.' We took the bag, delighted, and thanked him profusely. It was a kind gesture from a stranger to a mother and her daughter, a moment of human empathy. At home, while baking a blackberry crumble, we discussed having never seen him before. Jackie declared, and meant it quite literally, 'That man was a guardian angel in disguise.'

These interventions by supernatural forces were everywhere. I was distraught one afternoon to discover I had lost my crucifix. The chain must have snapped. I prayed and prayed, and a few days later the necklace turned up in the laundry. I knew exactly what had happened. My necklace had been taken by Satan, and Jesus had intervened and placed it among the dirty clothes for me to find.

Praying didn't always work, but we made excuses. When a friend of Bernice's gave me a pair of beautiful sky-blue trainers, I was dismayed that they were a size too small. I wore them all day but they pinched my toes badly. I so rarely had new shoes, and never trainers like these. It seemed a great injustice that my good fortune should sour so fast. That night, I prayed and prayed (directly to Jesus this time, reasoning that he was the younger deity so would find my problem more relatable than God would, who perhaps had greater works to care about than a little girl's ill-fitting shoes). *Please, please make the shoes fit me in the morning*, I begged, like a poor orphan in a fairy tale. The next day I held my breath as I slid my foot into the pastel shoe, hoping to be Cinderella. It would be a perfect fit, because Jesus loves me and I deserve new trainers. I cried a little when the rubber and canvas had not magically grown overnight (I would also have accepted a shrinking of my feet), but Jackie told me that perhaps Jesus had other plans for the trainers, for someone even more in need. This was comforting and sensible, so I turned my disappointment into benevolence and gave the shoes to the even littler girl next door.

Strongly encouraged by the stories of perhaps the most fundamentalist member of our church, Eileen, whose style of belief was a sort of hysteric's fire and brimstone, it was normal for Jackie or me to look for a religious explanation for every unexplained happenstance. Demons could not only inhabit and manipulate objects, but people too. Jackie had once confided in me that one of her greatest fears when Mike would fall asleep downstairs was that she would go down in the middle of the night and find him floating above the settee, taken over by demons. But, equally, she had once believed that some unexplained marks on his hands were stigmata, the power of Jesus speaking through him. It was shortly after the stigmata episode that he had finally relented and, two years or more after the rest of us living and breathing the Holy Spirit, finally agreed to convert too. The only photo I have of the four of us together, the most informal of family portraits, is from a church picnic at a nearby lake, a year or two before Mike's conversion. We are participating in a three-legged race. Mike, in a burgundy jumper and jeans, has his ankle tied to Emily's; she is in a pink jumpsuit. Next to them, in jeans and T-shirts, are Jackie and me, our ankles bound, mid-stride. It was one of our happiest days, and my dad's presence at a church event confirmed that it was a safe place to be. He was our family protector, yelling at the boys who congregated late at night outside our house, or telling Jackie that everything would be all right about the social workers or the phobias or the debt collectors.

But once Mike was dead, the demons had free rein.

15

DEMONS ARE FEARS MADE REAL. They are the physical embodiment of the anguish an empathic human feels at experiencing or witnessing cruelty. Demons explain why people do horrific things to each other, why good children turn bad, why God doesn't simply make everything perfect all the time.

I had heard people describe alcoholism, depression, criminality, even infidelity as a personal demon that should be battled. Exorcized. Fought and dominated. But in our Christian world, demons were real. The Lord was the hero, Satan was the villain, and demons were Satan's minions, possessing our things and eventually my body and making me scream pure anguish in the night. What other explanation for my behaviour could there possibly have been?

The catalyst for the exorcism was my bedroom mirror. It was a heavy round ornate metal piece that had once belonged to my great-grandmother. She had died years before and, after a while, the mirror had found its way to me. Jackie had painted the filigree metal frame lilac to match my bedroom. The mirror was hung on a nail in my plasterboard wall, rather than fixed securely with a screw, but it hadn't budged the whole time I'd had it. Until one day, when I went into my room to discover the mirror had fallen off the wall.

Bernice suggested Mike's death had attracted the ghost of my great-grandmother. I told Jackie, and together we told Eileen, who said both I and the mirror were likely possessed. This explained my behavioural problems, my screaming night terrors and daytime hysterics, my refusal to attend school. I had noticed a tendency for people to act as if Jackie and I should be over our grief, even though it hadn't even been a year.

In that time we heard the following advice:

'Pull your socks up, Jackie.'
'Kids are resilient.'
'Isn't it about time you all moved on?'
'She'll be fine. Children bounce back.'

Children don't bounce back. It is a dangerous generalization to claim they do. Trauma causes physical changes in the brain, scars that affect you for the rest of your life. Trauma, if untreated, can cause lifelong problems. A child who experiences trauma *may* grow up fine, sure, or she may have serious mental-health issues that try their best to ruin her life. The way to minimize the risk of this happening is to help the traumatized child properly.

There had been superficial attempts to help me, limited to the GP prescribing sleeping pills and a few sessions with a very passive child psychologist, but it's likely that in the late eighties there simply wasn't enough understanding of childhood trauma to help me in meaningful ways to readjust back into school and a normal social life. There were more mistakes than help. Mistakes that made everything much worse.

Adults I trusted told me I might be possessed by a demon. And so, one evening, Adam and Bob came round and performed an exorcism. This was an area in which Adam had experience, and he was reassuring in his calmness. Demonic possession was serious and frightening, but exorcism and the power of Christ were far more powerful. Adam just needed to say the magic words and Satan and his minions would be banished.

I wondered what it would feel like when the demon left my body. I had already spent countless nights struggling against whatever was inside me, so it made sense to give it physical form. I imagined it as a little goblin-type creature, dark red and leathery, or an entity made of smoke as thick and black as treacle. It felt real and not real, in the same way that my childhood elf friends BeeMee and JaJa really existed, even while I knew they didn't.

As Adam commanded the demon to leave my body, I fell back into Bob's arms. I thought, *Oh, I'm supposed to fall backwards now*, and, feeling no demons whatsoever leave my body, knowing I had to go along with the ritual, played my part perfectly. After the exorcism we all prayed, and Adam and Bob left, satisfied.

I was relieved. I had accepted the possibility of demonic possession. But after the exorcism, I no longer believed I was or had ever been possessed. I remember faking the fall, and I remember the little nudge in my brain as doubt entered.

If life after Mike's death had adjusted into a healthy normality, that nudge of doubt might have meant more, but I had far bigger problems to worry about than whether or not my religion was true. The police had stopped coming round once we'd been told there would be a single manslaughter charge, and the church was our only support. The trial date was set for almost a year after the arrests, an unbearable wait, not Limbo but Hell. Meanwhile, from the local authority's perspective, history repeated itself and Tracy King developed a 'school phobia' just like her older sister.

After the long stretch of summer holidays, during which I parted with my appendix, I had started a new school year. Fourth year, the final year of middle school, meant I had a brand-new teacher. Mr G was kind and young and tried his best, but by this time I had convinced myself I didn't want or need to be at school with my peers. I needed to be either with Jackie or on my own with my thoughts and prayers.

If I slept badly or had a night terror (which was often and usually about demons or spiders or Armageddon), I didn't go to school that day. If Jackie and I had stayed up half the night talking, I didn't go to school that day. If I overslept by ten minutes, I didn't go to school that day. If I felt sad or overwhelmed or scared or just didn't feel like facing that damn phone box or those other children or risk seeing one of the gang of boys, I didn't go to school that day. If I was anxious about leaving Jackie alone, I didn't go to school that day.

And, of course, that was most days.

Where was Jackie in all this? It's a parent's job to get her child to school. She tried, just like she had done with Emily. But this time she had nothing left with which to fight and no ally. Even without the tranquillizers she was easily defeated. I wore her down. Sundays were the worst. The unspoken dread mounting as the evening progressed, and then eventually, a note of fear in her voice for the impending fight, Jackie would say, 'Are you going to school tomorrow?'

She didn't have the strength to issue an order. We'd tried that. It was too late. I would say my earnest 'I'll try,' and I meant it too, even while knowing it would probably be impossible. The dread was too strong. She would get upset or panicky about how much school I was missing, and we'd have a screaming argument, which would inevitably end in us both sobbing. 'You promise you'll try?' she would say and I would promise, and we'd cry, and I'd lie awake all night in terror of the alarm clock.

But I did try, over and over. I'd go back to school for a few weeks, then stay at home for a few more. Then it was just a few days at school until I could no longer cope, and then a few hours. When the bell rang for lunchtime I would go home and stay there.

At one point, the headmaster, Mr N – a usually kind and patient man, very popular with pupils – summoned Jackie and me for a crisis meeting about my attendance. He was losing patience and kept saying it was the law for me to attend school, as though I could be scared into complying when the problem in the first place was overwhelming fear. He had been Emily's headmaster too, and Reece Webster's, and some of those other boys' whose names I had memorized and whom I might bump into at any moment. I didn't see why the law about school should matter to me at all. It seemed like a law for optimum conditions, not exceptional circumstances. Didn't he know that the law was on *my* side, that the police were working on getting justice for my dad? Surely it didn't matter that some other smaller law said I had to go to school. What was that crime compared to the murder committed a stone's throw from where we all sat?

He asked if I wanted to try a new school. I didn't think I needed strangers and questions and bewilderment. I needed the comforting recognizable safe things: my home, my church and Jackie. Anything else was too draining and petrifying to contemplate and my thinking had been distorted by too much responsibility – to Jackie, to my religion, and to the new, misplaced sensation of adult leadership. But I was not, despite all of that, unwilling to try. I was aware that the end of this particular road was me being taken away as Emily had been. For the sake of everyone, in tears I promised again to try to go to school.

Mike had had no life insurance, and no will or anything to leave in one. We inherited only debts, some of which were forgiven and some paid off by friends, family or church members. The Criminal Injuries Compensation Board is run by the Ministry of Justice and exists to give money to victims of crime or their families. Although the eligibility criteria are very strict, it's still paid out billions since its inception in 1964. This is because there is a lot of violent crime, and therefore a lot of physical and psychological harm and related loss of income. Or, in our case, loss of the sole (albeit infrequent) breadwinner. Mike had been on unemployment benefits a lot, and his commission-only computer-salesman roles paid a pittance. A few days after he died, a letter arrived for him to confirm he'd been awarded the government grant he'd applied for to start his own computing business. My aunt Sarah wrote back so the grant could be reallocated to someone else.

The idea of the criminal injuries compensation scheme is not to measure the value or worth of a man's life but to recognize, on behalf of society, the harm victims of violent crime endure. It's part of the 'system' in 'criminal justice system'. Over the years the compensation scheme has been criticized for, among other things, being needlessly complex, but we didn't have to navigate it ourselves. Someone did the paperwork for Jackie, and we waited.

Eventually, a cheque arrived for a few thousand pounds. Some of the adults around me thought it was low, but I thought it was an incredible amount of money. I rarely encountered money any bigger than five pounds. Hundreds was a fortune, so thousands must be several fortunes.

I felt rich. Jackie called it 'money for murder', finding the award bittersweet or tainted, but by now we were staggeringly poor. Jackie had turned to charity when she couldn't afford to buy me any Christmas presents that first year, and was provided with a second-hand Barbie doll and doll's clothes, including the most wonderful pair of miniature brown cowboy boots. Jackie was completely honest with me about what was happening, trying to apologize for her shame, but I absolutely loved the gift. I didn't have a Barbie house, so I cleared out my bedside cupboard for my new doll to live in, washed her hair in my bathwater, and made furniture from old yoghurt pots.

So the money was a major change in our fortunes. It took away so much stress that I even managed to attend school for a few days. Walking across the playing field one lunchtime, I told Michelle of our plans to buy a second-hand piano for Emily.

'After all,' I boasted, having not yet learned how quickly a fortune can be spent, 'we can afford it now.'

In reality, the bulk of the money went on paying off debts. But Jackie gave Emily and me a hundred and fifty pounds each to do what we liked with. We went into the town centre on the bus and I proudly opened a bank account, which came with a cashpoint card. This meant I had easy access to my money. Because we 'had money' now, we found excuses to head to the big town shopping centre more frequently. My main haunt was a modest branch of a large chain that sold books and board games. My weaknesses. Over the year following receipt of the money, I spent it, cautiously at first, withdrawing a crisp five-pound note from the cashpoint with which to buy a volume of Asterix or Sweet Valley High or another story by Nicholas Fisk. Having money represented freedom to buy things. Owning books instead of borrowing them was extraordinary.

Book-buying was always the most special of family treats. Once, when Mike must have been flush with cash, he had taken us to a shop to choose a book each. Jackie chose a fantasy game book, of the 'roll a dice and turn to page eleven, you've been killed by a wizard' type. It was called *The Warlock of Firetop Mountain*, the now legendary first book in the Fighting Fantasy series by Ian Livingstone and Steve Jackson. Although Jackie had enjoyed the fantasy elements, she wasn't as keen on it as I was, so it became mine. I was glad to have it not only for the story but because it had been a gift from Mike.

The Fighting Fantasy books had the same attraction as video games, offering a modicum of control over the plot and gameplay, with plenty of magic spells, evil goblins to slay, and creepy skeletons that might or might not become suddenly alive should I choose the wrong page number. (I will not confess whether I kept my finger in the page to go back should I find myself accidentally dead.) I spent some of my new riches on half a dozen other books in the series, and loved how their spines matched each other nicely on the shelf of my newly expanding bookcase.

I also bought *The Demon Headmaster* by Gillian Cross. The protagonist was a girl who was into computers and could code, just like me. I added it proudly to the shelf next to my other books, no hint of its impending fate. I spent the rest of the money on board games for Jackie and me to play, or to take to Bernice's. She was a volunteer at an old folks' home and would take me with her, so I started bringing games like Rummikub and Jack Straws to play with the old people, who were somehow more relatable than my peers.

Board games were one of the main ways in which Jackie and I entertained ourselves, a continuation of the family hobby when there had been four of us. We never played mah-jong again, because only Mike knew how to calculate the complicated scoring, and Scrabble was too sad on his homemade matchstick board, but I introduced new games, purchased with my special riches, to fill our empty days and evenings and try to regain some of our old fun.

I could argue that books and board games help develop a growing brain, but I wasn't really getting an education. I missed most of my final year of middle school. The time I missed erased me from everyone else's normal life. My friends moved on. My once-longed-for thirteenth birthday, a milestone after which I would be allowed to wear makeup and get a paper round, came and went, despite everyone's best efforts to make it happy. My year-long birthday plans with Michelle fell by the wayside. I missed enough lessons to lose track and then it became too frustrating or exhausting to catch up. I would sit in a lesson I didn't understand, among children who were barely my friends, and zone out.

I decided to go in for the last ever day, because there were no lessons, and I wanted to say goodbye to Miss T, the teacher who had been so kind. I bought her a box of marshmallows that had been reduced in price because they were past their sell-by date.

It was a school rite of passage everywhere that on your last day your friends signed your white school shirt with marker pens, but I couldn't afford to lose a shirt and I no longer had the sort of friends who would want to sign my sleeves anyway. I was no longer sure what was relatable, so I went around with a copy of Douglas Adams and John Lloyd's pocket comedy book *The Meaning of Liff*, which I had also recently purchased and was utterly obsessed with. I only gathered a handful of messages and signatures on the flyleaf of the book, and most of those were teachers. Miss T wrote, 'I shall be floating in pink marshmallows all summer!'

And then my tenure at middle school ended. A full six weeks of summer holiday stretched out before me, at the end of which awaited a 'fresh start' at a brand-new, bigger, bus-ride-away high school full of strangers, also attended by Reece Webster and the other boys.

16

WHILE I NO LONGER believed I'd been possessed by demons, my nightmares and conflict-triggered hysterics didn't improve. Clearly Satan was getting to me somehow. Influencing me. Making terrible dreams in which I was covered with spiders or the world was ending or Mike turned up alive but I wasn't allowed to see him, causing me to wake up screaming, halfway down the stairs, not knowing who or where I was, no chance now of getting up for school tomorrow.

One night, when Emily was home for the weekend, she had been peering out into the dark back garden through the dimpled glass pane in the kitchen door. Suddenly she screamed and jumped back in terror. A demonic face had come flying through the garden at her. Panicked, the three of us prayed together and Jackie reported it to the church so they could add their strengthening prayers to ours. As long as I wore my crucifix I was protected, but I still had to fight to avoid those satanic assaults, so my Christianity became more and more devout. I had to protect myself, my home, my sister and my mother, and the Lord would protect me.

That meant closing any potential doorways through which Satan could enter. We had been taught that fiction about demonic servants, such as witches and wizards or zombies and ghosts, could give something for Satan to latch on to (this was an imported cultural belief now called Satanic Panic). Unfortunately for my book collection, that meant no more Fighting Fantasy, no more *Warlock of Firetop Mountain*, no more *Demon Headmaster*.

The idea was something like this: fiction (or music like heavy metal) containing demons or magic was the work of Satan, an attempt by him, through the author, to influence the reader. A young mind might enjoy the demons in the story and seek out satanism in real life. Anything that celebrated demons or evil spirits was obviously blasphemous, but it wasn't just that the themes of the book were demonic, the physical books themselves were. The story might be fiction but demons and curses and evil were very real, and could work through the pages, hypnotizing the reader, possessing her. We couldn't give the books away or even sell them because that would be spreading blasphemy. Why would we unleash demons on unsuspecting readers? We were in a war against Satan and needed to use whatever weapons were at our disposal.

Fire. A healthy fear of fire is sensible, but mine was extreme. I couldn't even strike a match.

My fingers smelt of cigarettes when I was too young to smoke. I'd take the dog ends of my parents' recently extinguished Benson & Hedges and smush them even harder into the glass ashtray, to disintegrate the filter, paper and remaining nub of tobacco. This was to ensure any tiny sparks still nestling inside the smoking ash were obliterated, because I was afraid of the house burning down.

We didn't have smoke alarms, even after we had a fire.

One evening in the early 1980s Jackie had put Emily and me to bed, still young enough to be sharing a room. She had deep-fried a batch of chips for our dinner and left the chip pan of fat on the hob to reheat when Mike got home from the pub, switching off the cooker at the wall. She did not know the wiring was faulty and the electricity still flowed to the bright red ring of the cooker top. While we slept and she watched TV, the chip pan ignited first itself and then her brand-new beloved cork wallpaper.

I remember being woken, Emily and I bumping down the stairs on our bottoms because the hall was full of smoke and Jackie didn't want us to trip and fall. She tried not to let panic sound in her voice as she hurried us. Outside in the dark in our nightclothes we were ushered into a neighbour's house as one of them dashed inside with a wet tea towel to try to extinguish the growing fire. Walking home from the pub with his neighbour, Mike heard the siren of the fire engine and joked, 'Well, I hope that's not my house!'

The fire fighters came but the neighbour had already put out the fire, which on the whole had not done much damage, although the cork wallpaper did not survive. The damage to my psyche lasted longer, and I considered fire something to avoid at all costs, until . . .

'Shall we burn them?' I don't know whether it was Jackie or me who said it, although I think it was probably me. I was convinced Satan could manifest in the pages of my fantasy books and get to me.

So we burned them. We made a wretched bonfire in the now overgrown back garden as it was getting dark. Jackie struck the match. The pages of Steve Jackson and

Ian Livingstone's books burned into ashes, which flew away across the garden and out into the world. I imagined the demons screaming in frustration and fleeing back to Hell. Jackie and I prayed. It felt good to be with her in the garden exorcizing demons from books and our lives. We were in control here. Bad things could enter our lives but we would recognize them and send them packing. The political symbolism of burning books didn't occur to either of us. It just seemed like the only way to purge the world of the satanic influence.

At the same time as I was banishing the forces of darkness into the flames, I began to have doubts about the benefits of spending so much time with the church. Our congregation was very small: the Sunday-morning service attracted anywhere from ten to thirty people. There was a core group who turned up to everything. Adam and Denise, the church elders Bob and Adrian (in our denomination only men could be elders), Adrian's wife, a few women whose husbands did not get involved, and the fanatical Eileen and her quiet husband, Tom. It was Eileen who had told us the story of the Satan-worshipping woman who walked through fire, almost whispering the punchline with her eyes wide, as though it was the most precious gossip only to be shared in hallowed tones with the most deserving confidants. Jackie quickly became part of this core group, attending every church event. One afternoon, sometime before Mike died, she had gone to Adam and Denise's house for 'a special surprise'. I had chosen to stay at home with Mike, but half an hour after she left I felt badly homesick for her and decided to follow. I cycled to the minister's house. Denise let me in and led me to the living room, where the church members were sitting, various plastic bowls of warm water in front of them on the floor, washing each other's feet. Adam was on his knees, cleansing Jackie's bare feet as she laughed uncomfortably.

It was meant to be an exercise in humility and privilege, but I was horrified. I went outside to play with the younger kids.

After Mike died, that same group tried to intervene in my behaviour. 'You're giving your mom an awful lot of trouble'; 'She's going through enough.' And so on. Jackie had no say in this, of course. She would have been horrified at the idea of anyone telling me to put my own feelings aside and not bother her with them. But they might have had a point, had their alternative not been worse.

I did not respect any of them as parental figures: Adam and Denise, who never showed any personality to me outside their religiosity and who disciplined their children by smacking them with a wooden spoon; Bob, whose children seemed afraid of him; Eileen, who was hugely supportive and kind but who took me aside to encourage my growing fundamentalism with stories of Satan's dark works. None of them had the excessively close relationship with their children that I had with Jackie. We were more like equals or friends, while they seemed to lack mutual respect. But they had to interfere because they knew best.

'I don't want to go!' I cried. Emily didn't want to go either, but our dad was recently dead and our mother was on Valium and that meant other people got to tell us what to do. The church had arranged for the two of us to attend a week-long Christian holiday retreat for children during the summer holidays. I didn't understand why we were being sent away, particularly as our grief was still so fresh. 'It's to give your mom a break,' explained Bob.

A break from what? Her bereaved children? Were we that bad? Bob's daughter was going too, so it wasn't entirely terrible, but the thought of leaving Jackie made me sick. I asked her why we had to go, but she wasn't lucid. The church had decided some time away from us was the best thing, and that was that. Ordinarily Jackie did not like to let me out of her sight if she could help it, nor I her, so this seemed odd, but perhaps our co-dependency was part of their concern.

The retreat was in the East Midlands, but as we had no way of leaving once we were dropped off there it might as well have been on Mars. The girls' dorm had wooden bunk beds stacked with strangers. Emily and I had borrowed sleeping bags and she let me take the top bunk. Being away from home wasn't unusual for her, but neither of us adjusted to the place. I hated the communal meals, the earnest holding hands and praying, the enforced fun of obstacle courses, one of which involved eating cold home-made custard blindfold, a solid wobbly lump on a paper plate that made me gag just to think about. If you didn't eat it, the custard-holder was allowed to mash it into your face. I refused to participate but I did enjoy the singing, a chance to express some of the volume that filled me. In the evenings we gathered in a circle in the communal hall. An adult with a guitar taught us a whole new portfolio of fun Christian tunes, which we sang in the round and all the way home at the end of the week.

Oh, you can't get to heaven,
In a baked bean tin,
Cause a baked bean tin's got baked beans in.
All my sins are washed away, I've been redeemed.

I sang as much as I cried that week, consoled only by
Emily, who was feeling much the same but with the added
responsibility of looking after me. I felt like an unrelatable
freak, unable to make new friends. Even when I laughed
and enjoyed myself, I was a fraud. I still believed in God
and Satan but the other children there somehow seemed
more Christian than I felt. In the back of my mind I knew
there was no permanent comfort to be had from a moment
of amusement in a song about baked beans. Even laughing
was hard work. It felt more like school than a holiday.

When I was eight, Bernice won a hundred pounds at
the bingo and used it to rent a self-catering chalet for a
week in a seaside holiday camp in Wales. Jackie, Emily
and I piled into Bernice and Symon's car, with my cousin
Dani, who was fourteen. (Don't do the maths on car-seat
numbers: needs must, and in those days children routinely
sat on laps in cars. I travelled in the boot more than once,
with the shelf removed and strict instructions to duck
should we pass a police car.)

This was my first holiday since I was a baby, when
Jackie had got into debt to take Emily and me to Jersey for
a week with her family. Mike was in Saudi. I don't think
they ever went on holiday together after we were born.
Mike didn't come to Wales either, as his job offered no
holiday pay. The chalet was clean and bright, and Emily
and I shared a twin room with a view of nothing in

particular. The holiday village had a swimming pool (I was too afraid to go in it) and a play area of wooden climbing frames, although I preferred the donkeys that wandered the site. My granddad Symon cut an apple into quarters and I shyly let a donkey nibble one from my hand, its hairy mouth tickling my palm.

The site had a social club with a bar and a dance-floor. During the day it hosted activities and competitions for children, and at night typical holiday-camp entertainers were followed by a disco. This was what I thought a holiday should be, not scheduled Bible study and making dioramas of Noah.

After the Bible camp, the idea of a holiday didn't come up again until the church announced one of its famous weekend retreats. I didn't want to do another religious holiday, because the week-long camp had been so awful, but Jackie and Emily would be there, and I wouldn't be expected to eat any cold custard. There was trouble about the money, as always, but eventually Jackie scraped together or borrowed enough to cover the cost for the three of us. It felt like things happened because Mike had died. If he hadn't, we wouldn't have been going. Everyone felt sorry for us, wanted to help us, do something nice. I wanted to stay in the safety of our house for ever, but instead we packed some wet-weather clothes and got a lift to the remote rented farmhouse in Wales that the church used for spiritual bonding.

There was a hierarchy to the group that dictated the sleeping arrangements. Adam and Denise had their own room, as did the church elders. The rest of us had to sleep on the floor of the attic, under high wooden beams that were absolutely chock-full of spiders. I was more afraid of spiders than anything, so when we went to bed and I looked up, I screamed. And screamed. Jackie tried to calm me, but couldn't. She's afraid of spiders too but did her best to placate me, reassure me they wouldn't fall on me in the night. Nothing worked, and the other people in the room started to tut because they wanted to sleep and the child lacked discipline. I woke the entire house, and eventually Bob came into the room, told me to calm down, and when I said I couldn't sleep in a room with spiders, pinned my arms to my sides, picked me up, and carried me downstairs. That made me scream more as I struggled against him, 'Let me go!' He deposited me on the sofa and proceeded to give me what I assume he believed was a stern talking-to but I understood as a threat to behave.

Jackie joined us and tried to explain to Bob that I overreacted to stressful things because I missed my dad. My hysterics were getting more frequent, but this was the first time anyone outside the family had witnessed them. My shame – of the irrational fear of spiders and my hysterics – manifested as defiance. I was already afraid of Bob because of how I saw him treat his own children and his lack of warmth, and now he was on the side of the creepy-crawlies. This was the first time I had shown rebellion against a church member. Eventually I must have fallen asleep, because when I woke up I was back in the attic room under the spiders.

17

I N THE HOT SUN of the summer of 1989, the building
housing Birmingham Crown Court looked overwhelm-
ingly orange. I hadn't been to that part of the city centre
before but I'd seen it on the news plenty of times: it was
where suspects for the most serious crimes had their trials –
murder, manslaughter, robbery and rape. To me, the broad,
curved terracotta steps leading into the imposing building
were famous. Jackie held on to the railing as we ascended,
my entire family behind us. Inside, we were directed up a
glass staircase into a wide, glass-balconied corridor that
doubled as a waiting area. Along the wall, the closed
double doors of the courtroom. At the end of the corridor,
a small breakout area of tables and chairs with vending
machines for cans of pop, chocolate and hot drinks.

   There were other people in the waiting area, strangers. Men in suits, presumably solicitors. DCI Burns was
there, and a few other police. An odd politeness descended,
like the milling about at a wedding when the family are
off having photos taken and everyone else is left to make
small-talk with strangers: 'Are you with the bride or
groom's party?' The manslaughter trial equivalent is the
victim's family introducing themselves to the accused's.
Mr and Mrs Reynolds, Andrew's parents, seemed kind,

well-dressed and well-spoken. They were visibly distressed behind their politeness, knowing their son could face years in prison if convicted. A guilty verdict would mean Andrew would be taken straight from the court to prison; they wouldn't have him home again for a very long time, and by then he would be indelibly changed.

When teenagers are accused of terrible crimes, the public likes to wonder what the parents did wrong. Certainly there was a correlation between poverty, at-home violence and neglect, and juvenile crime. But Andrew's parents weren't poor, and they didn't fit any of the stereotypes formed by television and my own experiences. They seemed ... nice. Not defensive, not aggressive, not the types to have a gang leader for a son. I could see they were suffering, and I felt for the first time a sensation of empathy for the other side.

I did not expect to see any of the gang, even though I knew that the four youngest were witnesses and only Andrew was on trial. Because they had all been arrested for murder, I still thought of them as antagonists. Innocent of participating in the actual blow, but participants in the verbal abuse that preceded it, goading their friend into action and running away afterwards. DCI Burns had painted them as malicious, marauding, feral. He had told us that some of them already had criminal records for petty offences. Juvenile delinquents, later called ASBOs or hoodies, who were only escaping charges because they had agreed to cooperate as witnesses. Those four boys were complicit in Mike's death and surely responsible for the violent rumours I had heard.

Emily, Dani and I went to the vending machines for a

can of Coke. Two of the boys were there, laughing and joking. A hotness descended over me. Do we say anything? Will they say anything? In any other circumstance this would have been a fun meeting of three teenage girls and two teenage boys, with the usual dynamics that that entailed. But this was a manslaughter trial. These boys had been there when Mike was killed. They had called him names, the last words he had heard. What was there for us to say to them?

'All right.' Dani nodded to them.

'All right.' They nodded back, and left with their drinks.

At thirteen, I was too young to be allowed into the courtroom. Jackie said it was for the best anyway, as the trial would have been too upsetting, but I couldn't stand being left out. I felt entitled to be present and hated hearing everything second-hand. But she was right. I hadn't really understood what her being a witness meant. All of Jackie's family trooped in to sit in the gallery while Emily sat in the corridor outside with me, yet more chairs for us to wait on as time passed without us. She was old enough to go inside, but didn't want to. I didn't understand that, was desperate to know what was going on. We talked, read books, a strange tense boredom. I paced. Sometimes a family member would take a break from the proceedings and sit with us. Then suddenly the courtroom doors burst open and Symon stormed out, furious, distressed.

'Character assassination!' he cried. The defence barrister had done what he was paid to do – discredit the victim so that the actions of the accused seemed defensible. 'They said horrible things about your dad! Made it sound like he deserved it, like he was the one on trial.' Jackie had broken down on the witness stand, and – knowing how fragile and vulnerable his daughter already was – Symon had walked out in protest, believing this experience could destroy her.

We had been told the trial would likely last five days. On the second day, Emily and I had settled into the same waiting-room chairs as though they were ours. We had been so primed by the police about the events of that night, I didn't expect anything but a long trial and a guilty verdict. I hated those teenage boys, was petrified of them, but I had seen Andrew's parents in their distress and struggled with the police's image of him as the malicious violent gang leader. Perhaps, I reasoned, that is why the charge was reduced from murder to manslaughter. Maybe Andrew was showing off and wanted to hurt Mike but didn't actually believe his lethal karate chop would work. Perhaps, if it had all happened spontaneously enough, there hadn't been enough time for him to form such a clear motive. I had no idea how to reconcile any of this.

Murder is a difficult accusation to get past, and the downgrading to manslaughter did nothing to lessen the pain of a violent death. 'My dad was murdered' had been in my head for a long time. There is no equivalent phrasing for this. 'My dad was manslaughtered': it's not a thing. Someone had hit him on purpose and he'd died, but that someone hadn't meant to cause his death? That didn't tally with the police's description of a malicious karate chop, the jump from the wall, a martial artist knowing full well a blow like that could cause instant death. The motive was, we had been told, the entire point of the arrest.

But then another sudden burst of activity, like the day before, as the courtroom doors flew open again, and this time my entire family streamed out, livid with boiling disgust, half shouting, almost mob-like. Dani led the charge, furious at something, unable to hold back her distress. Emily and I jumped up, confused. What was happening? I heard words like 'Bastards!', 'Disgrace!' and 'Shambles!' Someone told me that the case had ended prematurely. 'The judge has thrown it out!' Andrew was free.

But why? What had happened? 'They were guilty on paper!' stormed a man in a suit to Jackie, angrily slapping the official folder he carried. Police like to get their man, and the investigation had been lengthy and expensive. Everyone around me seemed utterly horrified at what must surely have been a grave miscarriage of justice.

This was a lot of nuance for a child. That someone could hit a man who then dies but not be guilty of any crime was a new concept. It was the fault of the four other boys and their solicitors, the adults told me. Because the case had taken a year to come to trial, the legal team had had time to create a defence strategy in which each of the four boys, 'hostile' witnesses, would contradict each other's testimony. In the absence of compelling independent-witness testimony, this strategy had paid off and Andrew walked free.

I saw him as he was released into the corridor, joined his parents and left the court, a boy much smaller than his age, his parents visibly overjoyed as they accompanied him down the stairs and out of the building. I would never forget his face.

PART THREE

18

ON THE FIRST DAY back at school after the six-week stretch of summer, children are often asked to write an essay called 'What I Did on My Holidays'. Mine was usually about visiting Bernice and Symon or going on a church picnic. The year I was thirteen the essay would have been about how I attended a manslaughter trial and spent the rest of the summer contemplating death, injustice, and why God would allow any of it. That was the mood in which I started a new school year, and it went predictably badly. Fresh starts require a complete reset, not simply shifting the same problems a few miles down the road and removing what little support network and familiarity I had left.

By now Jackie was a new word I had learned: she was 'destitute', and relying on a lot of external financial help. I contributed as best I could, first with a paper round for the free weekly classifieds (I would skip delivering to Reece Webster's house, scuttling past as though he might jump out at me at any moment), then a Saturday job on a fruit-and-veg stall in the town-centre market. These cash jobs paid pence per hour rather than pounds, so were not enough even to cover my school uniform.

On the first day of high school I – like every other

pupil – carried a knot of anxiety. I also carried Mike's mini copy of the New Testament in my blazer pocket. My uniform was mostly new, having been paid for by a benevolent great-aunt under a veil of secrecy. Symon was not to know that his relative was paying for my school clothes and equipment, presumably because of his pride. But she could spare the money far more easily than my grandparents could.

I loved the uniform, loved wearing it. The knee-length navy skirt, white shirt, school tie in my 'house' colours, and the optional blazer onto which I had sewn an embroidered patch featuring the school crest and Latin motto. I had arranged to meet one of my only remaining friends, Carly, at the bus stop. We had spent most of the summer together, playing with her many kittens, writing short stories, or talking about Jesus, avoiding talking about the trial. We were thirteen, an age that for many of our peers was the beginning of sexual awakening or even activity, but Carly and I stayed in our innocent bubble. We didn't even talk about boys, neither of us having any prospects in that regard, but also because teenage boys were, to me, the vessels of the Devil, tools through which he caused chaos and pain on Earth. I didn't want any part of that.

It's not that I still felt like a child, unready for young-adult pursuits. Quite the reverse. I felt so mature, I was above such things. Boys and kissing and going to discos or parties was immature, banal. I had bigger ideas.

Although I'd missed the majority of my final year of middle school, I was keen to try again, despite misgivings. I wanted to learn, and kept promising myself that things would be different this time. Some of my old friends, including Michelle, were going there, as well as Carly.

The high school divided children in two ways, first into 'houses': Lancaster, Windsor, Tudor and York. My house was Tudor, and our colour scheme was red. I immediately developed a mild and irrational competitive bias against the others, which, of course, is the point of such arrangements. If I was in Tudor, then Tudor was obviously the best house. I hadn't the faintest idea what an actual Tudor was. But my friends from middle school had been placed in other houses, which meant I would see them only at break times.

The new first years were divided into 'sets', assigned via the results of exams. I loved exams and, because they tested things like logic and reading comprehension, rather than the general knowledge I'd missed, I had passed with flying colours. I proudly took my place in the top set, the only pupils who got to learn Latin. I was particularly excited about that because I was a huge fan of the Asterix comic books (thankfully not satanic so they had survived the bonfire), which contained many Latin puns. Perhaps I was the preppiest kid in the school. Certainly, I noticed on my first day, I was the only one who was wearing the optional school blazer with embroidered crest.

At first I embraced the formal trappings of education, thinking they reflected some deserving intelligence. But I was performing aptitude without any social knowledge. I didn't know what was considered cool or embarrassing, what was peer-appropriate and what singled me out as a weirdo. If I had ever cared about that, I quickly learned not to. My peers were largely unreliable anyway. The worst betrayal was their blossoming interest in teenage boys, my enemies, but our interests started to diverge in most ways.

I wanted to dress like Jackie, in nice skirts, blouses and high heels, not in jeans and trainers. I started to wear a huge amount of makeup and pin up my hair with combs, because it made me look older. None of the other girls did this, and they began to speculate on the reasons for my excesses, but it was simply to reflect the adult I felt like. I needed to look as mature and unlike my peers as possible so adults would take my ideas seriously. I couldn't stand to be treated as a child.

Things started to go wrong fairly quickly. I knew most of the boys from the gang went to that high school, and kept up a constant vigilance for them, as I did around the estate. Because I'd seen them all at the trial, I now knew what they looked like. One morning, walking from the bus stop down the long concrete path to the school, I saw a figure coming across the sports field. It was Chris Hendon. I did the only reasonable thing a panicked body could. I turned around and rapidly walked back the way I'd come, waited for the bus, and went home.

Because I got away with leaving the premises once, I did it whenever I was upset, angry or distressed, which was often. The much-anticipated Latin lessons became impossible when the teacher insisted on each of us in turn saying, in Latin, what our fathers did for a living. I couldn't bring myself to say, 'He's dead,' or 'He plays the harp on a cloud,' and knew I shouldn't have to. Instead, I refused to answer. I sat, mute, stubborn, until the teacher lost his temper and kept me back after class to lecture me on insubordination. I left the classroom and once again walked down the long path away from the school and out of the gate.

Jackie worried about me arriving home halfway through

the school day, so to avoid the questions and arguments, I began to hide my truancy from her. Instead of getting the bus, I'd walk the two miles home to kill time, diverting via fields and industrial estates. A nomad in a school uniform, I avoided the town centre and main roads (for fear of being spotted) and slowly developed a love for solitude. At home, Jackie and I were co-dependent, but my solo wanderings were an opportunity to think for myself.

The more school I missed, the more isolated I became when I did attend. Eventually, Michelle and most of my other middle-school friends stopped speaking to me entirely (or perhaps I stopped speaking to them), the catalyst coming one afternoon when, as we were all hanging out in the playground, Michelle's boyfriend came up behind me and teasingly hit me around the back of the head with his folder.

This was not ideal. I already had problems with teenage boys, so for one of them to hit me on the back of the head – the very thing that had killed my dad – was poorly timed. I lost my mind. Screaming at him that I would have him arrested for attempted murder, I ran off with tears streaming down my face.

There wasn't any coming back socially from that, so I spent my break times walking in squares around the perimeter of the playground, reading Mike's – my – New Testament.

Some days, as with middle school, I simply couldn't face it, or hadn't slept. I'd silence my alarm and wait breathlessly in bed to see if Jackie would wake up in time to try to get me to school. As often as not, she didn't, stymied by the medication she was on and suffering from exhaustion. After a while I began to think it was my choice whether or not to attend school, as she simply didn't have the strength to make me. By now, the rumours were flying. 'Her mother keeps her home from school', 'She's not allowed to do PE because of her religion', but it was pointless trying to argue. I didn't do PE because I hated PE and saw no good reason to participate. I didn't go to school very often because it was unbearable.

The rumours stripped me of what I thought was my autonomy, blaming my beliefs or family for behaviours and decisions I was certain were my own. Everyone wanted me in school, in PE, and out of my unique rebellion, but I would not comply. The rumours showed me that my friends couldn't conceive of me simply doing what I wanted or refusing what I didn't want. No thirteen-year-old is supposed to be allowed that, so it must be something that was being done *to* me. But I really was certain I was different, entitled to my superiority. I was only really happy when writing or reading. Emily kept my letters from that period; they are mostly comedy doodles and *Beano*-style exclamations to amuse her, but also inadvertently reveal my attitude to, and increasing isolation from, my peers. Their rebellions seemed banal and immature, even while my own youth showed. One letter says:

Guess what happened at school the other day! We woz in Tutor Period (posh name for registration), and the Tutor had to leave the room for a mo. Anyway, they all started throwing digestive biscuits at each other, except me, and this other boy. Anyway, there was biscuit EVERYWHERE,

and me and this boy saw a figure loom up in the doorway.
Guess who it was!

No, it wasn't the Tutor, it was Mr Saunders, the
HEADMASTER!!

Erk! You mightn't think that's so bad, but it is, when
you have over a thousand pupils in the school and you've
never ever even said one word to him, face to face. He is
reeealllllly strict. Anyway, whenever the HM enters a room
we all have to stand up. We did, and do you know, he
hadn't even noticed the biscuits!! Or if he did, he never
mentioned it. He just said, 'Keep the noise down, 3C' !!!

The school, concerned about my frequent and increasingly lengthy absences, sympathetic to our recent family
history, realized pretty quickly that Jackie and I were co-
dependent. I was afraid to leave her; she was afraid to leave
me. The solution? Take her to school with me. The authorities could see that I was a bright child and willing to learn
if I felt safe, so asked Jackie if she'd be happy to accompany
me to school in the morning and, as she could type and do
filing, spend half a day in the secretary's office doing admin
work as a volunteer. She was delighted. It gave her something to do and somewhere to be, and it got me to school.
We travelled there and back together, and she got used to
the environment quickly enough (or perhaps for my sake)
to overcome her anxiety. If I had any emotional problems
during the day, I could simply go along and see her. Instead
of spending the morning break-time alone in the playground, I would go and sit on a chair in the office and
talk – as I had with Michelle and Miss T two years

before – but this time with the secretary and her new unpaid assistant, my mother.

At lunchtime I would go and meet her and we'd head home. These half-days were intended to keep my education going, and it worked well from that perspective. The weird Christian girl in too much makeup was now bringing her mom to school, so it also achieved an increase in social isolation and rumours, but I was way past caring. I had a decent compromise and an emotional-support person. I was nowhere near understanding that this meant I was not dealing with my problems but avoiding them.

For around two months, Jackie and I had a stable routine of mornings at school. But one day she broke the news to me that the office simply didn't have any more work for her to do and she should no longer come with me. I would have to face school on my own again.

That wasn't going to happen. As soon as she stopped going, so did I. The school didn't give me detention or send truant officers, because there was no malice in my misbehaviour. Everyone understood it was trauma. I can't imagine being given detention but I would have had a breakdown there and then. It wasn't in anyone's interests to try to correct my behaviour with boilerplate punishment, but God help them if they'd tried. Jackie would have been a furious hurricane through the school corridors and straight into the headmaster's office. Instead, I was summoned to crisis meetings with, first, the school, then the local education authority and a social worker. They were stern but clearly worried, while I was contrite and eloquent. They made notes and wouldn't let me read them. I promised to go to school. I tried. Again I failed. And again. And again.

I had been violently pulled out of my world. Adults were whispering in other rooms, strangers pitied me. No one wanted to talk to me about my dad, but everyone wanted to gossip about what had happened. My friends couldn't possibly understand, and even if they'd wanted to let me talk about it I resented their innocence too much to bother. They could simply go home and not be affected by it. I would never have that luxury again.

I didn't trust anyone else, but I trusted myself completely. Once the social worker started leaning on me with mild threats, I couldn't skip school entirely. I'd turn up first thing for register, which meant that as far as the authorities knew I had been in school that day. When the post-registration bell went for us to go to lessons, I'd hang back until everyone had dispersed, then quietly slip away. I knew that walking out of school was the right thing to do. I was certain that the best thing for me was whatever I wanted at the time. I couldn't be persuaded. I was dead set on complete autonomy and wasn't burdened with the usual teenage self-doubt. I was not safe or happy at school. I wanted to be alone with my thoughts. I felt alone anyway, barely present and utterly divorced psychologically from other children, so why endure the false company of the classroom? I would walk across the playground, behind the geography block, ducking as I went so I wouldn't be seen through the windows, and out of the back gate. The second I was away from the school grounds I felt my freedom return, and off I'd go, back to the safety of my thoughts, on my terms.

19

THE YEAR I WAS fourteen, something wonderful happened. Jackie had worked various cash jobs around the estate, but when their respective budgets ran out she was short of options to make money. Her safe radius was tiny, and she couldn't leave the estate because she couldn't get onto a bus by herself. Close to the end of her tether, she went back to the doctor for help with her agoraphobia. But this time, instead of another prescription for tranquillizers, she was offered graded exposure therapy.

Jackie was referred to a therapist at an NHS outpatient facility in the nearest town centre. At first I went with her, because she couldn't get the bus into town on her own, and waited on the dimpled hard plastic chair with a book while she had her appointment. Her therapist was a pale red-haired man in perhaps his late twenties. Her guardian angel, she would later come to call him, because his gentleness and empathy were so much greater than any she'd experienced before from a mental-health professional. His name was Sean.

Although her therapy took place over a period of months, in my memory it all happened very quickly. I'd been used to her one way my entire life, and compared to that a few months was a flash, a rapid-fire montage of scenes of progress. Within weeks, Sean's therapy progressed from talking to doing. He taught her how to acknowledge and then overcome panic attacks as they arose, with the goal of eventually not having them at all.

Panic attacks had long been part of her identity. The local newspaper had somehow learned about her and reported on the estate poet who couldn't leave the house. They printed a poem she had written about Adam and Eve, alongside a photo. She looks beautiful, smiling warmly as though her psychological problems were sufficiently compensated by her art. It is an odd story because agoraphobia is, with enough resources, support and expertise, curable. Not entirely, but enough. If those resources had been available when the article was published, it would just have been a story about a housewife who writes.

That was the new goal: just a housewife . . . a widowed single mother who writes. And gets buses, and goes to new places by herself. And who maybe has a good job, a proper income, a second chance at a life. She must have seen that I would need the opportunity to have my own life, too. She couldn't depend on me to get buses with her for ever.

It's hard to imagine the amount of willpower and sheer grit she must have summoned to achieve her goal. I don't think even she knew it was possible to fix, but after a few months of intensive work she was transformed. Her phobias had always been driven by an overwhelming fear that one of us would spontaneously disappear: first Emily and next Mike were indeed taken away. She could have become a shut-in, too afraid to set foot outside in the estate, and I don't know why that didn't happen. Maybe she had simply lost enough, and wanted freedom. Her future, and mine. Poetic, for the poet.

Sean came to our house. It was odd to have a man from a clinical setting in our living room, breaking the fourth wall. We walked to the bus stop to meet him and he came for a chat and a coffee. Really, what he was doing was a recce of the bus journey from the town centre to our estate, and the walk from the bus stop to our house, so he could plan Jackie's exposure therapy accordingly.

Her therapy was a joint effort, as she included me as much as she could, and I wanted to help. I would develop little reassuring mnemonics or aphorisms for her. I knew how she thought and could say the right thing. When she told me that walking down a long path made her feel like it would never end, I suggested she focus her gaze on a lamppost a few feet away, and make that her destination instead of the pointed V of the path on the horizon. My idea was that she would reach the lamppost quickly, and could then focus on another small visual marker a few feet away, until eventually she reached the end of the path. It made perfect sense to me. She tried it, and it worked.

Eventually, she got on the bus by herself and travelled one stop to where Sean was waiting in advance. A week later she went three stops, to the estate shopping centre next to the phone box, where Sean met her and walked her home. At first, he had accompanied her on the bus, sitting at the back while she sat at the front. I've often thought of Sean on the bus with Jackie, whether he kept the tickets to claim back on expenses, what they talked about at the bus stop and if anyone overheard. I must have been having one of my increasingly rare days at school, as it wasn't something I could have gone along to as well, but neither would I have been left at home alone. I remember Jackie excitedly telling me about it, her eyes shining with achievement and ambition.

One day they arranged for her to walk to the bus stop, board the bus, and do the entire fifteen-minute journey into town by herself. Sean was there to meet her at the other end and accompany her home. 'I did it!' she screamed. Then she smoked three cigarettes in a row.

The final step was for her to get the bus into town alone, and then come home alone. She told me that she was scared she would panic and forget which bus stop was ours, so I made up a rhyme:

Three stops
Past the shops.

She liked that, and repeated it to herself on the journey. Alone on the bus, she carefully counted the number of stops after passing the phone box, and disembarked in the right place.

Jackie relayed to me each new leap of progress, then to Emily on the phone, and Bernice, and my aunts, everyone's pride and relief swelling along with her confidence. Eventually she didn't have debilitating agoraphobia any more. What was left of her anxieties was manageable. Everyday life could change, and change was what we needed most.

She got a job as a pub cook in the town centre. This was unprecedented freedom. We needed money badly, and the pub advertising for a lunchtime cook was not one of the rougher ones. It was up the hill from the high school, so Jackie would be close by if I needed her. In this new dream, I would start attending school regularly and Jackie would have a life and an income.

I tried, for as long as it took for something or someone to upset or scare me, and then I bailed. It was mid-morning. Jackie was just up the hill, preparing for lunchtime diners, and I was worried about her. I wanted to see her. I needed to see her. While she was trying to rejoin the wider world, I was retreating from it. I was upset and scared and wanted my mom. I walked up the hill, across the main road, around the back of the pub and into the kitchen.

I spent the majority of my days there for the next six months. Some days I would be at school for 9 a.m. as I should have been, but invariably I'd get overwhelmed at something in class or the wilderness of the playground, and by eleven thirty I'd be off up that hill towards the safety of Jackie and the adult world. Most of the time I sat on a metal stool in the corner of the pub kitchen, reading. When it was quiet, Jackie and I would talk. If it was extremely busy, usually a Friday, I would help, cutting sandwiches or stirring microwaved garlic butter into mayonnaise. Our dinner most nights was the day's unsold food, destined otherwise for the bin. Baked potatoes, still warm from an entire day wrapped in a foil blanket, and great wobbly slices of catering-sized quiche, lukewarm and sweating from their clingfilmed hiding place in Jackie's bag.

After one of our crisis meetings, I had promised the increasingly impatient panel of professionals that I would try a different high school. This one was further away, and I didn't know anyone there. I was almost fifteen and had barely attended school in three years. I stood in the strange classroom and stared at the strange children who all stared back at me. I must have looked odd, in a full face of heavy makeup, bronze and green eyeshadow up to my brows and dark copper lipstick. My hair was long at the back and arranged in a sort of split bouffant at the front, pinned back with two white plastic combs. I had invented the style one afternoon while experimenting, and I stuck by it stubbornly for months, even though I looked like a cross between a fifties housewife and a vampire. The combs needed to be adjusted every few hours. The drama of the hairstyle was precisely why I liked it, but I looked nothing like the clean-faced teenagers opposite me in rows of wooden desks.

After register, we had a business-studies lesson. I hadn't encountered this subject before. We were learning the difference between a limited company and a public limited company but, as it was the middle of term, I had missed some crucial information and struggled to concentrate. Instead I imagined myself in a suit, with a briefcase, going to work for a faceless giant utilities company, and the thought made me panic. I couldn't even go to school regularly: how was I meant to upgrade to an office job, which, after all, was much the same routine, uniform and hierarchies? Is that what school was training us for? I wanted to write or act or sing, or be a lawyer or journalist so I could argue all day and figure out what was wrong or right, or a librarian so I could talk about books.

I was relieved when the bell rang. I had the familiar ocean of anxiety, disorientation and anger in my stomach once again. I could feel myself not fitting in, and I wanted to run. Instead I went to a French lesson and was given a desk on the front row. Even I knew that wasn't cool.

I had never had a lesson conducted entirely in another language. At my old school, foreign languages were not taught in that way, but at this new school as soon as we were seated the teacher started speaking to us in French and we were meant to know what he was saying.

I did not know what he was saying because I had barely attended school for the last few years and my French was very behind, so I did nothing while the other children opened their textbooks. He noticed my inaction and kindly stopped so he could embarrass me in front of my new class-mates. He stared at me for a minute and said, 'You are wearing too much makeup. Please go and wash it off.'

It is true that by the standards of the other kids in class I was wearing *more* makeup, but I didn't know what *too much* was, when the uniform requirements included entirely decorative things like ties and mottos on blazers. Girls had to wear skirts but not too short, as there was such a thing as too much leg, but no one had said anything about makeup rules. This man I had never met before had simply decided that, however much eyeshadow was accept-able, I was over the limit. It was, I was sure, none of his business, so I lied and said I could not remove it as it was waterproof.

Because he didn't know the first thing about makeup other than what was too much, he accepted this.

'Make sure you don't do it again tomorrow,' he told me. I knew I was prepared to fight for my eyeshadow, but I wasn't sure what my options were. What if I just didn't come to this French lesson ever again? I didn't understand him anyway, and he clearly didn't understand me, so let's say *au revoir* before things get inevitably messy.

The makeup issue stretched before me, a vision of detentions or visits to the headmaster's office, and the fight exhausted me before I'd even had it. I had absolutely nothing in my power except self-expression and apparently that was 'too much'. Don't do it again tomorrow.

Somehow I got through that French lesson and the rest of the day, but there was no way I was going to get through the rest of my legal school years or even the rest of the week at that place.

Every rebellious teen has deeply held internal justifications, even if they don't yet have the words. I couldn't show everyone my face without the makeup that helped me look older, so I stopped going straight away. Jackie despaired and we fought. We were both exhausted, scared and broken, so went back to our one-day-at-a-time-tomorrow-will-be-better-I-promise-I'll-try routine. Sometimes she came to wake me in the morning in time to fight about school, but other times she would sleep in, because of the strength of her pills or perhaps the knowledge that my will was far stronger than hers. I would lie in bed, praying for it to be too late to get up for school.

The social worker suggested I try the same pupil referral unit that Emily had attended. I knew from Emily's stories that it wouldn't be the place for me, but I was willing to try. I wore my favourite outfit, shiny purple trousers with a purple silky blouse and purple fake-suede high heels, and took my place in a classroom of five or six other teenagers, all in jeans and trainers, all there because they had been expelled from school. They did not want to listen to the teacher, or to be taught, and I was scared of them. I found myself asking the same question as Emily had a few years before. Why can't I just learn at home, where it's safe and inspiring? I was scared and lost, and the pupil referral unit made that worse, so I stopped going there too.

20

W E HAD ALWAYS LEARNED together as a family. Jackie was the fastest typist, having been a secretary back in the day. Mike, Emily and I took it in turns to read out lines of code from the back of a BASIC coding book. BASIC was the programming language of the eighties, and with it you could make anything from games to digital art. Mike taught us to say 'string' instead of 'dollar sign'. We would swap jobs when it started to get boring, the kids doing one-finger typing and Jackie reading the code in her best posh telephone voice.

That voice, an approximation of Received Pronunciation, a.k.a. 'how newsreaders and Shakespearean actors talk', once attracted a wannabe phone stalker who became besotted after accidentally calling our house. Jackie told him he had the wrong number, but shortly after he called back to say what a lovely voice she had. And kept calling. After the fourth or fifth such call she put on her most authoritative voice and informed the caller, 'My husband is a policeman and if you call again he will have your number traced!' He never rang again. She would re-create the tone and vehemence when telling the story over the years, always with the same posh voice. I could almost hear the sound of the telephone slamming down at the punchline.

I'm glad Mike was a computer salesman rather than a policeman, though. It meant we always had computers in the house in an era when almost nobody did, let alone the lower classes. The explosion of home computing in Britain brought the Commodore 64, ZX Spectrum, and in our house the Amstrad 464, simply because my dad worked for Amstrad at the time it was launched.

Quite a few families on the estate had acquired a home computer by the late 1980s, usually on hire purchase from Rumbelows or Dixons, and for some, off the back of a lorry. We were fortunate in not having to pay for or steal any of ours, but that also meant they didn't belong to us permanently.

A few weeks after Mike died, two women, colleagues from the Amstrad office, came to collect his company car and the computer. They were crying, which I found odd given they didn't know us (it didn't really occur to me that they'd known him). It seemed rude to get upset in front of his widow and children. I also found it odd – unjust, I guess – that they were taking the computer. Surely the company could afford to let us keep it, I thought. I don't know where that sense of entitlement came from, other than the importance of a computer to our lives and my self-education. But the Amstrad bosses weren't to know that, and neither was it their problem.

It was, however, Jackie's problem. By 1990, once Emily had gone back to her boarding school where no computers or even a TV were allowed, our new normal was well and truly in flow. Our days were filled with board games and reading, mostly, but also writing. Jackie encouraged me to write, in part because she thought I was good at it and also because she loved to write poems and stories, and this became something we could do together.

She realized that computer games provided essential escapism for a depressed child. Plus, we had always played games together as a family. Coded together, learned together. It was more important than a television. My favourite of all the family computers had been the Amstrad 464. I had a dozen slow-loading games on cassette tape, and access to Amstrad BASIC for coding, but nothing on which to type a story or – optimistically – homework. But by 1990, that machine was long gone.

This was also the era of credit. Three decades ago, there were options to rent electrical goods from shops like Radio Rentals, an attractive proposition to families who didn't own their own home so were used to the feeling of living with someone else's property. Why buy something that might break or become obsolete when you could rent and simply swap it later for a newer model? Alternatively, there was hire purchase, credit with extortionate interest rates but the promise of ownership (unless you stopped paying).

One afternoon, I was worried about not having anything to write on. We had been looking over some of Jackie's old stories and I'd volunteered to help her rewrite one, a Christian sci-fi parable about the last man on Earth. I'm not sure what I thought qualified me to edit her writing, given I was fourteen, but we were both excited at the prospect, despite the small obstacle of not owning a typewriter or word processor.

Before the internet, getting credit required the store in question to telephone a centralized credit company and read out the details from a form we'd completed instore. Name, address, previous address, employer, that sort of thing. This meant giving a large amount of private information to a random sales assistant, then having to stand there while they read those details out loud over the phone and waited for the call-centre operative to give the yea or nay to a line of credit.

We had arrived at the electrical-goods store not long before closing, it being a spur-of-the-moment trip and a bus ride away. It sounds irresponsible to buy a computer on credit when the household barely had any income. Jackie had her widow's pension and the statutory family allowance. None of that was enough to justify a spending spree, but . . .

A commonly weaponized trope against poor people is the ownership of apparently indulgent 'massive tellies'. Few people who haven't lived in comparative poverty understand why we spend when we're poor. Ignoring the fact that most televisions look massive if the room they're in is small, that any family would choose to prioritize an entertainment device should be understandable with a moment's thought. You can't stare at the wall. There is, simply, little else with which to fill time. A television is solid, dependable, visible, the centre of the household, a window into culture, company for the lonely, and a connection to the wider world.

Jackie's version of this, towards the end of 1990, was to buy me a new computer, as we hadn't had one for more than eighteen months. The salesman in Dixons was excited to present the brand-new Amstrad 464Plus, an upgraded version of the one we used to have.

The salesman claimed that Amstrad would be releasing lots of amazing new games on this cartridge format, so of course I wanted to be ahead of the curve. Amstrad would do no such thing because (as fourteen-year-old me did not know) this particular computer was out of date before it began. Buying an 8-bit computer in 1990 was as behind the curve as it got, because the 16-bit era was just beginning. Mike would have known this.

Jackie and I did not know, so we fell for the sales spiel. The assistant had made a sale, and was inclined to push his luck. Surely we also needed a printer, for homework and such, he suggested. He was right, of course. What blossoming young writer didn't have a printer? Such a thing would elevate me. And Jackie was also a writer; perhaps she should have her own machine too. He showed us an electronic typewriter. Jackie was smitten with it. She told him she was a widow. The typewriter would be, he reassured us, just another few pounds a month.

He totted up our purchase total as we filled in the credit application – 'No job, I get a widow's pension.' Then we waited by the till for the judgement while he phoned the credit centre. The answer came back: yes. This had never happened to us before.

I have a photograph of that Amstrad, because it was important enough to warrant taking one. We set it up in the living room, the new centre of the household, rather than in my bedroom, and I would spend my days playing games, trying to code without access to any instruction, or writing stories.

Jackie was very involved in my gaming and writing, and asked me to help with hers.

The new electronic typewriter usually lived in its mottled grey case, but some afternoons we would set it up on the big table and she would help me improve my touchtyping while we worked on her stories and poems.

Every minute we spent on those machines had a cost. I don't believe we properly understood the nuances of buying on credit, and certainly not how compound interest worked, but as long as we were making the minimum payments at the post office every month, it didn't feel like debt. It never does, until you miss a payment and a red bill arrives. Then anxiety sets in, which turns into a psychological burden that can overwhelm.

It seems irresponsible for a widow to get into debt, but she was providing for me as best as she could while I refused to attend school regularly. We didn't spend money on new clothes or trainers or the other things parents bought their kids. We spent money on my future. I don't condone buying on credit, and I'd go as far as condemning the sometimes exploitative sales tactics and lack of clear information for the financially illiterate. But I also think it's not right that a working-class family can't access the same culture and educational tools as middle-class families. When I was growing up, under Margaret Thatcher, you could get a free telly from the council because TV was on an 'essentials' list. Telephones weren't, because those were a luxury easily replaced by letters. If you were too poor to afford a TV, even the government was sympathetic.

While my preference was to spend my days on the computer or reading, when the weather was good I walked. Explored, really, as I spent the time imagining I was a spy or Frodo Baggins. I'd spend the whole day walking around the estate and its wider areas, roaming for miles. No one knew where I was. Jackie believed I was at school. I was told by teachers, by Social Services, by family and church, you must go here, to this building, for these hours. You must do this and that. But when I wandered by myself around the estate or even further, my world truly opened up. I could go anywhere, do anything. I was in a tug-of-war between my education and my freedom, and freedom won, even if that meant I was locking myself out of so much.

Alone with my thoughts, I'd make up stories or imaginary conversations. I'd construct elaborate arguments for both sides, debating with myself (not about anything important; I was largely ignorant of the news beyond the BBC evening bulletin). I developed a huge sense of injustice and would rant about the ozone layer (I won a *Blue Peter* badge for a drawing of global destruction) or nuclear weapons (I wrote a terrible poem that, alas, did not survive the blast). Jackie was distressed by what she called my 'crusades', and didn't know how to help me channel my furious sense of unfairness and helplessness. My crusades were the product of having to navigate a system I had had no hand in designing. I was trying to *change* things.

Fortunately, I was a reader. Without my library card, the book tokens I got for Christmas and birthdays, and the literature Emily brought home from school, I don't know what I'd have done with that aggressive sense of injustice. As it was, I found what I needed in books. My reading moved up a notch. I invested in copies of *Animal Farm* and *1984*, and – because Emily was reading *Jude the Obscure* at school and had told me how tragic, how *unjust* it was

191

('done because we are too many' had us both in floods of tears) – I acquired every Thomas Hardy novel the Wordsworth paperback range offered. These 'one-pound classics' were the foundation of my education. I could buy ten works of literature, everything from Homer to Tolstoy to the full family of Brontës, for a tenner. That's a lot of books for a little money. Printed on cheap paper with pastel-toned covers, the books – so many of which make up the British canon – could be produced and sold so cheaply because they were out of copyright.

In those three years of self-guided learning, English was taken care of, and Emily had developed a passion for Ancient Egyptian history and art, which she, of course, passed on to me, to which I added Greeks and Romans. Latin was fine, I hadn't returned the Cambridge Latin textbook to my old school. Maths and science were more challenging. I had a set of jumble-sale *World of the Child* encyclopaedias from the 1950s that were woefully outdated but at least contained enough information that I could fill in some knowledge gaps. Otherwise I had to rely on snatches of insight from Open University shows on BBC2. I enjoyed mental arithmetic, in part because of Mike's teaching, so would look forward to the maths part of *Countdown* in which I would race the contestants to the answer. I usually failed, but the thrill of succeeding could sustain me for a week.

The older I got, the harder it was to fit back into school. Not only because I was socially isolated but because, by the age of fourteen, education was focused on GCSEs and had no flexibility. If I missed a month of school, then went back for a day, I was expected to pick up halfway through a subject. This was basically impossible for some disciplines. English was fine, because I could read the book and write the essay without needing to have been present the whole term. Maths was mostly okay, because I found it fairly intuitive so was motivated to catch up on whatever rules and terminology I had missed (even while being aware that it was deeply uncool to like maths). But everything else was a lost cause.

Some of it was like a waking nightmare. I would find myself in the middle of the sports field in my PE kit, expected to participate in a team sport that I did not know how to play. One afternoon, I turned up after a lengthy absence to discover I was expected to sit a German exam. I had attended precisely one German lesson over a year before, but I liked the quietness of exams so decided to do it anyway. I had nothing to lose and, you never know, it might be possible to fluke my way through it.

Write a conversation in German the exam instructed me. I had had to skip most of the paper because I didn't have the foggiest idea what any of it meant, but here I was invited to freestyle. Easy. I remembered my one German lesson well. We had learned basic numbers (*eins, zwei, drei*), basic drinks (*Bier, Cola*), and basic manners (*bitte, danke, nein* and *ja*). It was memorable because the teacher had played a language tape of a barman getting a drinks order wrong, to the great amusement of the underage class.

'*Zwei Bier und drei Cola, bitte,*' I wrote, my imaginary grown-up self buying drinks at a Frankfurt bar, probably panelled with wood and elaborate *steins*.

'*Drei Cola und ein Bier?*' the hapless fictional barman replied.

'*Nein! Zwei Bier und drei Cola, bitte!*' I insisted. But the barman got it wrong again. So I corrected him, again, back and forth until I had filled the page.

I wasn't there to get my results, so we can only guess at the outcome. I have since successfully ordered drinks in Frankfurt without miscommunication, so let's say I passed.

21

I F YOU MISS ENOUGH SCHOOL, the bogeyman will get you. Every truant knew that. I knew it because it had happened to Emily. Eventually, Jackie and I were called to a meeting with Social Services and the local education authority and given a final ultimatum: go to school or we will take you into care, just like your sister. And then Jackie will be alone, said no one in the room, but they didn't need to. This had been threatened a few times over the past few years, and every time I had tried to go back to school and eventually failed. But this time, it was made clear, I had run out of chances. If I didn't start going to school, I would miss out on GCSEs and then I wouldn't amount to anything at all.

If they couldn't make me go to school, then like hell could they make me leave my mother. She didn't have anyone else and neither did I. This scheme felt designed to punish rather than help me. There was absolutely no way that I would allow the authorities to take me into care. Emily had 'aged out' of care, reaching sixteen and no longer legally obliged to be educated or parented. She had a handful of GCSEs, and was now doing A levels at college in the city of Birmingham. She had moved in with our aunt, uncle and cousin Dani, and was now living a normal teenage life of pubs, clubs, friends and study. She had wanted to come back to live with us, but didn't want to attend the town's college, which in any case didn't offer the subjects she needed. She didn't confide to anyone in her new life about her strange past, and no one could tell.

Jackie was doing incredibly well, following her therapy with Sean. She could now get a bus by herself and therefore access training, and an office job. All of this felt like it was building towards an inevitability. Birmingham had a different local education authority from our small town's. If we moved, I would no longer be under the jurisdiction of the borough's Social Services or LEA and could have an even fresher start than those I'd tried before. I could go to a brand-new school where absolutely no one knew me, and Jackie could get a job and make new friends. Emily could come and live with us again.

My aunt and uncle lived in a suburb of Birmingham, in a small stone-clad mid-terrace house they had bought in the 1960s. Emily had recently taken possession of their tiny box room. Her bedroom in our house was the largest, and we kept it exactly as she had left it for when she visited, but her box room represented necessary distance from the estate and its traumas. Her ability to let go and move on gave me strength to do the same, even though our red-brick house – the King family's home – was the only one I'd known. My only two friends now were girls from the church, although as we all turned fifteen we seemed to be growing distant from organized religion. I had stopped going to church, but I still socialized regularly at the houses of the elders. I would miss the family church gatherings and barbecues in nice back gardens, where Mike had once joined us. Even the shops and the scene of his death were tied to me. Leaving that would be leaving Mike behind, for good.

But there was a part of his past, if not ours, that was newly available. The suburb Emily now lived in was the same area where my parents had bought their lost home, where Jackie and her twin Miriam had grown up and attended school. We would be a ten-minute walk from the pub where Jackie and Mike had had their first (blind) date and where they had done their courting and started a family. Jackie's happy memories lingered on every corner – 'This is where we went to pick bluebells!' If we could live in that area, Jackie would retain a link to Mike, and we'd have family near by. It felt like it could be home. All we needed to do was find a council tenant in the area who wanted to swap houses.

To start the process, we had to visit the Birmingham suburb's Neighbourhood Office, a branch of the local council where residents could get help with household repairs, benefits claims and sundry issues, to place a postcard listing in the ringbound album of 'exchanges wanted'.

Three bedroom terraced house available, upstairs bathroom and downstairs toilet, front and back gardens. We are seeking a two or three bedroom house or flat.

We scoured the pages of listings to see if anyone would consider a move outside Birmingham. No one would, and we left dejected. It was a slim hope that a local family would want to move to our rural town, although it was possible someone would consider the move from a two-bed to a three-bed. Emily desperately wanted to live with us again but we all knew we couldn't pin our hopes on three bedrooms. And yet within a few days our phone rang. A woman and her children urgently needed to leave Birmingham. Their home was a maisonette in a rough estate but it had three bedrooms. They seemed desperate. We were also desperate, and said yes there and then.

The plan somehow came together. I still shake my head in wonder when I think about how, the year I was fifteen, we ran away to Birmingham so I wouldn't be taken into care. We couldn't believe our luck. The house swap proceeded so rapidly and seamlessly that we didn't stop to consider why the other family was so keen to leave.

The Birmingham estate we moved to was more than rough, it was *notorious*. When I told people where I now lived, their eyes would widen in silent horror. Now long-demolished, our new home was a ground-floor red-brick maisonette in a block of a few dozen, facing other blocks in a square. The small wasteland in the middle was a no-go area of broken glass and abandoned syringes. Whatever attempt at landscaping had been made when the estate was new was long gone, shrubs torn up by the roots, leaving large holes that neighbourhood children poked at with sticks as I had done in the woods back home. But this was home now.

It was a very different sort of estate, on a busy main road into the city centre. I wasn't used to the lights or the sound of traffic at night but I quickly found I liked it, a reassuring ambience compared to the suspense of the night-time silence I had known before. I was determined to like my new home, particularly as my bedroom had its own radiator. I'd never been able to control the temperature in my room before. Bernice paid for a new carpet for me and one afternoon she and I fitted it (we always laid our own carpets, saved a fortune), discussing how everything would be okay now we were nearer to family: Jackie could get a job and, crucially, I could start at a new school. It was Jackie's old school and she had been fairly happy there, so, of course, I was bound to be. I wasn't going to be scared of traffic or of school; that was behind me now.

But everything else scared me silly.

The tiny gardens were full of litter, car parts, broken washing machines, long-abandoned toys, the cliché of a stained mattress. We kept our garden neat, removing the beer cans and discarded crisp packets that found their way in almost daily. Jackie had always been incredibly house-proud, so we quickly gained a reputation for snobbery, in no way helped by our actual snobbery. I had barely been to school for three years, dressed like a thirty-year-old Parisian secretary, cared only about books and computers, and had absolutely no idea how to talk to other children, let alone big-city estate children.

Just down the road there was a sprawling comprehensive, like the one in *Grange Hill*. I knew it by reputation, but Jackie's stories were from the 1960s. It was now the early nineties and the school had grown along with the local population. It was a terrifying prospect: low sprawling buildings I would never be able to navigate; classes twice the size of those in my tiny town, and a sort of social hierarchy I had never encountered before. I had barely socialized with anyone of my own age for the past three years, so I didn't know how to fit in anywhere, let alone at a city comp. I was bound to get into trouble straight away.

The class was having an informal discussion, something I hadn't really encountered before. I had been used to a formal learning style, where the teacher presents facts and questions students individually or asks for raised hands. It was new for the whole class to be welcome to pipe up at any time, although I realized quickly that in part that was because there was no way of stopping them. These were pupils who spoke their minds, without concern for discipline or repercussions. Perhaps here I could finally have a voice.

We were discussing the ancient world. The textbook had an illustration of Jesus that I thought was wrong, so I loudly said so. The class stared.

Wrong. I mean not wrong, as there is plenty of debate about portrayals in Western art that might make for an interesting class discussion. Wrong to say it.

The bell went and we filed out. A girl came up to me, furious. She wanted to know why I had opened my mouth. She told me I should keep it shut from now on. And then I felt the blow against my cheek as she hit me as hard as she could. No one had hit me before.

I ran to a stairwell and huddled there, crying. Children crowded round, some concerned, others enjoying the drama. Someone fetched a teacher, a man.

'What's the matter?' he asked.

I couldn't answer. I was paralysed with fear and shock.

'Did someone hit you?' he wanted to know. I said nothing, just carried on crying and hugging myself.

He had no patience for this. 'Well, if you won't tell me, then I can't help,' he said angrily, and left.

It felt like punishment. How could I possibly snitch on a girl who had just hit me for having a big mouth? I didn't know the rules of this school and those children, but it was very clear I had just been taught a lesson, and I'm a fast learner.

Eventually everyone left me alone, so I got up and went home. I developed a bruise on my face, near my eye. I had overstepped the invisible boundaries of teenagers, and had been punched in the face for it. The fresh start wasn't going too great. Jackie's furious trip to the headmaster's office resulted in my being moved into a different class, and I made friends.

I attended for about a month, and started to learn to socialize. But the school wanted me to remove the silverplated locket containing photos of my parents that Jackie had bought me for my fifteenth birthday. It replaced the crucifix I had stopped wearing and I was incredibly protective of it. They wanted me to wear a gym skirt for PE when I thought I should be able to wear shorts like the boys. I defended my corner and exhausted everyone.

The other schools I had been to had had small pupil numbers, so bullying and violence on school grounds were dealt with quickly and effectively. But this place seemed out of control, and some of the pupils seemed to have an authority I didn't understand. There were frequent fights among boys in the playground or classroom that scared me. A boy threatened me with a small kitchen knife, so I started skipping school again. The only safe places were home with Jackie and Emily, or the solitude of my wanderings. I had a whole new territory to explore. Birmingham airport was not far away and surrounded by fields. The bluebell woods of Jackie's courting days were now another council estate, but I was as happy to explore urban sprawl as nature. Little cut-throughs and gullies, dead ends leading to unattended blocks of garages, unexpected corner shops in residential enclaves.

I never went back to school.

A truancy officer knocked on our door one afternoon and was surprised to find me at home with Jackie. From there, a child psychologist came round to the house, and I was given a bunch of psychometric tests to figure out what sort of disobedience they could diagnose me with (I still have the tests; they're not supposed to be used on children). This was already more mental-health support than I'd had in the entire last three years. They immediately recognized that I was extremely keen on learning but was very unlikely to do it in a school. If I'd been younger it would have been too expensive to provide me with a personal tutor, but as I was way too late to start preparing for GCSEs, the best way for the LEA to fulfil its obligation to educate me was to send a home tutor for an hour at a time a few days a week.

She was a retired teacher, and we got on extremely well. She listened, and told me things, and laughed, but in an encouraging way, at my big ideas. I had maybe a dozen of these hour-long lessons over the next few months, covering everything from maths to ancient history to why I didn't want to go to school, and then I was sixteen and it didn't matter any more. The LEA was free of its obligation to educate me and I was free of the legal pressure to do things their way. I would do what Emily had done and go to college. But while she had gained a handful of GCSEs and gone straight to A levels, I had nothing except mental-health problems and an attitude like a brave but inexperienced kitten recklessly taking on a dog ten times its size.

22

I N THE FIRST WEEKS after we moved to Birmingham, Jackie and I visited friends from church a few times, but we were both uncomfortable being back on the estate. We stopped talking about religion at home almost immediately. I was a young adult without any idea what I was looking for, but I knew the church had not delivered it. Perhaps the city might. Even before we had packed away the last of our things for the move, I already knew I wouldn't be looking for a new church, although Jackie said she was considering it.

A few months after the move, Jackie and I went back to visit Mike's grave. Afterwards, we headed to a church social event, an afternoon tea at one of the elders' houses in the private bit of the estate. Going there felt like a step backwards. I found no trace of my old loyalty and wasn't comfortable answering questions about school and whether I was keeping up with my faith. I started to feel embarrassed about it, because I hadn't had anything in common with the church elders except our beliefs, and mine had been straying from the prescribed path for some time. We left and headed for the bus stop, and I knew I wouldn't be involved with the church again. It belonged to the old life, and new, believable possibilities were emerging. Memories and familiar spaces became an acceptable trade for a blank slate.

I put Mike's New Testament into the box under my bed. I was far better guided by Judy Blume, Diana Wynne Jones and Lloyd Alexander. And, sure, some of those morality tales were Christian allegory (C. S. Lewis, Madeleine L'Engle and George MacDonald remain favourites), but the morals were human, universal and asked for no belief. I did not think Aslan had literally to exist in order to accept his lessons of patience and kindness, and eventually I realized that was also true of God.

I lost touch with my remaining friends after one phoned me to say she had run away from home to join what I realized must have been a cult. She had phoned me with the strange glowing excitement of the recently radicalized and told me that smoking drugs made Satan enter your body through your feet. By then I was sixteen and could see her fundamentalism with the same eyes that others must have been able to see mine. I ended the phone call.

I had already stopped praying and seeing everything through the narrow lens of religion, but hearing someone my age breathlessly describe her new cultist beliefs made me realize how incompatible the whole thing was with being a teenager. I was meant to be 'coming of age', and my world had already opened up – geographically and socially – while hers had narrowed to an even tinier, more restrictive one than our estate church. It was the first time I really noticed how concerned religion was with morals. Sex, drugs, alcohol, certain types of rebellious music or film, individuality, independent thought and rejection of familial norms and tradition: all of these things were the story of teenagehood.

By the time I was sixteen my religious beliefs had faded away completely. It wasn't revelatory, I simply stopped thinking that if I didn't believe and worship I would go to Hell. I had lost countless nights of my childhood to fearful insomnia, feverishly praying for Jesus to protect me from satanic forces. I had been exorcized to banish demons from my immature brain and body, treated as a potential vessel of evil. I wanted to find other ideas. As religion lost its hold on me, I started to become interested in other explanations of how the world works.

I had once believed in religious healing, and had often tried to pray my pain away. I had been convinced by tales of the blind seeing, old ladies throwing away walking sticks, wheelchair users suddenly able to stand up and dance. God could, with sufficient prayer power, remove cancer and even bring the dead back to life.

But Jackie didn't trust our health to miracles: if one of us was ill, she made an appointment at the NHS surgery at the shops and we spent ten minutes with a doctor who had known us for years.

We had our vaccines on schedule, went down with chicken pox and the usual run of coughs and colds, but on the whole we were physically healthy children. We managed to avoid the nits that plagued estate schools, although on more than one occasion we caught the worms that everybody's pet had. The cure for this was a pink powder, which Jackie mixed for us with water in her special metal goblet to make it more like a chalice of magic potion than a bitter medicine.

Other healing options were available, too, although it wasn't until Emily went to boarding school that I learned alternative medicine existed. It was the obvious choice for a school of that type, in line with the no-computers-or-TV ethos that was really about rejecting technology and science. If Emily had period pain, she was given homeopathic remedies. Her house mother would sneak her paracetamol in a sensible breach of rules, but everything else was alternative. Medicine, food, even the festivals they celebrated, which included Lanternmas, Candlemas, and a St John's Day ritual in which a magnifying glass was used to start a bonfire; when the fire died down, the children took part in a ritualistic jump over the embers. This type of thinking was baked into the lifestyle and indeed the education.

The school's cleaning products and even toothpaste were proudly 'chemical-free'. In one lesson, Emily was taught about homeopathy: 'Imagine you take a herb or flower and put it into gallons of water. Then you take a tiny drop of that water and dilute it in gallons more water. The water retains a memory of the original flower or plant and it becomes a gentle restorative way to heal. You have to hit a vial of that water against a Bible a special number of times.' She didn't question the logic or plausibility of water retaining a memory of one specific thing, let alone whether that herb or flower has healing properties in the first place. And because she didn't query it, I didn't either.

This made for a straightforward teenage segue from mainstream religion into alternative remedies and spiritual practices, which seemed to offer something for mental health that the GP did not. Really what I needed was therapy, but instead I invested in flower remedies suspended in what I later learned was simply alcohol (no wonder a few drops on the tongue felt nice). Most of these things had been considered if not outright satanic, then certainly dangerous in my previous religion, so their temptation now formed part of my transition from born-again Christian to a new word I had recently learned: agnostic.

I felt like I had autonomy. I had potential, and now I was going to fulfil it. First, I would need a proper education.

'What do you want to do for a living?' said the admissions officer of the local college to sixteen-year-old me. My role models in that regard had been limited. Most of the families I knew had not been to university, had jobs to pay the bills rather than wealth-creating careers. The future was supposed to be parenthood. Everything else was a nice-to-have. I didn't even know what my career options were. Jackie, free of her limiting phobias, had gone to adult education classes to get an NVQ in office-admin skills while she worked part-time in the local supermarket (until she was held up at gunpoint and never went back, even though she had been well aware the gun was a fake and had bravely told the would-be robber to sod off).

Office admin was a possibility for me, as I was confident handling computers and could already touch-type. I'd been working in shops and on market stalls since I was fourteen, but shop management didn't appeal. Jackie's lifelong ambition was to run a milliner's, and we talked about our dreams often. We were both teetotallers and joked about opening a soft-drinks bar called High Sobriety. These businesses were pipe dreams anyway – might as well make them enjoyably ridiculous. In reality, I had to pick an ambition that would bring in enough money to stop future me being homeless, which was always just a bit of bad luck or one foolish choice away.

But what did I actually want to *do*? Emily was studying art, and doing very well. Her college life was fun, and as she shared her learning with us I began to see myself in further education. I was no longer legally obliged to *be* educated. Instead, I could *get* educated. One downside of not doing GCSEs is they give you a little taste of lots of subjects, so you have some clue about what you like doing or are good at and can shape your ambitions accordingly. I only knew in very limited terms what I was good at. But I did know what I liked doing, and that didn't need any GCSEs. From the very first play in primary school to my winning turn in a talent contest, I had wanted to be on the stage.

Stage acting requires training and opportunity. I had no idea how to get into theatre, but I did know it wasn't going to happen without a qualification of some sort. I didn't realize that the local college only offered technical subjects. The admissions officer insisted that a BTEC First was equivalent to five GCSEs, so I should do one of those. A 'vocational qualification', these courses were meant to be attractive to employers who were looking for more specific skills. After the BTEC First, I could do a BTEC National, or A levels. After that I could even go to university, although no one in my family ever had. It was a good plan, and the feasibility of actually becoming a stage actor didn't really factor. Until now.

'Ah,' he said, a bit amused. 'Well, we don't do the arts here. What else do you enjoy?'

Oh. I faltered. I hadn't really thought that there might

not be an option to train in the arts. On the spot I had to pick a new career path. But what else did I enjoy? I'd always wanted to be a librarian, the only career in books I knew existed, but he had nothing for that.

'Computers,' I said.

Correct answer! Thank goodness. I could see visible relief on his face. The college had the perfect course, a BTEC First in Information Applications, which was basically coding plus a couple of modules on graphic design and, optionally, a foreign language. I chose German because I had once done brilliantly in an exam. He enrolled me there and then.

All the other students on the course were also sixteen, and male. I hadn't really engaged with boys my own age for four years, except to scorn them when they chatted me up, or to cross the road if they were in packs. Now I was the only girl on a computing course. But these computing boys didn't scare me like most estate boys did, although they were from the same demographic. They, too, hadn't sat GCSEs, either because of bullying, illness, or problems at home.

We were all in love with technology. Crucially, none of us had many friends or any romantic interests, and we were the oddball corner of the college compared to the cool, trendy lads on other courses, so a few of us became a team. We bonded over video games, science fiction and coding. In the German class, I did a presentation on the filmmaker Wim Wenders and no one took the mickey. Unpopular, socially or physically awkward, our group was a union of the bullied. None of us particularly had social skills, being loners or outcasts, so we developed them together. After a few weeks, a third of the class had dropped out, leaving eight of us, then six. We must have made a strange sight, five unfashionable, awkward sixteen-year-old boys in creased trousers, hand-me-down jumpers and unbranded trainers, plus one aloof, skinny girl in cheap market pastel jeans, a tiny crop top exposing as much mid-riff as she could, giant hairsprayed coiffure and a full face of makeup. Alone, each of us would have been a target, had always been a target. Together, we could discuss our ambitions and interests without being mocked or ostracized or punched.

My new best friend was a tall, kind boy named Tim who helped me cope when my granddad Symon died. We took to visiting the runway of Birmingham airport to spot planes. He came to my house for lunch most days, as it was ten minutes' walk from the college. We hung out chastely in my bedroom, sometimes with a few of the others, play-ing games on my now outdated computer. None of those boys ever made a pass at me, unlike the lads on other courses who would sit in the canteen and stare, then occa-sionally send a brave volunteer to wander over and say, 'My mates think you've got a boyfriend. Are they right?'

They were not right. I did not have a boyfriend and had no idea what I would do with one. But I did have a group of proper friends for the first time since I was a child, and I was much happier. Jackie was happy for me, despite the presence of teenage boys in her house. She mothered my new friends with tea and toast, and trusted them if I did. Teenage boys had been my source of fear for four years, but now I better understood why they hung out in packs.

I also discovered subculture. Birmingham has a rich

history of rock and heavy-metal music. Everyone had a Judas Priest or Black Sabbath story, and, of course, Robert Plant of Led Zeppelin was from just down the road in the Black Country. Emily had become friends with the alternative-music kids at her college and started going to rock pubs and clubs. In 1993, when I was seventeen, they invited me to see Metallica at Milton Keynes Bowl. On the coach there, these slightly older, black-eyelinered teenagers played mix tapes and enthused about music in a way I'd never experienced before. Some of them were in bands that seemed to channel angst and joy at the same time. The venue was packed, and in the tens-of-thousands-strong crowd I felt unity and kin-ship. Tim was in the rock tribe too, and for Christmas bought me a book about Guns N' Roses, the first gift I'd ever received from a boy. I still have it.

Rock music and culture often played with themes of black magic and Satan, not because we believed in it but because we knew it was made up. My new friends were as much into the *Lord of the Rings* as Iron Maiden's satirical blasphemy. No wonder rock and heavy metal inspired a Christian moral panic. When I was a believer, I could tell we were being disrespected and were threatened by what we thought was a genuine demonic force working its way into the world. The Antichrist would come because Satan's servants – heavy metal bands – had let him in. If demons can be exorcized, they can also be summoned, which was what we believed those long-haired leather-clad musi-cians and their fans were doing.

But now that I had friends in heavy-metal bands and saw things from another perspective, I finally let go of my lingering worries about Hell. I realized that if I no longer believed in God or Jesus, I no longer had to be scared of Satan or his evil doings. I could just enjoy the iconography and lyrics, like I enjoyed Greek mythology or Disney musicals. I was doing well.

I passed the BTEC First, and now had what I had been assured was a qualification equivalent to five GCSEs. This meant I could go on to a BTEC National, which was allegedly equivalent to three A levels. Another college, two bus rides away, offered a brand-new vocational qualification in Performing Arts. I could train in acting, singing, dancing, scriptwriting and stagecraft. I got a part-time job in a deli and became a drama student.

Studying the performing arts is a gift to the traumatized. For the first time, I had mentors, educators who became friends, and they took an interest in my potential. I had to learn to control my face and body to channel and communicate a whole range of emotions. I learned to write scripts, and started to develop a sitcom about Arthur Dent and Ford Prefect sharing a bedsit. I had the longed-for singing lessons, and we took a comedy musical to the Solihull Library Theatre. Emily painted scenery for the set and Jackie sewed my costumes. I don't think they missed a performance. I also learned to control my breathing, which tells the frightened body that there is no threat. I inhaled all this new knowledge as if I was desperate for oxygen. I turned eighteen, becoming an adult for real this time, and no one was looking over my shoulder to tell me what I should be learning. I read everything. Not with humility, but with a sort of righteous fury that there was knowledge to be had and it was being kept from me.

I was free from the limitations of religion, but over the

next few years I looked for as many things as possible to think and read about. I bought Eastern mystical objects, like meditation balls, tarot cards, and several books on astrology from a heavily scented shop specializing in Zen merchandise. I tried to develop psychic skills, telekinesis and divination. I went through phases of studying spiritualism, numerology and Nostrodamus, but nothing stuck for more than a few months. I'd get bored and move on to the next idea. The poet Wisława Szymborska said, 'People speak of incompetent writers, but never incompetent readers.' I read without knowledge, and still thought that if something was published in a book, it must be true. I didn't even know I was allowed to question something in print. Doing so felt like blasphemy.

My boyfriend and I were driving to band rehearsal, which was how we met. Liam was the songwriter and rhythm guitarist in a rock band, and I had recently joined as a backing singer. We became friends immediately, both driven by our dedication to the band and our impending huge record deal, which was surely just a demo tape and a few gigs away. We quickly fell in love.

Liam was two years older, an electrical apprentice by day, a rock god by night, and somewhat my protector the rest of the time. I'd confided in him about Mike and the various traumas of my childhood, and he wanted me to have normality. In his world, one of four strapping sons with parents whose gender roles were as traditional as in any 1950s home, there was a home-cooked meal three times a day that he didn't have to think about or plan. The few times I went there for dinner, his mother would also prepare the next day's packed lunch for her husband and sons to take to work, and she always offered to make one for me. Of course I always refused. I found the secure domesticity of their family intimidating rather than comforting. Here was not an underclass family marked by trauma or poverty, but a classic blue-collar upwardly mobile working-class family. They worried about bills, but not bailiffs. I felt awkward and out of place, a dark stain on their chequered tablecloth, and I didn't want his picture-postcard family to know what the estate I lived on was like.

My family couldn't escape crime, death, or chaos – the sort associated with 'problem' areas. The neighbourhood children terrorized us. The quiet, vulnerable widow and her two bookish daughters were easy targets. No man about the house, no real kinship with the other residents, and therefore no loyalty towards us. We hadn't grown up on that estate, so were outsiders. When the council had to do essential work on the roof of the maisonette, they erected scaffolding against our house. At night, the local kids would climb it and try to enter our bedrooms, or bang on the windows to scare us. We huddled together in Emily's room, petrified they would get in, listening to them taunt us through the windows.

Petty crimes against our home escalated to crimes against our persons. The same kids would throw rocks at me and Emily, once striking her head. They would follow me down the street, shouting abuse. We were clearly afraid of them. This was different from the old estate. Worse, because we were new, and we didn't have the hum of my dad's legacy around us any more. We weren't Mike King's widow and kids now. We were just that weird, different family on the corner, and kids hate weird and different. So they attacked us, and we didn't fight back because we did, indeed, think we were better than them.

The children who lived next door even broke into our house, stealing my portable stereo – the only thing of value I owned – and some of my clothes. The thought of them being in my bedroom, rooting through my belongings and laughing at me made me sick, but the police said there was nothing they could do.

The chaos of that particular block was not confined to us, and many times I was simply witness to other people's hell. In 1994, I was lying in bed writing my diary late at night. My room was dimly lit by my bedside lamp. My curtains were closed to block out the bright light of the main road outside and to stop children seeing in and shouting abuse, as they had done so often before. I heard a car, so, of course, I immediately made a small gap in the curtains and looked out.

My window became the screen of a television showing a horror movie. Two men, Sam and Graham, had been trying to run away from the car, while the driver – and this is not something I will ever be able to explain – accelerated and deliberately ran over them.

Sam, a man who lived in our block, was still alive but with serious injuries. But Graham was tangled in the car and dragged to the top of the road, dead.

The killer was a taxi driver. Rumour next day said they were trying to dodge the fare, as though that could possibly qualify as a motive. I never learned what makes a taxi driver snap and deliberately run over two men. Rage? Psychosis? As a child I would have been told – and believed – it was Satan working through him, but by now I had figured out that the terrible, violent things that happen are not acts of demonic possession but failures of human autonomy.

The family of the man who died went through something I understood, but no one should have to. A senseless death, the knock on the door, the police and the crime scene, the autopsy and the agonizing wait for, first, the funeral and then the trial. The gossip and the strange looks and the failure of most people to know how to treat you; and then, after far too short a time, the realization that they've just got on with their lives and forgotten about the man who died or the crime in their neighbourhood.

I never forgot the man who died outside my bedroom window, as witnesses to awful things rarely can, but I had no choice other than to put a stranger's death behind me. I was already vulnerable, petrified I would be called to give evidence, like Jackie had in 1988. My diary entry the next day says:

I hope I don't have to go to court, I don't think I can handle it. I need to see a doctor or something.

I had told the police what I saw, but as there were other, closer witnesses, my testimony wasn't needed. I felt guilty about my relief until the perpetrator was convicted of murder.

23

To escape the escalating crime and violence, Jackie and I moved to a first-floor concrete two-bedroom flat in a safer area, while Emily moved into a bedsit with her long-term boyfriend.

Liam would pick me up from college and take me to McDonald's on the way home. We'd discuss books or films over a Big Mac and fries, or in the car on the way to band practice, and I thrived. He encouraged me to write, and liked to read as much as I did.

About a year into our relationship, he recommended a non-fiction book that he had just read about ancient humans. It sounded fun.

I learned that technologically advanced civilizations with great secrets had existed before modern history, and had left clues around the world. I found I could understand the book's claims and I accepted them as readily as I'd accepted my horoscope or that water has magic memory. I felt educated.

I read a few more books along similar lines, and discovered that aliens had once existed and still might. Alien civilizations or lost technologies were warmly familiar after the multiple viewings of *Close Encounters of the Third Kind*, *Cocoon* and *Batteries Not Included* we'd enjoyed as a family. One Christmas, Mike had acquired a bootleg copy of Spielberg's film *E.T. the Extra-Terrestrial* on Betamax. His present from Bernice and Symon that year had been a pair of tan leather driving gloves, and he spent quite a lot of the afternoon poking a gloved forefinger around the doorframe and saying, 'Phone home,' in a shaky voice to entertain us.

I read unsolved mysteries and resolved never to fly over the Bermuda Triangle. I found arguments for the Loch Ness Monster and Bigfoot if not compelling then something to consider.

The authors set out the arguments and evidence to support their theories. This wasn't helped by my avid fandom of *The X-Files*, which I took not as a brilliant work of fiction but as a sort of dramatized version of reality, in which such things were not only possible but, in a world where crazy things clearly happened (to me), probable. I was still seeking explanations for life's inexplicably cruel randomness.

If you have believed in an interventionist God, it's really easy to believe in a secret conspiratorial cabal pulling the strings, particularly if you haven't yet learned that just believing in things without further query is not necessarily a good idea. I knew the lads in the gang had conspired to get their mate off a manslaughter conviction. If that sort of injustice was possible, then anything was possible. The alien conspiracy theories were like the anger phase of grief, helping to contextualize the innate injustice that had cut my childhood short. A teenager angry with the world in general can find a lot of comfort and company in 'the truth'. It never occurred to me that conspiracies always have insidious, nefarious motives. You don't get internet rumours of a secret society of billionaires planning to make everyone happy. Good things aren't credited to government cover-ups, only bad things. Conspiracy theories are, by nature, bad faith. But I thought I had discovered the truth in those books.

Really what I had discovered was non-fiction. I just didn't yet know that non-fiction didn't always mean true.

After college, I'd had a vague plan to move to London and look for a theatre job. But my band was beginning to do well and trying to get a record deal, so that took priority. Liam had recently moved in with me, and I couldn't imagine leaving my life and moving to a frightening capital city that would swallow me whole. The other option was university. A few years later, tuition fees would be introduced, but for now it was free for those who couldn't afford to pay. I wasn't sure if I wanted to go to university at all, but I knew I was supposed to. When I was nine, my favourite teacher had told Jackie so. When I was fifteen, Louise the social worker had also told me so. She said I would finally find my 'people' there. But I already had my people.

Birmingham had two universities – a traditional red-brick in a wealthy area, and a former polytechnic three bus rides away in one of the roughest parts of the city.

I wanted to do an English degree. The BTEC in Performing Arts had given me a wealth of experience in multiple non-performance disciplines (from sound and lighting to stage management to budgeting), by far my favourite of which was writing. I had produced essays on Ancient Greek theatre or the influence of Stephen Berkoff, plays of just about every genre. I had written comedy sketches, tragedy scenes, even plays for children, but neither university would accept a BTEC National in Performing Arts with an English module in lieu of an English A level. This was disappointing. I'd been promised by the college that the BTEC was 'equivalent' to A levels and that employers and universities knew this. But it simply wasn't true. English degrees were hugely popular and oversubscribed, so the university had no reason to take anyone who didn't have good A levels. My second choice was a law degree, but those were A levels only too.

The head of the law department at one of the universities invited me in for a chat, and offered me a place on a new, under-subscribed course, BA Government. It was a mix of politics and law. I knew nothing about politics and had no political affiliation, but it sounded challenging and interesting and I didn't have any other option, so I said yes.

There were a dozen other people on the course, mostly teenagers but a few mature students. Most had either a law A level, a politics A level, or both, and I quickly learned why those were useful. I knew nothing. The UK was in the middle of a general election, and it was the first time I had been eligible to vote. We were supposed to have strong, lifelong-held opinions about politics, policies and parties. I didn't know who the then chancellor of the exchequer was (or what that job actually entailed). I didn't even know what the difference was between the main parties. Unlike books, computers and theatre, politics had not been a part of my life. I fell into a spiral of self-doubt. Formal learning instantly revealed how much I didn't know, and that was a strong demotivator.

My knowledge gaps were too great. I simply didn't have the necessary skills. The Fortean books I was reading had presented ideas as a packaged deal, no scrutiny required. I enjoyed the law lectures and did well with history essays, but contemporary political debate required at the very least a historical knowledge of formal logic and politics. I had none. I made friends, but told them nothing about my early life. I sat in the union bar in bemused silence as they talked passionately about things that were simply above my head.

Maybe if I'd admitted I didn't know what they were talking about, I could have opened a door to catching up. But I didn't feel I was on the path to a career. One afternoon in a law class we had to discuss the difference between murder and manslaughter. I tried to argue, but got overwhelmed and upset. Unable to tell anyone why, I left. I found myself wandering the campus, walking aimlessly with my racing thoughts as I had done for so many years on the estate.

Eventually I went home and called the English department of the university to request to switch to an English degree, but without a relevant A level they still wouldn't consider it.

If the university hadn't been multiple expensive bus rides away every day, or if this, that and every other thing had been different, maybe I would have stuck it out. Over the next few months Liam and I split up, and while we remained friends and continued the band, my life changed. I was living alone, completely skint, and the university course I didn't like wasn't worth the poverty. I was so tired of it, of living on microwave pizza and scraping together bus fares. I'd worked part-time in shops and pubs the whole way through college, but maybe I just needed to quit trying to get a proper education, and instead get a proper job. So I stopped going to university and went to the local job centre.

Job centres in 1997 were a hybrid of computer technology and the old school notecards my dad had spent so much time perusing there in the eighties. In the middle of the fluorescently lit, grey-carpeted room was a bank of ridged noticeboards, each ridge holding a small lined notecard with handwritten job details. When I was on the dole, it was a condition of the benefits to choose three notecards per week and apply for those jobs. The noticeboards were divided into sections for each job type. Retail, hospitality and entertainment, manual labour (factory work made up the bulk of the job adverts), sales, admin, secretarial, and so on. White-collar listings were rare, and usually required secretarial qualifications or were for commission-only sales. But today, magically, something I had never seen before:

PA AND MARKETING ASSISTANT
– computer literacy
– graphic design
– customer service

Hello. What's this, then? No real idea what a PA is or what marketing is, but I seem to be qualified for it. I took the little white card from the ridge to one of the booths, where a staff member looked up the job details.

'It's for a classic-car company,' she said. 'They want

someone to help in the office, run the computer, and design their adverts and brochures. Do you want me to give them a ring?' After a brief chat with the business owner, she handed the phone to me. I spoke to a very sweet, very posh old man and told him I had a BTEC First in Information Applications, which suddenly sounded very grand and relevant. He sounded impressed. I heard him repeat the information to his wife, with whom he ran the classic-car business from their house.

'We did have a young man interested,' he said, 'but he doesn't have any computer experience.'

Sorry to that young man for gazumping his job, but it was nice to be the qualified one for once. I went for an interview the same day, puzzled and delighted by the rich chaos of their large house in one of the fanciest areas of Birmingham. They gave me the job, and my new marketing career began.

My two bosses, delightfully quirky (one was a morris dancer), treated me like an adopted niece, giving me full creative control of branding, copywriting, catalogue and advert design, and sometimes dog-walking and hoovering their house. They thought I was an IT wizard. Working on an ancient CRT monitor with a twelve-disk copy of Harvard Graphics and Word for Windows, I taught myself how to design a product catalogue. Eventually I persuaded them to trade in their old dot matrix printer to an inkjet, and to upgrade from a 1980s floppy disk database to a new PC. I taught myself how to use customer relationship management software and build databases, and they proudly showed off my work to their customers.

Being given the space to develop my own career was a

perfectly timed gift. Perhaps a university degree would have been as useful, or differently useful, but a few years' work experience with a thousand facets was valuable in ways formal learning was not. As my skillset and experience grew, so did my confidence. Eventually I had handled every type of person, query, problem or even catastrophe the weird world of vintage motoring could throw at me, and had been a passenger in some of the most beautiful vehicles ever designed. It was a good time.

And those always end. Eventually my bosses wanted to move to the coast for their retirement, and I was out of work and back on the dole, but this time with a CV full of skills.

24

A FEW MILES FROM MY FLAT, there was a large suburban village. It had a second-hand bookshop that I'd passed on the bus many times but never visited. The village had lost its charm but the bookshop endured, an olde-world anachronism with a painted wooden sign and crates outside full of ragged hardbacks in cloth bindings. All second-hand bookshops should look like this, of course. It had always intrigued me, partly because bookshops are rare on estates, and partly because it had erratic opening hours, which gave it the air of one of those magic shops from short stories that disappear after you've purchased a mysterious, life-changing manuscript (ideally leather-bound with strange runes on the cover and a tingle when you touch it).

I had run out of books on conspiracy theories and aliens, finding their quality had quickly dwindled and not opened up any interesting new avenues of learning, so had an eye open for old books on similar subjects. I thought I had discovered something, and it made me feel clever and informed. Everything that hadn't made sense about the world suddenly did, and I knew the great secrets of the universe.

These beliefs were a better proposition than religion,

which had taught me that every little thing I did mattered if I wanted to get to Heaven. It had been exhausting centring God in my every move and thought, and I was long done with it. Our particular form of Christianity had conspiracy baked in (there's an evil force fighting for control of the world, cleverly manipulating human hierarchies for his own ends), and I was a little lost without an overarching power and creation myth justifying the existence of humanity. But the knowledge that secret powers were pulling strings and suppressing alien technology inspired me.

The inside of the second-hand bookshop was as clichéd and chaotically perfect as the exterior. Overcrowded mahogany shelves ran from floor to ceiling, books of all heights and designs, faded colours and dated typefaces all crammed in together under hand-laminated genre badges, like NEW AGE and WORLD HISTORY, leaking the chemical smell correctly known as lignin but more familiarly called 'musty books'. There wasn't a CONSPIRACY THEORY section and neither would I have known to go looking there, but I wandered to the label marked SCIENCE and it seemed the right ballpark. There weren't many books in that section, which wasn't even a shelf but merely an uncurated messy pile on top of a box. Some old textbooks, a few non-fiction books by authors I didn't recognize. The one on the top of the heap immediately grabbed me.

The Demon-Haunted World: Science as a Candle in the Dark.

It was a paperback, well-thumbed, with pale broken creases down the dark spine that hinted someone had found it worth reading from cover to cover. It was black and had the sort of design and typography only seen on American editions of books. A picture of Planet Earth, blue and green, dramatically lit from behind. Perhaps it was about aliens. Across the top in large letters, the author's name: Carl Sagan. Never heard of him. I flipped the book over. The author in the photo smiled out at me, a pleasant man with seventies-style hair, a roll-neck jumper and a suit jacket. Whatever an 'astrophysicist' was, it sounded like it would involve UFOs or ancient alien civilizations. Up my street, I thought. Plus, demon-haunted? That could be interesting. I'd had a few demons myself.

The book was two pounds, much cheaper than the original cover price of seven ninety-nine, so I bought it, and started reading it on the bus home.

Sagan opens with a preface about the relationship between science and poverty:

> In 1939 my parents took me to the New York World's Fair. There, I was offered a vision of a perfect future made possible by science and high technology.
>
> The 'World of Tomorrow' would be sleek, clean, stream-lined and, as far as I could tell, without a trace of poor people.

And then,

> My parents were not scientists. They knew almost nothing about science. But in introducing me simulta-neously to scepticism and to wonder, they taught me the two uneasily cohabiting modes of thought that are central to the scientific method. They were only one

step out of poverty. But when I announced that I wanted to be an astronomer, I received unqualified support – even if they (as I) had only the most rudimentary idea of what an astronomer does.

Sagan goes on to say his childhood education was deficient in many areas, in particular 'no soaring sense of wonder, no hint of an evolutionary perspective, and nothing about mistaken ideas people once believed':

> There was no encouragement to pursue our own interests or hunches or conceptual mistakes. In the backs of textbooks there was material you could tell was interesting. The school year would always end before we got to it. You could find wonderful books on astronomy, say, in the libraries, but not in the classroom. Long division was taught as a set of rules from a cookbook, with no explanation of how this particular sequence of short divisions, multiplications and subtractions got you the right answer. In high school, extracting square roots was offered reverentially, as if it was a method once handed down from Mt Sinai. It was our job to merely remember what we had been commanded. Get the right answer, and never mind that you don't understand what you're doing.

I had been filling the gaps in my education with literature, but it had never crossed my mind to revisit science or maths because I had no idea there was a philosophy to them, or a science to my interests. I had experienced them as rote teaching, a set of principles without application and processes without understanding. When, aged about ten, I had correctly used a method in maths that Mike had taught me, I was chastised by the teacher and told to use the textbook method instead, without explanation of why I should find the answer one way and not another. No one had ever said, hey, actually science and maths are a way of *thinking*. Maybe the textbook method was better than Mike's method, or maybe there was a totally different method superior to both, or perhaps all methods were equal, but it had never occurred to me it might be fun to find out.

I'd been interested in many ideas. Possession and curses, ghost hunting or mysticism, conspiracy theories about the Bermuda Triangle, looking for a lens through which to examine my life. Sagan talks about some of those same ideas, and explains their flaws and the counter-evidence. He teaches the reader how to do the same, and how the scientific method works. I learned about pseudo-science and how to spot it, and suddenly understood a lot more Terry Pratchett and Douglas Adams jokes.

I felt a stir of excitement that I might now have a way of working things out for myself. It had been much easier to excuse my educational gaps when I believed that the most valuable knowledge was paranormal. I could have been disappointed or even angry, but instead I was fascinated. It's possible to . . . think better? Surely thinking was thinking.

I found the humility of Sagan's science more compelling than the certainty of pseudoscience, in part because Sagan includes the caveat 'But I could be wrong.' When Mike was helping me with my homework, he always said that being wrong is an opportunity to improve.

I discovered that astronomy is the science of the stars and planets, and astrology is the pseudoscience of them, as homeopathy is the pseudoscience of medicine. The bits that cling when science has moved on. Science, when done well, values being wrong as much as being right. Otherwise no progress can be made.

I learned about the concept of a 'testable claim', and the basic principle that extraordinary claims require extraordinary evidence.

Homeopathy, psychic abilities, astrology, statues crying blood, photos of alien civilizations on the moon are all testable claims. And they had been tested, in some cases to exhaustion, and consistently found wanting. Yet they persist, not because they somehow transcend proof but because they give big answers without it.

For my eighth birthday, Jackie and Mike had bought me Usborne's *First Guide to the Universe* by Jane Chisholm, to encourage a growing interest in science. I'd promptly set about writing an essay about my favourite chapter, 'What's in the Sky?', carefully drawing illustrations. When I'd proudly showed my family they'd been delighted. Jackie was happy to learn why the stars twinkle, while Mike, who already knew, admired my art.

I didn't return to *The Demon-Haunted World* again for a very long time, but read Sagan's other work, alongside other science authors. Over the decades, I filled some of the glaring gaps in my education and learned how to tell fact from fiction, even in the non-fiction section. I worked on my career, which I had decided was going to be many things at once. I couldn't see myself as a scientist and couldn't afford to start my schooling all over again; besides,

I wasn't someone who wanted to do just one thing. I had lots of ambitions and ideas, and was interested in the intersection of art and science. Both, I observed, start with the wonderful question 'What if?'

I wanted to work at that intersection and develop new skills. I taught myself animation software, became a producer. I wanted to make educational cartoons and do stand-up comedy about science, so I did. Over the course of my marketing career I had learned so much, including how to collaborate, so I took my skills and ideas, moved to London, and went into science communication. I had to take some frightening risks, but had had a complicated relationship with fear ever since marching up to that police officer to ask what was going on. What did I have to lose compared to what I'd already been through? Besides, Jackie, Emily and I had always supported each other in our goals, however out of reach they seemed, and Birmingham wasn't that far away. I spent years on projects that made me feel the joy of learning. I made many mistakes, and had a lot of therapy, but finally got to a place where the past could no longer hurt me.

Perhaps it's because I had so much else to think about and do that I placed my traumatic childhood in its own special untouchable file for so long. I no longer believed or needed to believe in any of the spiritual, religious or paranormal claims of my youth, and it was all muddled together in a way that prompted no examination. Where religion and the rest had focused on the past, science looked – and worked – to the future. I'm done with the past, I must have thought. Or, more likely, I didn't really think about the facts at all. I had emotional scars from Mike's death, the gang's arrest for murder, the subsequent collapsed trial. I told very few people over the years, just a few close friends and partners. The circumstances of Mike's death became a private story that had once dominated my psyche and mental health. If I thought about my dad I thought about those boys, the trauma, our religion, my exorcism, the suicidal feelings, the anger and pain. The story of his death overshadowed the joy of his life. Our family life. For a long time, it was better to keep that particular book closed. But as the decades passed and I became a writer, eventually I began to wonder if I should put some of that life on the page. By now, if I was an expert in anything, it was surely my own life story.

When Carl Sagan said, 'But I could be wrong,' he was talking about pseudoscience. In a chapter entitled 'Science and Hope', he wrote:

Science is more than a body of knowledge; it is a way of thinking. I have a foreboding of America in my children's or grandchildren's time – when the United States is a service and information economy; when nearly all the key manufacturing industries have slipped away to other countries; when awesome technological powers are in the hands of a very few, and no one representing the public interest can even grasp the issues; when the people have lost the ability to set their own agendas or knowledgeably question those in authority; when, clutching our crystals and nervously consulting our horoscopes, our critical faculties in decline, unable to distinguish between what feels good and what's true, we slide, almost without noticing, back into superstition and darkness.

I had proudly believed myself well-equipped to avoid that slide because it is possible to distinguish between what's true and what feels good. What I hadn't considered is that this principle – one that underpins personal and societal progress – applies as much to the past as to the future. I hadn't thought to question the difference between what is true and what feels *bad*. I hadn't ever told my story and added the all-important, thoughtful caveat . . .

'But I could be wrong.'

PART FOUR

25

'Poverty tramples honour underfoot
and brings some to the gallows and
others to the hospital.'

CERVANTES

LITTLE THINGS REMIND ME of that night, small details
forever tapping at my psyche. Chinese food, karate,
public telephone boxes. Without my consent, the shape of
Mike's death and the essence of the boys frozen in adoles-
cence intrude, at first painfully, then merely habitually. For
many years I tried to avoid such anxieties, then learned to
deal with them and accept that some things come with a
side order of emotional baggage.

As the decades passed, I thought about the boys from
the gang as little as possible. I had no feelings of anger or
even blame, having long made my peace with the chaos of
it all. I wished them well, and wondered if Andrew Reynolds had given it any thought in the years since, whether he
had even seen the little girl outside the courtroom or heard
the shouts of my family. Someone yelling, 'Bastards!'; the
man in the suit insisting, 'They were guilty on paper!' I

wondered if he ever thought about us at all, and what sort of person he'd become.

We had never met, so I had no real sense of him. But that wasn't true of all of the boys in that gang. I had known Reece Webster.

It's a bright, sunny day as I swing my bag of loot over the handlebars of my bike and push both bike and bag down the garden, out of the wooden gate my dad had built, turning a sharp left in the direction of the woods. I mount my steed, away on an adventure with our treasure. Halfway down the path I encounter a boy outside his house. It is Reece Webster, Emily's sort of friend. Some boys make me a little afraid, some make me boast, and some make me shy. Reece Webster is the shy-making sort. He is carefully kicking a football against the wall of his house.

I stop my bike with my heels instead of the brakes and start fiddling with the contents of the bag over my handlebars. This is to get his attention, not for me but the prizes within.

'What you got there?' He comes over, curious, football now in hand.

I remember him as one of the nicer kids. Emily says the same. A bit rough around the edges, but that was common for the boys in our street. We didn't know him well enough to be aware of what – if any – trouble he was in at home or at school, but he was not a bully, never teased us or called Jackie a witch, as other kids sometimes did. We played together. He was not a stranger to me before the night Mike died. He was not a stranger to me at the trial. Perhaps he wasn't a stranger now.

In early 2020 I found a way to contact Reece Webster. I reassured him that I wasn't harbouring any ill will or blame for the past, that I was trying to piece together a few things. I said it would be amazing if he wanted to tell me, but understood if he didn't. He agreed to answer my questions, and we arranged a video call.

I'm beyond impatient, my usual confidence abandoning me. I rehearse the hello in my head, worried the butterflies in my stomach and chest will flutter up into my throat to choke me. I'm nervous that we won't communicate well, or that we simply won't like each other. Perhaps I will immediately be triggered by his face or voice, the recognition of the boy from the estate, or, worse, the teenager from the trial. I start to get uncharacteristically paranoid, critical thinking fleeing under panic. What if he's setting a trap, what if he's working with the others to tell me the same lies they told on the witness stand? He had said he'd be happy to talk to me, but what if he has an ulterior motive? What if he's a sociopath, or a con man, or simply evil? I acknowledge the flood of adrenaline and reassure myself these things are extremely unlikely.

The screen suddenly flickers into life and there he is, sitting in his home. Reece Webster. A man I have known since we were both children and whose fate as a boy was horribly entwined with my family's and my own.

I stare at the man on the screen for signs of the neighbourhood boy or the courtroom teen, and am puzzled to discover I can see neither. His face is familiar, yes, but in the way that you can't figure out where you know someone from. There is no triggering, no stabbing pain in my heart, no sickening lurch of recognition. There is just a slightly familiar, serious but otherwise ordinary man. Not a stranger, not a friend, not a foe.

He is slender, his face unshaven but groomed. He's wearing a navy sweatshirt, inside which I can see the occasional flash of a thick silver chain. The room he is in is painted the same shade of dark grey as the room I'm in and has similar furniture. I like his art. I wasn't expecting to have the same taste in decorating.

'Hello!' I say, putting on an upbeat tone to disguise my nerves.

'All right,' he replies. His accent is way more Brummie than mine. It surprises me, but that accent always feels like home and his is particularly warm. What I took for a serious face suddenly appears kind and unthreatening.

'How you doing?'

'Yeah, fine, how about you?'

I'm assessing him through the camera, sizing him up, having absolutely no reason to trust him but very much wanting to. This conversation is a leap of faith for us both. Only clichés come to mind: looking into someone's eyes to really trust them, seeing how they move, listening for truth in their voice. And yet. I have writtens articles about the pseudoscience of body language, lie-detector tests, and the pseudoscience of criminal profiling. I knew there was no in-person test for trust, that such subjective tests can be gamed by anyone who studies them. Looking into someone's eyes reveals precisely nothing about whether or not they're lying. And if Reece is sociopathic and scheming enough to have been lying this whole time, he'd certainly be able to fool me in person. I'm sure sociopaths have no trouble telling lies directly to someone's face.

But I don't think he's a sociopath. I just want to talk to him via video, to remove the final barrier between us and remind myself that he is flesh and blood, not just a traumatic memory.

I am very nervous, and the talk is small. In my career I've worked with some extraordinary people, but this is the most challenging conversation of my life. I need to hear what Reece has to say about Mike's death, but he has to relax and trust me. You can't just go straight into 'So, tell me about when you were arrested for the murder of my dad.' We make more small-talk for a few minutes, but when he refers to 'the incident' I realize he's as keen to start talking about it as I am. Why else would he be here? He's not in this to make a new best friend. We chat for a few minutes about the impact of that night on our lives. I tell him I thought he was a nice kid, back when it happened. That's our cue to just go for it. Still in my slightly formal upbeat tone, I say, 'Tell me every single thing you remember about that night.'

The story he tells me is not what I expected. It's not what I expected at all.

26

REECE WEBSTER HAD RECENTLY turned fourteen, but had never been involved in a fight before. He and his friends spent most of their time playing football, or video games on the home computer Reece's dad had acquired from a dubious source. As the local boys grew into their teens, their home lives became too chaotic to spend much time there, so they wandered the estate or hung out on the wall outside the community centre at the shops, where all the bored youths of the estate would congregate. Reece's mother had recently left, and his father was frequently absent.

The night of Mike's death, Reece Webster and Anthony Mears, without anywhere else to go, headed to the shops with their friend Ian Barrows, a small, quiet boy. They'd all been in minor trouble with the police, but nothing unusual for the estate. Talking about 'whatever', they were sitting near – but not with – another boy, Chris Hendon, also fourteen, who was talking to an older boy, Andrew Reynolds—

'Wait. You didn't know Andrew?' I interrupted Reece as he was telling the story.

'Not at all. He was nearly eighteen then. He was doing well in sports and was, you know, it's Andrew Reynolds. What the hell would he be doing hanging around with us? That's why it was so odd he was even there that night.

'I mean, why would he talk to us? He never spoke to me. He never engaged me. I didn't know where he lived. I didn't know about his family. We didn't know anything, really. Apart from he was into competitive sports, and sometimes he was around the group, which could have been forty or fifty kids on any particular night or a selection of that. So it's an odd one. Why was he there? I don't know. I can't even think why he was there.'

What happened to the marauding gang of five, the older boy as ringleader? It was suddenly nowhere. The gang did not exist. Instead, there were five individual boys along the wall, each with their own reasons for being there: Andrew, talking to Chris, and a little way along Reece, Anthony and Ian. As they chatted among themselves, Reece noticed a man he knew, Mike King, approach the phone box. The boys were being noisy; there was an exchange of words. Chris Hendon, sitting a little distance away with Andrew Reynolds, said something to Mike, and Mike stopped in his tracks . . .

'So we've all turned around as your dad doubles back and punches Chris straight in the face.'

When I review the recording of that first Zoom interview with Reece, I am struck by how calm my reaction is. Partly because I'm trying to keep a little emotional distance from the story, partly because it's so shocking I don't really have time to process it and react, and partly because, somehow, it doesn't surprise me as much as it should. Reece's version of events already contradicts the story I've always carried, the malicious marauding gang with the controlling ringleader. None of them even had the bikes I had been told they fled on. They left on foot. Why would it not be true that Mike threw the first punch? Chris was sitting on the wall, said something unforgivable to Mike, who doubled back and, as Chris stood up, punched the boy in the face. This is not the scene that has tortured me for decades. And yet, somehow, without knowing why, I don't disbelieve it.

'So whatever Chris said must have been pretty damn . . .' My voice trails off.

'Yeah. And I promise you, I don't know what it was. Chris never, ever spoke about it. I don't remember ever speaking about the incident, ever. And because Chris was a bit older, you know, we never pushed speaking about it.

'So, anyway, your dad, he punches Chris in the face and it was a pretty decent, you know, pretty hard shot. I remember Chris's head going back and him coming away from the wall and he tried to hit your dad back. He tried to, but he didn't really connect with him. And your dad's momentum now has taken him past Chris, towards Andrew Reynolds.'

To Reece it was an instant. He saw Andrew throw out his arm in self-defence, his fist connecting with the side of Mike's head. I immediately see it in slow motion.

I had been told, over and over, by DCI Burns and everyone else that Andrew – a black belt in martial arts – had stood on the wall and deliberately jumped off to land a karate chop to the back of Mike's neck. A clumsy punch in the side of the head, in the heat of a street fight, is not that. It's not even close to that. But. It seems more likely to be true.

I think I'm doing really well handling this. I'm not even sure these revelations are showing on my face. I'm listening, and handling this new version with an open mind. Not so open that I stop thinking, but I have to be amenable to what, so far, is actually a much more plausible version of events. A clumsy punch from Andrew in self-defence caused instant brain death, not a malicious karate chop. But then, this.

'Your dad walked forward, which was weird at the time as he'd just got punched in the head. Your dad carries on walking, literally, like, away. And then I've got to tell you how it happened. Your dad kind of falls to his knees. And then he puts one hand out and just, like, hits the floor.'

I'd always been told Mike died instantly, had always visualized it that way. He fell where he was hit. His brain was dead before his head reached the ground. Blackout. So that he never even felt a thing. That's what I knew, and my knowledge of Mike is precious little enough so I can't just let that go and replace it with something worse. I can at least keep that, can't I? To die instantly is to die painlessly and, more, it's to die without knowing your own tragic fate. I did not want Mike to be a witness to his own death.

I can speculate for ever inside those two or three seconds where he walks away and falls to his knees, where Emily and I are sitting happily on the windowsill and Jackie is downstairs readying the plates, but madness is in there. His final thoughts are impossible to know, and the speculation makes me want to be sick. I have been done with that type of demon for a long time, so I try not to dwell on his last thoughts or feelings, and replace them instead with the memory of the four of us falling about laughing over a game of Scrabble.

I spent two hours on Zoom with Reece Webster that

evening, and he told me his version of what happened after Mike stumbled away and hit the ground. A couple of adult men came over and one told the boys they 'had better scarper', so they did. Reece was certain they would not have left the scene otherwise. And the next day the four schoolfriends, Reece, Anthony, Ian and Chris, met at Chris's house; his dad had arranged to call the police. As none of them knew Andrew, they did not contact him.

The four boys were arrested on suspicion of murder, held and questioned separately for several days, then released without charge (not on bail as we had been told). Reece said that he was physically and verbally abused in custody. He shook when he said this. After he was released, he tried to go back to a normal life, but an arrest for murder sticks. His grandmother stopped speaking to him, having called him 'a murderer'; his relationship with his father declined even further and he was eventually abandoned to live on his own, not even on the radar of Social Services. He stopped going to school and instead would wander the estate all day, at the same time as I was doing the exact same thing. Our paths never crossed.

And then he was called to give evidence at the trial. He told me that when his statement was read to the court, it had changed, and he and his dad had to raise it with the judge. Perhaps this was where the conspiracy theory about the boys planning their trial strategy had come from. A whisper network or mishearing, misunderstanding, bad faith interpretation. One of the bad boys was disputing his statement, must be malice.

So much of what Reece said made sense, and so much of it was unbelievable. If Reece's version was true, why would DCI Burns have told us differently? Was Reece making up the stuff about police misconduct to try to discredit them? But there I was, into conspiracy thinking again. Never mind ifs and maybes, of which there are more than there are stars in the sky, what does the evidence say? What would satisfy me that he was telling the truth? I would not be making the same mistake twice. If Reece was telling the truth about that night, I had to find proof.

I needed to speak to Andrew Reynolds.

I'm sanding a doorframe when my phone pings. Wiping my dusty hands, I look at my phone. My heartbeat makes itself known as I see his name. It's Andrew Reynolds, replying to my recent message. The first thing he writes is how sorry he is. It's a lengthy reply, incredibly kind and tactful. He says how difficult it is for him to be typing these words to me, how a week doesn't go by that he doesn't think about that night. And again, how sorry he is that we went through it.

I sit down, then immediately stand up again. My heart hurts. My head buzzes. I had waited thirty-four years to have a conversation. Now here he was, and he was saying he'd be happy to talk to me. I told him I am a writer and producer, mainly science and technology, a professional nerd, and reassured him of my good intentions. We typed back and forth for a while. He wanted a few days to process, but would give me a ring.

He might yet change his mind about calling, but even just hearing that he hadn't simply forgotten about my dad was a gift. Mixed up with my lifetime of him as a malicious, arrogant teenager was the knowledge that he was a human being with emotions and feelings. I had never been able to reconcile the two. He was a character in my life story, and therefore couldn't surprise me.

But the real Andrew did surprise me. I had not been expecting – didn't even consider – that he would reply and say how sorry he was, and how much it meant to him. No malice, no aggression, just a kind, thoughtful man. In Reece's reframing of Andrew as self-defender rather than aggressor, I had almost forgotten that, regardless of the legal ins and outs, if he hadn't hit my dad, Mike would not have died. He was sorry my dad had died. He was sorry I had lost a parent. He was sorry it had happened, not just to him but to us.

A few days later, my phone rings. It's a number I don't know, but I know it's him. Andrew. I look at the phone for a moment, then answer the call.

'All right, bab,' I hear myself say.

I was just as intrigued by what he didn't know as what he did. He didn't know anything about my family except that I had an older sister. He didn't even know that Reece Webster knew us and had lived a few doors down. I found this reassuring, more proof of Reece's assertion that they were not a gang, weren't even friends. The frightened quiver in his voice, the willingness with which he answered my difficult questions, the apologies, made nonsense of the old story. The last threads of the conspiracy floated away.

We spoke for over an hour. The first thing he said, again, was how sorry he was. He told me he had been at the shops that night because he was meeting his girlfriend for a date. That, although he was the oldest boy there, he was by far the shortest. And that, after Mike had punched Chris Hendon, he had also kicked Andrew in the stomach; Andrew had lunged forward and taken a swing in self-defence. His details were similar to Reece's, that they had tried to help Mike and that two men from the bus stop told them to run.

What did Chris say that was so bad Mike had turned and punched him in the face? The best Andrew could offer was something like 'Fuck off, old man.'

Would that have done it? Would that have been enough to make my dad snap and punch a teenage boy? Maybe. If he'd been drinking, if he was wound up enough. Or maybe it was something worse, more personal than that, and Andrew had either forgotten or didn't want to say.

It was a difficult conversation for us both, but warm and positive, and I liked him very much. He said he regretted throwing out all the paperwork he had had, as otherwise he would have given it to me. That meant a lot. We agreed to stay in touch.

I had to ask Chris Hendon his version of events, and whether he remembered what he'd said. I contacted him, and after a while he replied. He was willing to chat, but only briefly, and I respected that. His version of that night was much the same as the two I had already heard, differing in ways that didn't change the thrust of events. But he didn't remember what he'd said to Mike that had made him snap.

Next stop, Anthony Mears. I had a moment of paranoia that these men were all conspiring, swapping strategies in secret. Obviously not. It would be insane to talk to me at all if they were lying. They could simply have ignored me.

Instead, all had been welcoming and kind and willing to answer questions. Anthony's version confirmed the other three, again with subtle but understandable differences. I couldn't find Ian Barrows online so assumed he didn't want to be found and chose to respect that. But I had plenty of testimony already, and a growing friendship with Reece Webster. With some allowances for time and memory, it was looking pretty likely that what he had told me in that first call was true.

Today is a new day, just as sunny as the one over thirty years ago when Reece Webster, now one of my newest but dearest friends, had approached me, football in hand, baited by my obvious posturing. 'What you got there?' the boy had said to the younger girl, which was exactly the question she was hoping for.

My granddad worked in the stockroom of a Birmingham department store, and occasionally gave me salvaged treasure. This time it was a bag of promotional badges for the instant-mashed-potato brand Smash, whose advertising featured a family of metal aliens. I loved Smash, although it was more expensive than real potatoes so we didn't have it that often. I liked to eat the crunchy dehydrated potato granules raw from the tin, and when my mother mixed it with boiling water and a knob of margarine to make mash, I'd fashion mine into a volcano and add ketchup for lava.

The Smash aliens were funny and cute, and branded merchandise was a great wealth. The plastic bag my granddad had given me contained a dozen small round metal badges, backed with sharp pins, and white fronts each with the face of a Smash alien. The pink alien displayed the legend 'My Mum's a Smasher!' while the blue said the same about the wearer's dad.

I knew these gems would be popular, and I wanted the older boy to take an interest, which he did. 'Those are cool, where'd you get them?' he said, and seemed impressed.

'My granddad gave me them,' I boasted. 'He works at Rackhams.' This was a big deal. The Birmingham department store was expensive, and far away. If you were very lucky, you got to visit Santa's grotto there.

'Would you like one?' I offered.

'Yeah, go on then.' He chose a blue alien, 'My Dad's a Smasher!', and put it in his pocket.

'Thanks,' he said, but I didn't know what else to say, so I cycled off as fast as I could.

On this future sunny day, which is in 2021, I'm talking to Reece Webster over a video app. We've been friends for almost a year now and talk regularly. I have learned that his mother was neglectful and abusive, and eventually abandoned him entirely. His father, while also violent, eventually repented and apologized, and Reece had given up his life in London to move to a small country town and care for his father in his last two years of life. He had died a few years ago, and Reece hadn't dealt with it well. It became one of the things we helped each other with. Our dads had been neighbours, mates, contemporaries. The same struggles, the same fears, the same hopes, neither man achieving as much as he might wish for his children. I have risked so much to trust Reece Webster and believe his version of things, letting him into my life and family because he has none.

I have just received a small package from eBay, the contents of which are on my desk as we chat. I hold up a small round metal badge, mottled with age, depicting a blue alien and the words 'My Dad's a Smasher!'

'Remember this?' I say, hoping.

'Oh, wow!' he says, eyes lighting up with nostalgia and recognition. 'I had one of those!'

'Yes, you did.' I laugh. 'I gave it to you!'

Reece looks puzzled for a moment, searching his memory. 'I don't remember that,' he says at last.

I recount the story of my bike and bag of treasure.

He shakes his head. 'No memory of that, sorry,' he says. And then adds, 'But I believe you.'

27

TRUST IS ENOUGH FOR ME to want to believe the new version of events – that my dad punched first, that the boys were told to run – but it is not proof. It is a type of evidence that would have been scrutinized at the trial. Andrew was acquitted, his self-defence argument a success, his name cleared. What was the other evidence presented to the court?

It's summer 2021. I sit in the passenger seat of a car, clutching a sealed A4 brown envelope with 'Tracy King' handwritten on the outside. Inside are the detail and facts of Mike's death. The hard proof, or as hard proof as I'm ever going to get. A copy of the original police report from 1988. It has taken me a long time to get my hands on it. Would it confirm what the four men had separately told me? Or contradict them and throw everything into doubt?

After a few minutes of silent reflection I unstick the heavy glue seal, withdraw the report halfway, and immediately push it back inside. I can't do it. It's not the right time, sitting in a car park on a sunny day against a backdrop of happy children playing on the perfect green grass in the nearby playground. I take a deep breath, put the envelope on the floor and do up my seatbelt. Feelings, you win this one. Facts, you'll have to wait.

Courage is not something I'm generally short of, unless it's dealing with spiders. (I have made my peace with them; they are excellent creatures. But it still takes bravery.) But today I'm scared of a brown envelope. Fear, rational or otherwise, is usually about a perceived threat, but the contents of the envelope are currently abstract: potentially the longed-for hard proof that I value so much, but also forensic detail that, were it anyone else's father, would merely fascinate. In my case, it could shatter me. Curled up on the sofa, almost foetal, I withdraw the bundle of papers.

The police constabulary logo, disproportionately large, towers over the hand-typed description of the contents. My hands are shaking and my fingers tingle as though the paper, a photocopy of a photocopy, is imbued with some material aspect of Mike himself. I begin to read the cover report, the summary and opinions of the case provided by DCI Burns at least thirty years ago. I had trusted Reece's version of events, that the story he had told me on that first video call and in a dozen subsequent conversations about that night was true, that Mike had punched first, that Andrew had simply acted in self-defence. The story that Chris, Anthony and Andrew had corroborated and added to. I want to believe them. But here, in my hands, finally, is proof. Would the police report confirm that they have been telling the truth?

The police report into my father's death is the most important piece of evidence I have. It's not gold standard or sacred by any means, but it does answer a great many questions that for most of my life I didn't know I should have asked. Here is what I learned.

<u>MOVEMENTS OF THE DECEASED</u>

The typewriter uppercase heading is underlined for emphasis, or, from where I sit, foreboding.

Mr and Mrs KING woke up at approximately 8 a.m., Mr KING was feeling unwell as he was complaining of flu symptoms. Their youngest daughter was also at home getting ready for school. The 14 year old girl was to return home from boarding school that evening.

What a scene. It provides a tiny clue into his mood that day, and perhaps therefore why we argued. If he was ill, he wasn't going to be too receptive to my insistence that I go with him to the shops. I find myself wondering what my day at school was like. It was so normal, so easy, it doesn't even register.

After their daughter had left home [for school] the couple then walked to the community centre where Mrs KING worked. At the centre they spent a short time together before Mr KING returned home for a bath.

Mr KING set about his personal business and was seen shopping in the town centre, while his wife remained at work. It had previously been agreed that they would meet at their home at 6 p.m. that evening as Mrs KING had arranged

```
that afternoon to collect her daughter
who was returning for the school
holidays.
     Due to traffic congestion, Mrs KING
did not return home until approximately
7.35 p.m. She entered the house with her
daughters and saw her husband asleep on
the settee in their living room.
```

These details are so strange to me. What do the parents of a child do all day while she is at school? Jackie worked part-time in the community-centre café, Mike was a travelling business-computer salesman. That was all I knew. These little details of shopping and having a bath sit wrong, somehow. He clearly wasn't working that day, perhaps because of the school holidays, but more likely because, according to Jackie's statement, he'd had flu-like symptoms and a headache. The police report is oddly detailed in some ways and utterly lacking in others. And then we're back to the bits I already know. He goes to the takeaway and orders a Chinese meal for four, which costs £13.40. He pays with a twenty-pound note. The report doesn't say that Jackie gave him this banknote from her purse, but she was interrogated at length about that on the witness stand. It haunts her, that note. He was trying to quit drinking but had money in his pocket, and the pub was right there.

The question of his alcohol consumption that day is largely addressed in the report. He did not go to the pub directly, but went to phone Jackie first. Burns writes:

There is no evidence to suggest he
consumed alcohol on the day of his
death.

This confirms Jackie's insistence that he wasn't drunk.

It is not possible to indicate what he
did during the day time except to say
that when his wife came home at 7.35
p.m. she was convinced he had not been
drinking because she claims to be able
to tell immediately. In the house on
this day were four cans of beer and
these were still intact after his
death.

I remember Jackie eventually giving those four cans of
beer to a neighbour so they wouldn't go to waste.

Certainly once he left home he could not
possibly have had a drink as he was tied
up getting his meal. There is evidence
from his associates which also confirms
he had not been in the public house that
evening. Blood samples have been taken
but the value of these is nil because he
remained in a state of unconsciousness
for some twenty-four hours before his
death, when the blood was finally taken.

But I am jumping ahead. He isn't in the hospital yet.

It's 8 p.m. and he's still in the takeaway, planning the rest of his evening.

> Mr KING left the premises and at this
> point he must have decided to telephone
> his wife before going into the Public
> House. Instead of turning left for some
> ten yards he must have turned right and
> walked some twenty yards to the
> telephone kiosks.

I remember those phone kiosks so well. One evening, perhaps a few months after Mike's death, after a church service Jackie had had to make a phone call from there. I stood in the kiosk with her, as close as possible. Over the road by the doctor's surgery I could see three teenage lads. I did not know if any of them were *those* lads, but they were clearly up to no good and were toying with what looked to me like a hand grenade. I started to cry and panic and tug at Jackie's arm. As she ended her phone call I gasped, 'They've got a bomb.'

She looked over. 'It's okay,' she told me. 'It's a water balloon.' We walked away hurriedly as they laughed and threw it at a passing bus.

> The kiosks are set against a brick wall
> and consist of the latest design, i.e.
> mainly glass construction and without a
> door. Anyone using such a kiosk could
> be entitled to question if they could
> hear very well should there be any

excess noise in the vicinity of such a
kiosk.

Unfortunately and tragically this was
the case on this occasion as the five
youths subject of this inquiry were
milling around this area and apparently
behaving in a rather loud and unruly
way.

Setting aside the incident for a
moment, it must be said that Mr KING
telephoned his wife and sounded in a
perfectly happy frame of mind. He told
his wife that he had spent £13 of her £20
note and laughed as he did so. When
questioned, 'On what?' he revealed that
he had decided upon a treat and ordered
the Chinese meal. The purpose of the call
was to ask his wife to warm the plates
and set themselves up for a meal. At no
time did he speak to his wife about any
aggravation he had encountered or was
encountering with youths in the estate
centre.

There's nothing in the report about my argument with
him. It suggests he was happy, celebratory, as he should
have been, given Emily was at home. But he was also anxious, depressed, trying to quit drinking. The report seems
to want a definitive mood, some certainty about Mike's
state of mind. There is none to be had. Many theories can
emerge, the clues leading wherever the reader wants to go.

He might have had a brain issue that contributed to his death and also explained his mood inconsistencies or the moment of violent temper. He might have had a bottle of whisky stashed somewhere. He might have been someone who got into fights and kept it from his family. There are as many options and theories and even conspiracies as there are days that have passed since. Very few of them are testable, so I must dismiss them as useless. I simply cannot know.

THE DEATH

Mike's death. It's about the five arrested suspects and whether they committed the crime of murder. They did not.

```
Evidence relating to the immediate
circumstances surrounding the death has
been obtained from witnesses who saw
certain aspects of a dispute. No one
person gives a complete account of
events except the evidence of the five
suspects subject of this report.
    However, the independent evidence
does suggest that their accounts under
caution are truthful, as any prosecution
case would have to concede at the outset
that the first blow was probably
delivered by the deceased upon one of
our suspects.
```

Probably. Mike probably hit Chris first, and Andrew defended himself in the ensuing chaos. Not definitely, not possibly, but probably. How much room for doubt does 'probably' give, and what is my reason for rejecting the probable in favour of the improbable? Well, that's simple. I don't want Mike to be someone who hit a boy, and I don't want him to have died because of it. Strong motive for the improbable.

But he probably did. And that makes what Andrew did next self-defence. Not murder.

> KING seeing these youths close to these modern open telephone booths was obviously concerned about making himself heard should he make a call. Consequently he told these youths to go away. I have no doubt he did swear at them which served only to cause them to remain purely to aggravate the situation. When the call was complete KING spoke again as he began to walk away, presumably to the public house.

Walk away, I find myself thinking over and over. *Just walk away, Mike.* He was walking away, the right thing to do. But then:

> These youths again responded with some back chat which caused KING to stop and respond to this cheek, he turned around and would have found himself confronted by two youths, namely: HENDON and REYNOLDS. Behind these were the three others: MEARS, BARROWS, and WEBSTER.

261

HENDON being the most verbose naturally attracted KING's attention. They developed what has been described as an eyeball to eyeball confrontation resulting in a straight punch being delivered by KING upon the jaw of HENDON. This could not have been too heavy a blow as HENDON simply moved back a short distance. KING remained in an agitated state and he immediately kicked out at REYNOLDS who was also close by.

KING must now have felt very threatened by the presence of a five to one situation, although three of the five were behind what I would describe as the two main aggressors. Although it must be acknowledged it is KING who also responded aggressively by turning back to the verbal abuse.

Evidence from both the suspects and independent witnesses suggests KING was wagging his finger, HENDON goes on to indicate KING was going to poke his finger in HENDON's eye so he brushed his arm aside and punched KING in the face. Again this must have been a light blow because KING was heard to say 'Come on what was that meant to be?'

Suddenly half a dozen lost memories emerge. The finger-wagging-at-eyes reference. It was a martial-arts movie trope, a close-combat technique called a two-finger poke or scissor strike, and I had forgotten Mike teaching it to me alongside other self-defence techniques. He wasn't being serious when he did it; it was more a funny impression of martial-arts stars like Bruce Lee. But clearly it was also a genuine technique to him: he used it as a threat against Chris in that moment. It chills me because it's a fun memory, us all laughing and joking, an absurdity. Chris saw a grown man threatening to poke him in the eyes.

```
This eyeball to eyeball situation
remained, but REYNOLDS was now further
involved as he too had been struck
(according to him and his fellow
suspects). HENDON was still directly in
front of KING while REYNOLDS was
slightly to KING's right. This point is
important because the next blow was
struck by REYNOLDS who threw a right
handed punch to KING's head. The punch
connected because KING was heard to say
'Bloody hell that was a good one.'
```

What will my last words be? Something else, I hope. Not seven words of grudging, fearful admiration for a lethal blow. When Mike said that to Andrew, he must have known something was badly wrong. I hadn't wanted to let go of his instant, painless death when Reece had first told me Mike took a few steps before collapsing, but here it is again and this time with words. I must replace my conciliatory, naive, hopeful belief with the difficult, typewritten truth.

```
This final incident caused the youths to
back off as KING rubbed his cheek/neck
before staggering forward and collapsing
onto his knees and finally he lay flat
out.
```

That is the end. Not of the police report, which is only just beginning, but of Mike King's life. If he wasn't brain dead then, he would have been within minutes if not seconds. During our conversation, Andrew and Anthony both wanted me to know they had made efforts to revive him. Anthony says he got water in his cupped hands from the nearby public toilet and ran back to splash it on Mike's face. Andrew checked that Mike hadn't swallowed his tongue. The police report confirms this was their testimony at the time.

```
The only complete account of this whole
incident around the kiosk is that taken
from the five suspects. Certain aspects
are corroborated by other independent
witnesses.
```

The independent-evidence section illuminates the origin of some of the mythology. There were indeed two adult men who told the five lads to leave. DCI Burns describes one as having witnessed Andrew Reynolds

```
push himself off the sloping wall and
launch himself at KING. This youth aimed
a swiping blow at KING and it seemed to
```

```
land in the ear region of the man's
head. The witness says it was a slapping
motion rather than a punch (karate
chop).
```

Another witness claims Mike said, 'Fucking hell, that was bad,' before his collapse, and that the lads were laughing as they left, with Andrew saying, 'I didn't hit him that fucking hard.' That witness is the source of the 'karate-chop' claim. To the police, this looked like 'Andrew was a karate black belt who knew exactly what he was doing.' The third independent witness, who did not witness the violence, had overheard Mike saying, 'If you don't shut your mouths I'll smack you.' This, DCI Burns writes, *served only to cause the youths to laugh and humiliate KING.*

What did they say to him? What could possibly have been so bad that he turned his threat into action? I'm almost hoping the report won't shed any light on that, because I don't think there's a single alternative that wouldn't be devastating.

```
Once KING had completed his call he
renewed his verbal exchanges and again
told them to 'fuck off'. This prompted
HENDON, the tallest of the five, to ask
'Why?' And state such things as 'You
don't own it'. Unfortunately KING
threatened to punch them to which HENDON
replied, 'Oh we are scared.' Others were
calling KING names such as 'slap head'
and 'wanker'.
```

Reece Webster's witness statement reads, 'I remember Chris Hendon called him a bald-headed bastard, and at least Chris had hair on his head.' I'm not surprised he has since forgotten this detail, because it is, as a provocation, both absurd and banal. 'Slap head' is a peculiarly British insult, and has largely fallen out of favour now, along with the comb-over, but baldness had never seemed shameful to me.

Mike carried a small comb and he'd let me style the sparse patch that constituted his comb-over. He taught me the principles of static by rubbing a balloon on his jumper and raising those few hairs straight up like magnetic magic. The bald skin was tanned and leathery, and felt nice to touch. He would laugh uproariously at the legendary Hamlet cigar advert of the man in a photo booth whose unruly comb-over had a life of its own. But Mike's baldness could clearly be used as an insult as much as a joke, and perhaps that was what crossed the line of disrespect.

28

I N 1988, THE BEST coin was the fifty-pence piece. Everyone my age thought so. We were all enamoured with the novel *The Queen's Nose* by Dick King-Smith, in which a magic fifty pence granted wishes upon rubbing the edge towards which the regal nose pointed. I tried this myself so many times, but no wishes came true. I had failed to understand the 'monkey's paw' moral of the story, where wishes for personal gain always come at personal cost. The protagonist, a ten-year-old girl, experiences great physical pain and loss in return for time off school and a new bike. In the end, she uses her last wish to save her uncle's life, which we all understood to be the right thing to do, particularly as he gave her the magic coin in the first place – but I still coveted a brand-new bike, having never owned such a thing.

There were other pleasures in a fifty-pence piece besides wishes. It was the largest coin, so therefore seemed worth the most. It fitted satisfyingly in my small palm, its silver heptagonal body designed to receive the tight grip of my fingers. Fifty-pence coins *were* worth far more than their face value. Everyone on the estate had an electricity meter that required a regular offering. It would only accept a fifty-pence piece, not two twenties and a ten or a bagful of coppers. So the coin was prized by everyone, and hoarded accordingly.

In financially happy times, Jackie or Mike would put a stack of fifty pences on top of the black meter, which was high up on the wall of the downstairs toilet. Mike would lift me up to feed the meter. I loved the chink and clunk of the metal coin going into the metal slot, audibly sliding through a mechanism into the belly of the beast that supplied our heat and light. The stack of coins was on top of the meter rather than inside it because the money might, in a pinch, be needed for something else. Mike's rolling tobacco or Jackie's cigarettes, or a bar of chocolate each as a family treat after a bad day.

Sometimes the meter would tick down to zero and, its belly empty and no coins on top, angrily cut off our electricity without warning. The lights would go out, the television pop during an episode of *Boon* and the picture evaporate. There might be a scramble through pockets or Mom's handbag for a fifty pence, a child dispatched to a neighbour to borrow one. Everyone on our street did this.

And if there was no fifty pence to be found or borrowed, the only other option was to steal. Mike would carefully break open the meter with a large wooden-handled flat-headed screwdriver to retrieve a few coins and feed them back in. Everyone on our street did this, too. It was that or sit in the dark.

On my desk next to the lamp is the police report. It was – is – strange to see the detail behind the man's life contained therein. I knew Jackie had a tendency to play down his faults, glossing over some of his worries and failures, but until I read the report I thought I knew the key life events of Mike King. Of course, any man with a life as complex as his would have had secrets, but I wasn't expecting the police report to contain quite such a revelation. Page ten is headed Criminal History. It does not refer to Andrew or the four other boys. It refers to my father.

```
The deceased had two criminal convictions:-
    1. 11.3.1983 he was fined £50.00 for
abstracting electricity, and a further
£50.00 for theft of money from the
Midlands Electricity Board.
    2. 12.8.1986 he was placed on
probation for 12 months for making a
false representation to obtain social
benefits. He was ordered to pay £337.25
compensation. He had four offences taken
into consideration.
```

I did not know my dad had a criminal record. But the offences listed here are suddenly familiar, memories springing back to life, as if someone has just fed the electricity meter. I remember the fuel poverty and ensuing problems in the form of authority, arguments, panic and whispered conversations. There was a man who came to read the meter and empty it of coins. If the amount of money inside didn't match the amount of electricity used, there was trouble. I dimly remember such trouble, but I was never told how far it went.

The second conviction is straightforward enough. In 1986, after a massive increase in rent, a lot of desperate unemployed people took cash-in-hand work to supplement their benefits. Margaret Thatcher's government ran an advertising billboard campaign, encouraging people to inform on anyone who was committing such fraud. Mike had been working as a site labourer, hauling paving slabs for cash. Someone had 'fitted him up', and I had been puzzled as to why my lovely dad could have an enemy. I'd always assumed that incident had simply meant a drop in income. I had had no idea it resulted in a criminal record. No wonder he was depressed and anxious.

I understand poverty and complexity and depression, and I wouldn't have as much of a problem with what Mike did if not for how much getting caught had contributed to his problems. That's crime, though. It's a very short-term solution from panicked thinking that often enough exacerbates the problem it was intended to solve. I now know why he struggled to get a job. It's incredibly hard to come back from a criminal record. But by 1988, with his sales job and his impending government grant to start a business, he did seem to be on the way. Was his life really so bad that he would risk starting a fight with five teenage boys?

There are scant other clues to Mike's mental state in the police report. Nothing about his recent conversion to born-again Christianity after years of pressure from his family, and nothing about Emily's school problems (a paragraph simply states that his elder daughter is 'being educated at boarding school while the younger attends a local school'), but it does say that his new job as a computer salesman wasn't going well.

```
Evidence from his wife indicates while
in this new job he tried to achieve that
which can only be expected of a much
younger man. As a consequence, Mr KING
```

did suffer anxiety problems which caused
him to visit his family doctor.

As evidence, this is fairly useless hearsay, but of course
his GP was asked to provide details, which are included in
the report. As an insight into the man I barely knew, it's
invaluable. I had no idea he suffered from anxiety. Of
course he did, with a life like that.

I learn that he had previously complained of pains in
his chest and arm, but ECG tests were clear. He also had
regular headaches and sharp pains across his eyes. These I
remember, him lying in a darkened room with a damp
washcloth on his forehead, and the strange, careful quietness that descended on the house. So many odd little
insights into his life, mood, health. 'Mrs KING describes
her husband as a man susceptible to stress, he has never
slept well.' His alcoholism is addressed too:

The deceased was a person who smoked
some 30-40 cigarettes and consumed in
the region of four pints of beer each
day. On occasions this concerned Mr KING
who felt he may be an alcoholic. The
evidence of his wife suggests that the
effects of alcohol only served to cause
him to behave in a silly manner as
opposed to becoming violent.

This all checks out. I remember him trying to attend
Alcoholics Anonymous meetings, and various phases of
'getting on the wagon' in which he would switch to

non-alcoholic beer or powdered glucose in water. He tried to quit smoking so many times, made me promise I would never start. He was generally an introverted man, but not in an intense, brooding way. He was fun and extremely silly but he did not like a crowd. His handful of violent actions (the door punches, the dinner thrown at the wall) have gone from Jackie's memory entirely, but remain with Emily and me precisely because they were so out of character. Or, as I'm beginning to see, out of character for the husband and father. For the estate man in the rough local pub, surrounded by loud insolent teenagers, maybe not.

Mike's medical records confirm his worries about his drinking, and I'm proud that he sought help at a time when it was even more difficult to do so. He was referred to the Addiction Unit in Birmingham in 1984 but, his records say, he failed to attend. I can make excuses (it was expensive and not straightforward to get to Birmingham from our town without a car, for example), but he continued to seek help. In 1986 he was self-medicating for anxiety with 'ten pints of beer a week' and was prescribed temazepam. In 1987 he had chest X-rays because of pain, but these revealed normal health, and in December that year, just four months before his death, he was prescribed Zantac for stomach problems and 'revealed he was now drinking alcohol-free beer'. He didn't renew that prescription, and by March 1988 he was drinking again. Relapses are part of the process of recovery from alcoholism, and he was clearly trying. I am sad he didn't get the chance to succeed, if 'sad' can sufficiently describe the mourning for lost potential.

I had always known – or believed – that while he was

absolutely an alcoholic, he was always trying to fight it. I refused to drink alcohol for decades and would justify it as 'for my dad'. I felt a strong loyalty to his fight to quit the demon drink, and took it upon myself to succeed on his behalf. It made my life difficult at times: clubbing three times a week, playing in bands, throwing or attending house parties, taking advantage of all the excitement and hedonism of early nineties rock culture in Birmingham, all while stone-cold sober, made my peers feel awkward and judged at times, particularly as I was so uptight about it. Emily was experiencing a normal late-teens rite of passage, getting drunk and risking her safety, while I stayed sober and supervised her getting home safely or sending certain types of predatory men packing. She wanted to look out for her little sister, but I had already had too much experience in taking care of myself and Jackie. I had decided that bad things happen when alcohol is involved, so I set a hard boundary for myself. I finally relaxed it in my late thirties, got drunk precisely twice, and decided that one gin and tonic now and again is about my limit. But Mike struggled with limits. There's no way of knowing if he had been drinking that evening, and while some witnesses say they thought perhaps he was drunk, others disagree. I allow simply that it's possible.

Unlike his last conversation with me, and his last words in life, Mike's final words to Jackie were happy. Her second witness statement, taken a few days later, says:

```
Michael then told me he had ordered and
paid for a Chinese meal for four, and he
told me to get the plates ready. He told
```

```
me the food would be ten minutes and he
would just be popping in the pub for a
quick half.
     I said, 'Cheerio, mind how you come.'
I always say this after finishing a phone
call with Michael.
     Michael was speaking quite quickly
but I did not notice anything wrong with
his voice, and to me he seemed very
happy.
     Michael said, 'Cheerio.'
```

I always read newspaper stories about killings by teen-agers. Someone is killed by a gang of teenagers frequently enough for it to be considered a social problem, but not so frequently that it doesn't usually make headlines. The interest of the media tends to depend on the perceived innocence of the victim, because such stories are supposed to serve as warnings that this could happen to anyone. Marauding gangs of hoodies or ASBOs or chavs or juven-ile delinquents (depending from which generation you're looking down on young men), lying in wait on street cor-ners, ready to pounce on you just for walking past.

This 'random attack on a stranger' scenario happens, but very rarely. It is precisely why such crimes shock the press and the nation in a way that fights-gone-wrong do not. More common is the death of someone who was either involved with the gang or had escalated a verbal argu-ment, as Mike appears to have done. Sometimes the argument is about standing up for themselves, defending others or property, and sometimes it's about bravado or honour. Mike's death made the local papers, but no more than that.

There's a principle in law that says no words are acceptable justification for violence. I used to think that meant the boys had no right to hit Mike just because he told them to shut up. I now know it means Mike had no right to hit them for calling him names. I don't know why he did it. I barely know *that* he did it, other than the testimony of those at the scene, but it is, as DCI Burns says in the police report, the unfortunate but probable truth.

Aside from the statements of the other four boys, who by this time had been released without charge and were instead key, if somewhat hostile, witnesses, there are thirty-six statements, most of which are from people who were not present: the attending paramedics and hospital staff; family, friends and the girlfriend of Andrew; Mike's GP; and so on. What independent witnesses to the event there were make for frustrating reading. DCI Burns writes:

```
There is relatively little independent
evidence and those people identified have
chosen to see only parts of the
confrontation between the deceased and
these youths. It is indicative of their
mentality when one realizes that no one
actually set about getting involved to
resolve the dispute.
```

One of these says that the local shops were known for kids being noisy. Another says they assumed the siren and flashing lights were because one of the boys had hurt

himself. There is so much detail, yet so little actual witnessing. Nobody saw the events in their entirety except the
five boys, and no two statements really match.

> From where my mother and I had walked we
> had a clear view of this part of the
> shopping centre, although it was getting
> dark and I was able to see the man
> clearly as he was illuminated by the
> lights from the telephone boxes.

What a detail: Mike, in the orange-yellow glow of the
phone boxes. I watch the scene through the retina of that
witness, a twenty-one-year-old local woman who had been
walking home with her mother. She persuaded her mother
not to intervene in the unfolding altercation, 'in case they
had a go at us'. She was wise not to get involved, but I wish
she had.

> On that evening it had been raining and
> the ground was wet, or damp. At that
> time rain was not falling.

I knew it was rainy. That is, it must have been raining
on Mike, because it was raining on us too. The asphalt car
park outside the bedroom window was slick and dark, like
a black void, as the panda car pulled up. The witness who
wanted to get involved said this:

> At 8.15 p.m. I set off from my home
> address with my daughter.

When I was approximately 20 yards or
so away from the shopping centre and the
phone boxes I heard a man's voice. I
looked over and saw a man aged in his
forties in the phone box nearest to the
road. The man shouted something like
'you ignorant kids' and 'go away'. He
was directing this at four or five lads
who were stood opposite the phone box
outside the chemist. The lads were
saying something back to him, but I
couldn't tell what they were saying. It
appeared as though they were teasing
him.

From the moment I heard the man
shouting I stopped and watched them,
because I was annoyed at the lads
teasing him. I was going to go over
to them, but my daughter wouldn't
let me.

That word, *teasing*.

Enough to make him snap. Burns concludes that the
evidence of the five suspects

does suggest that their accounts under
caution are truthful, as any prosecution
case would have to concede at the outset
that the first blow was probably
delivered by the deceased upon one of
our suspects.

'Probably' is doing a lot of heavy lifting. In Chris Hendon's statement, he acknowledges that they were trying to annoy Mike while he was on the phone. Jackie says he was in a great mood on the phone, and indeed she was in a great mood after speaking to him. There's a big gap between that and being enraged enough to take on five teenagers. The difficulty with Burns's conclusion that the evidence of the five suspects is probably truthful is that their accounts don't always match, but that is a feature of witness accounts and the differences do not alter the main story. It all happened very fast, and emotions, hormones, fear and bravado were running at their peak. These are not optimum circumstances to make accurate memories. Interestingly to me, it is the differences in their statements that make them more believable. I would be suspicious of identical testimony, simply because eyewitness testimony is controversial in its reliability, so the chance of five children all having identical versions of events is implausible.

There's a theory called the Bystander Effect, which re-emerges whenever there's a crime in which witnesses are alleged to have insufficiently intervened. The idea is that if other people are around, individuals are less likely to help, perhaps assuming someone else will, or perhaps because the sense of responsibility is diffused. While there is safety in numbers, there is also apathy and denial. Or so the theory goes. It was coined following the brutal rape and murder of Kitty Genovese, a twenty-eight-year-old woman. Kitty was attacked at 2.30 a.m. by a man with a hunting knife who had followed her home. A few weeks later, the *New York Times* claimed that thirty-eight people had witnessed the attack, and they all did nothing. This claim is not true, and is unfair to those witnesses who did indeed try to help. The Bystander Effect has since been disputed in a number of academic studies. And yet in DCI Burns's report the paramedic states there were perhaps a dozen people standing around watching at a little distance, and he has to ask why none had helped the man lying there. I'm not sure the reasons for that are easily captured in a psychology study.

When I return to the witness statement of this woman, whom I shall call Mary, I notice something interesting. She, too, says there was light coming from the phone boxes, but that 'the lighting conditions where the youths stood wasn't very good. The youths stood in the shadows.' Her description of Mike is oddly wrong:

```
The man in the phone box I would
describe as white, aged in his forties,
5' 7" tall, plump build, with shortish
hair. I don't know what colour hair
he had.
```

During my science communications career I learned a lot about the fallibility of eyewitness testimony, although I never thought to apply it to the part of my life I had long ago shoved into a psychological drawer and left alone. But it isn't surprising that Mary got some key details wrong. Mike was much, much taller, and pretty skinny. He had almost no hair at all. I wonder if she simply didn't take in enough detail to be helpful, but her mind supplied an approximation. I also wonder if there's a difference between how witnesses perceive and describe victims and perpetrators. Or perhaps it was just too dark to see:

```
It's very difficult to describe the
youths I saw. They were all white lads
aged around 14 or 15 years old. I
couldn't describe them further or
recognize them.
```

She and her daughter didn't see what happened after the shouting as, fearful for their own safety, they had walked away.

Maybe he was dead when they left him, maybe not. There was nothing anyone could have done to save his life. Does it matter that a dead person was left alone for ten minutes? Is there dignity after death? Without a soul, a spirit, a ghost, does it matter whether anyone was with him while he lay on the cold concrete in the rain?

Of course it matters.

We can bear witness to his death now, through these pages. Every reader is there with him. We outnumber the bystanders.

The police report is full of small errors. I counted dozens, and those were just the ones I could identify. There are others, but I don't know how important any of them are. Most are typos, like road names or surnames, but it undermines confidence in the same way that the errors in the newspaper reports did. How can I know which bits to trust?

Many years ago, I met the physicist Murray Gell-Mann. He had a Nobel Prize for physics, but those who don't follow such things might know him better as 'the string theory guy'. He wrote a book called *The Quark and the Jaguar*, which I liked a lot and understood less. I thought it would be nice to ask him to sign it, which he gladly did. But when I handed it over, he said, 'Oh, this is the UK edition! It has a mistake in it.' I watched as he flicked through the book to find and correct the error, which I assumed would be some obscure or dense matter of physics. 'Here,' he said. 'I used a metaphor of a serpent opening its eyes to the sun. But, of course, snakes don't have eyelids!' He crossed out the offending line and made a note in the margin, then signed the title page and handed the book back to me.

I like this anecdote partly because of how much a simple error mattered to him even when it didn't materially affect the substance of the book (we can debate to what degree snakes have eyelids, but that is not the point). He just cared whether or not something he wrote was true, and therefore was in a position to care whether what others write is true, too. The author Michael Crichton coined the phrase 'The Gell-Mann Amnesia Effect', in which he describes the process of reading a news story on a subject close to you, and noticing the errors. Sometimes the facts may be so confused they reverse cause and effect. He calls them 'wet streets cause rain' stories. Then you turn the pages to a new and unfamiliar story and forget what you know. Your critical eye disappears and the assumption of accuracy returns.

The witness statements are no more or less reliable than a newspaper report, in that each witness has biases or an agenda, whether that's to protect themselves or be as helpful as possible, or they may simply be mistaken. One of the men who told the boys to run refused to give his name when calling an ambulance, while a teenage girl amended her original witness statement a few days later to say she had lied because she was afraid. Her testimony does not affect the facts of the case, but it is an interesting insight into estate life. I remembered my own fears around giving a witness statement five years later when a man was murdered outside our Birmingham home, and my relief that I would not be required to testify.

Of all the detail in the witness statements, the paragraph that changed my perception most is this:

```
While these youths did momentarily
disappear they returned once KING had
been taken away. They spoke to SMITH who
said he thought the man was dead, this
caused a great panic among the youths,
some were physically shaking while
others cried.
```

DCI Burns's report states his belief that Mike threw the first punch. His evidence for this is based on days of interrogation and testimony rather than the sort of hard evidence of, say, CCTV, but he has stated it as probable fact. There's enough evidential wiggle room for me still to choose not to believe it if I was being stubborn and over-loyal, but I think it is probably true. It is incredibly difficult for a bunch of scared teenage boys to maintain a complicated, consistent lie over days of interrogation and then again as adults decades later.

And then:

```
This behaviour by Mr KING served only to
encourage a continuation of abuse and
```

```
finally Mr KING was struck a single blow
to the head or neck which caused a
subarachnoid haemorrhage resulting in
his immediate collapse and death.
```

Head *or* neck. It would be good if the coroner and the detective chief inspector could get their stories straight, particularly as it was more likely the head. It matters because it tells me which way Mike was facing. The back of the neck tells a very different story from the side of the face. The back of the neck means he was walking away.

The report is a time capsule in which I relive the worst version of events as they unfolded. Murder. Gang. Karate chop to the back of the neck. The jump off the wall. It's all in there, unreliable snippets from witnesses who admit they couldn't really see what was going on. As I read, I see every piece of the original story and how, together, they look like something that, separately, they simply are not.

I recall Reece, Andrew, Chris and Anthony all telling me that a couple of adult men, whom I shall call Smith and Peters, told them to leave the scene, so they did. It is simply this that set in motion the murder investigation. DCI Burns says:

```
Had it not been for the irresponsible
behaviour of SMITH and PETERS, who
frightened these youths away from the
scene, there is no doubt that all five
would have remained at the scene to
explain the situation to the authorities
upon their arrival.
```

I have to conclude that the version of events I, and my entire family, had lived with since 1988 is not the truth. A simple principle of critical thinking is that you cannot prove a negative. Another is that absence of evidence is not evidence of absence. I cannot prove what did happen, but I can discount what did not.

The biggest clue to why we had that version of events in the first place is hidden in DCI Burns's tactful conclusion to his report:

```
As it develops [sic], the circumstances
presented themselves in a more criminal
and sinister manner than perhaps they
deserved.
```

Burns basically admits that the dramatic murder inquiry of fifteen CID officers and cancelled leave was simply overkill. But, for whatever reason we will never know, we didn't get the message.

29

'The ashes tether us to the man of the past,
while Mum is already reshaping him into the man
she will live with for the rest of her life.'

DAVID OWEN, *GRIEF ANGELS*

MEMORY CAN BE A LIAR. Memory will swear blind that the curtains were blue, but years later you find a photograph and discover they were red. Memory will insist that your sister was at your seventh-birthday party, but she reminds you she was in hospital having her tonsils out.

I'm not sure which of the details in my happy memories are accurate, but it bothers me that some definitely aren't. Most people have a strong emotional attachment to their memories, and rightly so. Memories are a personal history, a photograph and video album, a chronicle of the best and worst bits of our lives so far. Often memories are all we have. No wonder we get attached. But here's the difficulty: memories aren't facts, they're beliefs. And, like all beliefs, they can be biased, or even outright wrong.

That's not to say all memories are wrong, or even most. But without some way of verifying the memory, we should always allow for that possibility. In the course of everyday life, it doesn't matter hugely whether the curtains were red or blue, but if you were called to testify in a criminal trial about the colour of the curtains, it would suddenly matter a lot. And if someone was in danger of going to prison, it would be best if there was a photograph of the curtains so no one has to decide if the memory is credible or not. Someone would have to decide, though, if the photograph is genuine and, unlike memory, that is testable. Just like the paranormal, the more extraordinary the claim, the more extraordinary the evidence needs to be. If someone might lose their liberty, the standard of evidence should be very high.

I once had a friend who swore blind he remembers being born. When I pointed out that that's probably impossible, he got extremely angry. The memory of being born meant something to him, to the point where he needed it to be true. Parts of his identity and self-esteem hung on that memory being correct. And it's absolutely true that he was born, there is no doubting that. There's just currently no way to verify his specific claim about remembering it, even though his brain likely wasn't capable of forming the memory. Something being generally untrue doesn't remove the really strong feeling he has that, in his case, it is true.

My own beliefs were no less implausible. I believed that a person could walk through a bonfire and Jesus would meet her in the centre, take her hand and guide her out unharmed. I believed that Jesus could, if he chose, make my too-tight shoes or too-large feet change size. I believed, to the point of terror, in Satan, witchcraft and psychic powers. I burned my beloved books because I thought they were a portal to evil. Of course I would believe a police chief when he told me my father was murdered by a malicious gang of kids who then conspired to get away with it. But I'd grown out of the other beliefs, questioned them until they'd fallen apart, done my homework and interrogated my biases. Why had I never thought to do that with Mike's death? It never occurred to me I had fallen for my own personal conspiracy theory.

In *The Demon-Haunted World*, Carl Sagan said, 'But I could be wrong.' That was the flashpoint for how I learned to think, and I'm grateful for its liberating power. I had believed, sworn by and then conveniently ignored an elaborate story about Mike's death, and the truth – while no less devastating and in many ways harder to live with – is more mundane. Simply put, I was wrong.

Perspective matters. I did not know my dad was tall until I read his autopsy report, which described not his living height but the length of his corpse. He was over six feet tall. In my original draft of the opening chapter of this book, I had described him as 'diminutive'. Obviously I was always looking up to him, and perhaps a twelve-year-old girl, small for her age, is bad at judging height. Everyone was taller than me, so what difference would it make whether he was five foot six or six foot one? We usually start to figure out our parents' height when we catch up with it. I outgrew Jackie when I was fifteen.

But then I realized that the reason I had thought of Mike as diminutive was because of the story. The brick wall that Andrew jumped off, the karate chop. It was a very low wall, so even with a high jump, Mike would have to have been fairly short for the karate chop to land on the back of his neck. It never occurred to me that Andrew was much shorter than him. I was about four foot six. All the boys were taller than me. The story had shaped my memories.

But then I read in the autopsy report, 'height six foot one', and I *remembered* standing on my dad's feet while he held my arms and 'danced' me round the room. I never got too heavy for that. Him stooping under the up-and-over garage door. His hand casually at the very top of the door frame where I didn't see it, then his thumb accidentally crushed in the jamb. The ease with which he gave me a 'fireman's lift', or swung me onto his shoulders for a ride home, or lifted me up to let me put the fifty-pence piece into the electricity meter.

These memories make up my personal beliefs about Mike, his life and mine. Other memories, uncertain or dismissible by themselves, now serve to corroborate the new story. I can dimly recall Jackie recounting the story of his death to friends, saying dismissively, 'Maybe he clipped one of them round the ear'ole.' Ear'ole means earhole, which means ear. But she said it like that, 'ear'ole', a turn of phrase she'd picked up from Mike, his empty jokey threat when Emily and I were arguing. Jackie's own version of that, more often said in frustration than fun but never serious, was 'I'll bang your heads together in a minute.' I always wondered what that might feel like, but equally knew I would never find out. Jackie would no more bang our heads together than Mike would clip us round the ear'ole. I wondered what that felt like, too, and decided he meant a gentle rebuking cuff around the back of the ear. I had no reason to think differently. It never happened, and there wasn't even a threat in his voice when he said it. These were just funny phrases. So even when presented with the possibility of Mike striking Andrew first, the phrase 'clip round the ear'ole' immediately became a gentle ear cuff. It simply never occurred to me that my dad would throw a punch or a kick. I saw only a con-strained temper — but that was surely *instead* of punching people. It didn't signal to me that he had an out-of-control or violent temper, but that he could successfully divert frustration into inanimate objects.

But, of course, the enormity and injustice of his death distracted me from the reality, which is that attacking inanimate objects — a door, a wall — out of frustration indi-cates a problem. I wasn't scared by Mike, because even a child knows the difference between frustration and malice, and because his behaviour was common for estate dads in his situation. Half the bedroom doors on our street had holes in them. He was angry, yes, but not enough to over-power his love for us even momentarily. If I'd ever seen a flash of potential for harm against another person, I might have realized how significant that dim 'Maybe he gave one of them a clip round the ear'ole' memory was.

Not easily, but I can believe the version laid before me, that Mike, in anger, punched a boy who was insulting him, and kicked another. I can now see him doing it just as clearly as any of the other versions of the scene I've played and replayed. I asked Emily; she concurred. It is believable.

Other memories provide a breadcrumb trail leading to it. The holes in the doors, obviously. An argument Dani remembers when he overturned the dining table. And once, only once but enough to leave a memory, an argument with

Jackie during which he threw the plate containing his dinner at the wall. There was a stain on the wallpaper for years afterwards. Nothing compared to some other families we knew, but it does tell me that under extreme pressure or frustration he was capable of venting with his fists. I had previously interpreted these rare events as him maintaining enough control not to hit a person, but perhaps it was just enough control not to hit us. The only other clue I have is a memory of him coming home with small facial injuries. Jackie told me that a man he owed money to had tried to 'fit him up', frame him for shoplifting, and had tackled him to the ground. I accepted this explanation, because my dad could only be an innocent victim of other people's malice. That he might have simply been in a fight did not occur to me. Because he was trained in martial arts, he taught me how to throw a punch, but made it clear that violence was only ever to defend, never to attack. This was the sense of him I always carried. A man who was wise about violence, able to divert his temper towards inanimate objects, and compared to what men did in other people's homes, where violence against wives and children was not uncommon, a saint.

No one told me he hadn't died instantly, although everyone in my family who was at the trial would have heard the testimony to that effect. Perhaps they didn't believe a word the boys testified, or perhaps in their anger and grief they weren't listening to or forgot that detail, or perhaps they thought it was kinder for a twelve-year-old to believe her father had died instantly and painlessly and without any cause to the effect. Which is fine if you tell her the truth when she's old enough to handle it. The problem with that theory is I asked every surviving member of my family to talk me through what they believe happened that night, and all of them had the same story, including that he had died instantly. The wrong story. They had all, until I told them otherwise, continued to believe, as I had, that a gang of boys had conspired to evade justice for a malicious crime.

I had also been sure the boys were drunk or stoned. I wonder where that detail came from. It seems like profiling, an easily believable detail about teenage estate boys that helped to explain the unexplainable. Perhaps it also helped to minimize the potential contribution of Mike's own drinking. As far as the evidence in the police report goes, none of them, including Mike, can be said to have been influenced by alcohol. No one knows, and he isn't here to confirm or deny. I don't find any comfort in a conclusion either way. I won't ever know all the facts, and I can't ever truly know the truth. I have to be satisfied with that. I can continue to pursue the testable claims, but so much depends on memory and witness, and in turn that's subject to bias and error. It eventually becomes a fool's errand. I can't make it an obsession or a crusade, but I can use my critical-thinking skills to find a way to live with uncertainty.

I've got as much hard evidence as I'm ever likely to find, and enough anecdotal evidence to supplement it that I don't feel any nagging of unsolved mystery, a sharp contrast to the pseudoscience and religion of my youth, which all claimed to provide answers to unsolved mysteries. When I believed, I was satisfied with the answer, whether it was right or not. I could not remain satisfied with all the things I had previously believed in because they continually failed scrutiny. Things that were either not proven, thoroughly disproven, or just plain impossible.

It is clear from my own unquestioned belief in what happened to my father that the higher the emotional stakes, the fewer questions are asked. I now have to apply all of that critical thinking to my own life story. I have to interrogate my beliefs and ask if they stand up to scrutiny by not avoiding the pain of scrutiny. I ask myself why I didn't know all this sooner, and the answer comes back clearly: because I didn't think about it. I mean really, properly think about it, the way I think about other things. I did everything I could to avoid thinking about it, and when I thought about it without meaning to, when Mike's death or the boys or the trial popped into my head all by themselves, I evaded scrutinizing them, so I could get on with my life. There was no room for critical thinking among the grief and pain, and, later, no room amid the comfortable cushioning of emotional progress and survival. I moved on and away from the trauma and, unwittingly, away from the facts, too.

Realistically, I didn't know my dad. He wasn't around all that much, preferring solitude and the company of alcohol to anything else. My memories of him are so strong partly because there are relatively few of them. I think he knew to avoid us when he was in a low mood, perhaps protecting us from the worst of him but also protecting himself from the stresses of a young family.

I remember him as patient, kind, thoughtful and attentive, but clearly that was not the whole of the man. It's important to contextualize his life, like the content note recently added to the start of old television shows. 'This classic comedy drama reflects the attitudes of its time and contains references that may offend.' Nineteen eighties working-class Britain, as depicted in shows like *Boon* or *Auf Wiedersehen, Pet*, was full of casual male-on-male violence. A punch is easily thrown – sometimes literally as a punchline – and just as easily forgiven. Watching those shows now is partly nostalgic, partly instructive. I recognize Mike and other men from the estate in those characters – hustling, dancing around the law, fiercely loyal to each other, with an unwritten ethical code that says, 'We do what we must to survive and laugh at the rest.' There's nothing new in those depictions, and the classics about poverty-class melodrama I threw myself into, from Dostoevsky to Hardy to Dickens, are as familiar as *EastEnders*.

A saint with demons. It is hard to reconcile, but people are allowed to be complex and contradictory even when they are of the class for which much of society has no sympathy. There is nothing there that justifies the events of that night, but a great deal that explains them.

The tensions grew with our problems. His drinking worsened as the debt and unemployment did. When he did have a job, he hated the office life or the pressure of commission-only sales. Social Services, the great shame of parenting, had removed his child, and Emily and I were hurtling angst-first towards young-adulthood. His agoraphobic wife had found religion. He had a criminal record and a job he hated. He had a lot to be tense about.

It did not occur to us to question whether Social Services had the right to remove Emily and institutionalize her. It did not occur to us to question what the church was telling us. It did not occur to us to question the ticking-time-bomb theory, and when it was replaced with a malicious-punch theory and trial conspiracy theory it did not occur to us to question those either. If Jackie believed it, I believed it.

Other people's versions of the story were equally distorted. 'Your dad was killed at the shops by some kids on bikes,' a former neighbour told me recently. I tracked down a friend of my dad's, a retired doctor who met Mike through their mutual love of early computing. I hadn't seen him since I was about ten, so I took Jackie with me to his home for a reunion. I was hoping he had a more educated perspective on the events of that night, but when I asked him what he believed happened, he said he always thought Mike had been chased across the estate by a gang of kids, had taken refuge in a phone box, and had a heart attack from stress. A former church member told me they knew 'he'd been beaten up'. Someone else said they thought he'd been stabbed. None of those is true, yet all of those people had believed their own version of the story for decades.

A story cannot be contained by truth. It will be taken by everyone with even a passing curiosity, and pulled, stretched, torn into a different shape to fit an agenda or bias or fear. It becomes currency, whether true or not. I was protected from some stories (Mike's criminal record, for example), while harmed by others (a demon possessing me). In the absence of a way to confirm speculation, the most exciting version becomes the most believable.

I don't know what I don't know. It didn't occur to me

to ask if my dad had a criminal record, because I didn't know that that was within the bounds of possibility. I thought he was good at skirting around the law, doing whatever it took to survive or feel a modicum of control, like every other dad on the estate in those days, but I hadn't realized how far the pressure had taken him.

The newer, truer version is in many ways worse. Those boys were far more innocent than I had ever understood, far more harmed by that night's events. I had always thought of them as drunk or stoned or arrogant. Fear had crossed my mind but only as an abstraction. It wasn't till I spoke to them that I felt it. The fear still ran through them all as though it had just happened. It was a nightmare for them too. Underclass teenage boys are left alone to do their own thing, then blamed for the outcome, whatever it is. That isn't fair. Mike's death was not as instant, painless and peaceful as I had been told. That isn't fair either.

Andrew Reynolds had a lot to lose, so it was in his interest for Mike to have thrown the first punch, but the others, no. After their initial arrest for murder, they wouldn't have been charged. There was nothing to charge them with. If they managed to continue a conspiracy for three decades then they all have impressive acting ability and sociopathy. So I believe them, while accepting I will never truly know. The standard of proof I'd require doesn't exist. Memory will never cut it. I'd need video footage or to have been there myself. If we could peek into the afterlife to check it exists, we wouldn't need the leap of faith. The past is the same. There is no way to peek back in time to watch the events of 1988 unfold and know for sure. I had to take a leap of faith and say, yes, I believe you, even though I've spent my life believing something else, something easier to live with. It's much harder to believe something you don't want to be true. It threatens to distort happy memories.

I loved it when my dad sang. I knew his favourite Christmas hymn was 'Once In Royal David's City', suited to his baritone, so it was mine too, even though I was secretly loyal to good old soprano 'Silent Night'. I remember him singing 'Wooden Heart'. When the Flying Pickets were on *Top of the Pops* with 'Only You' he would sing along to the acapella bass: 'All I ever knew, only you, bada bada badadada . . .'

I can hear him singing far more clearly than I can hear his speaking voice. His sound floats elusively somewhere between my ear and my memory. I don't remember the sound of his laugh but I have strong memories of how he looked when we were laughing together, which was often.

These memories are valuable, particularly as Jackie has always struggled to talk about Mike, so Emily and I stopped too. Until I started writing this book, we hadn't talked about him for decades. Jackie can't remember anything about being on the witness stand, about the testimony she gave or what she said under cross-examination. In her words, she's 'blanked it out'.

'I don't want to remember' turned into 'I can't remember', and I can't blame her for that. The trial destroyed her and it took a long time to rebuild. She's had no reason to remember giving evidence at the trial for the manslaughter of her husband, and plenty of reasons to forget.

So, she thought about it as little as possible, until it was mostly gone.

Under cross-examination at the trial, she was grilled by Andrew's barrister about Mike's drinking. This was the most traumatic part for her. She left the courtroom and came to me, shaking and crying. 'They made out your dad was to blame,' she gasped at the time, and that part she still remembers now. This is how my family recounted it, too. A character assassination, victim-blaming, discredit the victim to make it seem like he asked for it, or was culpable, responsible. That is, of course, the defence barrister's job, to establish the facts in favour of their client. Mike *did* have a drinking problem. The barrister was right to try to prove that, because it was potentially relevant to the events. But destroying a vulnerable widow is not the way to go about it. Jackie couldn't take it, and broke down on the witness stand. Her father Symon was so upset at her treatment he had to leave the court. Witnesses as vulnerable as Jackie weren't protected in law until 1999, when new procedures, including giving evidence in writing or by video, were introduced. She said afterwards, 'I felt like me and your dad were the ones on trial.'

I see her pain so clearly. Her husband had been dead for a year; she was widowed before she was forty. All she had left of him was the knowledge he was a good man, a loving man, a kind man, who tried and tried. A man like that can't have had any part in his own death, can't have been anything but an innocent victim, in the wrong place at the wrong time. The good man against the evil gang. For the defence to paint Mike as anything but that was to paint over the only thing she had left. It broke her heart that anyone would even try.

When I told her everything I'd learned, from the

police report and various conversations, she said Mike throwing that punch is, for her, the hardest part to believe. Of course it is. The cost of believing it is much higher than the other version. But it being hard to believe does not mean it is untrue. The police believed it, the judge believed it, and it is more believable than a huge conspiracy. But it is also far more painful.

And, of course, our religion at the time meant Mike had to be a wholly innocent victim, otherwise he wouldn't have gone to Heaven, and I knew he had because of the elder's vision, of course. The elder had assumed a degree of innocence, too. Would he have had that 'vision' if he'd known the truth? Or would there have been a moralistic caveat? He knew Mike was otherwise a good, loving man, so therefore his place in Heaven was assured. Or would he believe Mike had good in his heart the whole time, so God would give him a pass? I'm pretty sure punching a child in the face is a sin in many religions, but maybe there was room for repentance after the regret.

I recently made contact with Eileen, the woman whose idea the exorcism had been. She had believed Mike had been calling us to see what we wanted from the takeaway, and as he left the phone box had been 'beaten up by yobs'. Of course. That is what everyone believed. When I told her that Mike had punched first in response to their taunting, she immediately forgave and excused him, saying, 'You can't blame him for doing that,' then called him a perfect gentleman and a lovely man. It was well-meant, like the exorcism in 1988.

I still have my demons. Trauma is stubborn and sometimes malicious. It tries to impede progress, wants to possess those around us, and my (sometimes exhausting) job is not to let it. I'm my own exorcist, and the trick of surviving to the end of the book is to know that I'm more than my demons.

What would my parents have been without theirs? Mike's drinking and Jackie's phobias. But it is as meaningless to ask that as it is to ask what I would be without my trauma. I accept, appreciate and love them both exactly as they were. When I think of the things I like and value about myself, I can draw a straight line between those attributes and their deliberate, careful, nurturing parenting. When I take a sideways glance at the ways in which I can be awful, or the things about me I dislike, I see a wobbly complicated jumble of lines attached to my entire life. In other words, I credit my parents with more than I blame them for.

I finally met Andrew in person in late 2022. The day before, I'd spent the morning on various trains back to the small town where the King family had lived. I looked out of the train window and listened to a Ruth Rendell thriller about a girl who didn't go to school. When I arrived, under the impending strangeness of meeting the man who killed my father, I did what anyone would do under the same circumstances.

I went and got my ears pierced.

Perhaps I wanted a small, manageable physical pain to distract me from enigmatic emotions, like my teenage rock days when I'd had six piercings in my right ear, all the way up to the top.

Maybe it was the memory of those cheap endorphins, or just some instinct to mark the occasion, or perhaps a grasp for control that made me walk into the accessories shop and ask to have my ears pierced. On the spur of the moment I chose pretty studs with pale pink gems that anyone who knows me would think are out of character.

The next day my newly pierced ears and I got a taxi to meet Andrew. The cab dropped me off at the exact spot I had met my dad off the bus one day. He had been to the job centre, and I had a five-pound note for my birthday that I wanted to spend on a set of doll's clothes I had seen in one of the big shops. Jackie had arranged for him to meet me, and it's one of the only memories I have of him and me doing something alone. The cab driver didn't know any of this as he said, 'Will here do?' and pulled over. I got out and walked through the town centre to meet Andrew.

He seemed nervous, so I kept up a stream of reassuring chat as we got soft drinks and found a seat. I felt no nerves. We had spoken on the phone several times and I trusted him. I had thought he'd perhaps want to avoid talking about Mike's death, but he jumped straight into the big-talk. Reiterating what he had told me on the phone, he spoke with sincerity and nerves. It had clearly affected him deeply his whole life. He told me again how barely a week had passed when he did not think about it, how it had all happened so quickly and how he had tried, in vain, to help Mike. He said when he bent down to make sure my dad wasn't choking on his own tongue, Mike had been groaning, and that when the men came over and told the boys to run, he'd thought he was still alive.

I looked at his hands as we talked, thinking about how simply a man had died from being struck, and how the karate chop that never happened had haunted my psyche.

The hands of the adult man were so different from the hands of that boy. The boy who maliciously jumped off the wall to land a deliberate blow, the show-off, the gobshite, the arrogant gang leader is not the man in front of me. That boy never existed. We talked about how tall Mike was compared to him, and the abstract image I had of the altercation between them suddenly came to life, my dad towering over this person in front of me. He said that after Mike had punched Chris, he kicked Andrew in the stomach, and that was when Andrew had lashed out and upwards, in self-defence. He said it simply, and with pain.

I asked how he had felt at the time thinking he would go to prison, and he told me how scared he had been and how the year between that night and the trial was now a blur. People had picked fights with him, he said, wanting to punch the kid who had killed a man, to prove they were tougher than a killer. He told me some of the rumours he'd heard about that night, similar to those I'd heard too: that he and the others had beaten Mike up, jumped on his head, brutal and visceral tales so far from the truth. He looked horrified and sad as he recounted the memories. He remembers little about the trial, but said he saw Emily and me – as we saw him – as he left the court. I was glad he noticed and remembered us.

He said again how sorry he was. I said I was sorry too, but that it would all be okay. As we stood up to leave, I thought about shaking his hand, but instead opened my arms for a hug. We parted as friends.

It's an old survival habit of mine, to push the weight of emotion off me. I'm not the sort to sit and have a big cry or call a loved one to get it all off my chest. I met the man who killed my dad: he was very nice. Now what? Obviously I would do what I did when I lived in this town as a girl. I would walk, and I would think.

I walked to my old high school and peered through the locked iron fence down the long driveway. I felt the old streak of rebellion rise, the one that had propelled me up that drive and out of the gates. I considered scaling the fence to go and look round, but remembered I'm an adult. I made a mental note to contact the school and arrange a visit another time, then made another mental note not to. What would I even say? 'Hey, I had a really bad time here but it wasn't your fault. Can I come and feel my feelings in your corridors?' So I left.

It was nearly two miles back to my old house from the school. I found myself starting to walk it without making a conscious decision to do so. Of course I would go back there. As I trudged through the autumn leaves along the tarmac path I could almost feel the pinch of my old uncomfortable cheap fashion shoes and the weight of my beloved white and purple Head bag that Bernice had bought me from her Kays catalogue. The two miles passed quickly, mainly because I walk so quickly. Everyone who walks with me tells me to slow down. Maybe that's why I prefer walking alone.

When I arrived at my old house, everything was very small: the patches of grass that had been makeshift football fields, the trees too huge to climb, all had shrunk to claustrophobic proportions. Everything was much closer together than it was in my memory. The house itself, now privately owned, was transformed. The cheap plastic house number and the council front door were long gone, as was

Mike's beautiful homemade wooden picket fence and the snapdragons Jackie had planted. I felt a momentary flash of annoyance at the trespass. Then I let it go and walked down the winding path to the skinny copse, the pretty stream and gnarled old trees where the four of us would pretend to be hobbits, and where later I would hide in solitude. There were two boys, typical estate kids, playing there. I remembered how I hated the sudden intrusion of an adult into my secret play space, so I walked away, retracing my steps.

I went down the network of gullies to the back of the house. The current residents had paved over the back garden, an improvement on the neglected grass and weeds. I went to the car park and stood where the panda car had parked. With great sadness I looked up at the bedroom window where Emily and I had looked down, and suddenly realized I was incredibly tired. But there was still one place left to visit.

The shops, you may remember, were just a few minutes away. Ten at a normal stroll, six at Tracy pace. Perhaps all truants walk quickly. But I took it slowly because I wanted to notice what had changed, and what had not. The estate was nicer now in many respects, in the main due to the privatization of the houses, which had brought with it more freedom and investment by homeowners; the few still obviously owned by the council stood out. I wondered how those families felt. I had once received hate mail from a neighbour who had bought his flat on the private market, and who felt the frequent and drunken need to tell me I was nothing but council scum. His hate and harassment escalated until one day he tried to set fire to my flat using a

303

homemade flamethrower (a can of deodorant and a lighter) as I frantically called the emergency services. I watched out of the window as he was pushed, resisting, into the back of a police car. I was apparently scum simply by merit of being poor. What was his excuse?

I left the past behind then, because I arrived at the shops. Remember the layout? The red-brick walls, the pub, the low-roofed buildings containing the Chinese chip shop, the newsagent, the supermarket, the community centre, the chemist, and – as if it could be possible to forget – the phone boxes. All gone.

I knew this already. I knew the local authority had demolished the old shopping centre and pub (the latter not to be replaced) and built a new, better, less enclosed and therefore safer set of amenities for local residents. No one needs phone boxes any more, so those weren't replaced either. I walked to where they had stood, and remembered worrying when Jackie left a red rose there because I knew someone would steal it. I thought about how inappropriate it would be to put up a memorial plaque – what would it even say? 'In loving memory of Mike King who got into a fight here and died, we will never know why but, hey, don't do that, okay?' Besides, these new shops were not the old shops. The cold ground where he had died had been dug up and tarmacked, and was now a pleasant road. I oriented myself via the few landmarks that remained. As I visualized the old buildings in place I felt them slipping away, being overwritten by the new layout. Very little from my memory was left there, and nothing of the Kings. But just a brisk six-minute walk away there were the happy ghosts of a family of four, making plans and playing games and laughing until tears came in the living room of our small but sufficient red-brick council house.

It was starting to get dark and a little cold, so I called a taxi. I went over to the newsagent to buy a drink, and when I came out I saw the cab waiting for me at the exact spot where Mike had died. I'm a coincidence theorist, but even I felt that was a bit spooky. I got in and asked the driver to take me to the station. I remembered the day Jackie and I had moved away, how it felt like it couldn't come quickly enough, and how badly we needed to escape, not just the area but the imminent threat from Social Services. We were relieved to be leaving an estate we had come to hate, and she never looked back. Neither did I, for thirty years, but when I finally did, there was no transformation into a biblical pillar of salt, no punishment or threat at all. This time I did not hate. I felt sadness, but also peace. I had finally met Andrew, had faced and perhaps exorcized some of the older demons, and returned to the scene of Mike's death with the capability and capacity to think about it all properly. For the first time ever I felt strong enough to let myself miss my old life, even as I got on with my future. It would be a long journey home, but I was going to be just fine.

Epilogue

I S THIS A CAUTIONARY TALE? It all happened long ago, and some things have improved greatly since then. But others are the same or worse. School phobia is still poorly understood and under-researched, and adults are still co-opting children into their life-changing beliefs, often leaving them with no route to disagree or exit. Children and parents in social housing are still treated differently, with prejudice. The experimental estates that peppered the UK in the 1970s are mostly still standing, but with little follow-up to see if the experiment worked or even yielded any useful data. Child poverty is back up to Thatcher-era levels and literacy is declining. Libraries are being closed. Teenagers are ageing out of care with their belongings in a black bin bag. Children are still being institutionalized. Decades later, I have middle-class friends who were also school refusers, but they were left alone to get on with their own thing. No Social Services, no psychiatric hospitals or special schools, it was just a given that they'd be fine in the end, which they were, because middle-class stability means options and second, third or fourth chances, maybe even an inheritance. The extreme interventions are for those who without the state-mandated formal education would be a future welfare burden.

Emily's incarceration at a psychiatric hospital was not an evidence-based decision. Even now there is scant research on school refusal. (She dislikes that term, saying it sounds like she had more autonomy and intent than she did. 'After all,' she says, 'you don't call yours Spider Refusal.') Armed with critical thinking, we could have demanded evidence-based interventions. Children in poverty are more likely to be removed. Rather than address the root causes of the problem (say, getting help for Jackie's phobias, Mike's drinking, unemployment and crime), the child is simply removed. 'The thing is that if you are living in poverty for long enough, it starts to look like neglect,' said the care-experienced campaigner Kenneth Murray, and he is right.

Vocational qualifications of the sort I did are under threat, another neglected experiment, and people are dying following benefit sanctions. Food banks are a rule now, not an exception. Critical thinking still isn't taught in schools, isn't embedded in journalism, isn't valued by campaigning charities or politicians.

A great deal is said about the risks of anecdotal evidence (I've said plenty of it myself), but humans are storytellers and social creatures, and wisdom matters. I found it much easier to understand my previous beliefs once I understood why I had them. Why did I need to believe homeopathy works? Why did I want fabulous science fiction to be true? Why did my family need religion at that specific time? Why did I need to grant myself psychic abilities, or to see history through a lens of alien intervention? What, in other words, are the problems these beliefs appear to solve?

For me, the problems were the obstacles and dead ends

of the maze I talked about at the beginning of this book, where children like I was are thoughtlessly experimented on without knowledge or consent. I have once or twice been deprecatingly referred to as 'a council-estate rat', which is meant to evoke a type of disease-ridden scurrying rodent of the sort you need to call in a professional to deal with. A pest, a problem, a scourge. In the early nineties Emily kept two pet rats and they were clean, intelligent, inquisitive and funny, so I'm not offended by the comparisons. Rats are survivors.

The King women have done more than survive. Emily got her A levels, then a foundation qualification in art. She spent twenty years as a commercial artist before changing careers to work in the charity sector while studying to be an art therapist. Jackie, after completing her admin qualifications, had a wonderful career. She's now retired and spends her days doing voluntary work, playing computer games, making art and reading. The three of us are well travelled, and once took a helicopter to the south rim of the Grand Canyon, where we rode horses together into the sunset.

One of the hardest things about writing a book on the search for truth is the fear of not being believed. Another difficulty is disguising identities enough to give privacy to others, and I hope I have succeeded. I've changed the names of the living (and one or two of the dead), and other identifying details. For the rest, I've done my best to service my memory (as Thucydides said, 'The closest possible fidelity on my part to the overall sense of what was actually said'), and fact-checked where relevant records or testimony were available.

I've had an unreasonably complicated life and I'm asking a lot of the reader to trust me that, yes, all this happened and, no, trauma like mine is not that rare.

What is rare is that someone like me has an opportunity to tell her story. Many people who grew up in poverty will recognize the chaos that surrounds us, the excess of crime or substance abuse or violence. While those things are not exclusive to the underclasses, they cluster there. It is not unusual for someone with my background to have experienced or been adjacent to multiple traumatic events, to know people with criminal records, or even to have committed crimes themselves. It's just that we rarely get to talk about it, and often don't even realize it's a problem until those of us lucky enough to get therapy discover what trauma is.

Crime and poverty are linked. Some people interpret that as 'poor people have criminal brains', which is not an opinion supported by data, or one that survives a minute of critical thought. If you remove the poverty, you remove much of the crime. There are also middle-class people who commit crimes, but they aren't accused of having criminal tendencies on account of class. The recognition that I was being stereotyped and therefore discriminated against on the basis of class is why I spent so long trying to 'pass' as posh. I tried to disguise my Birmingham accent, never admitted I grew up on a council estate as part of an underclass where petty crime was sometimes a necessary part of survival, that I had made mistakes and witnessed terrible things. That I didn't go to school. That I had a social worker. I wanted to be seen as the things middle-class people take for granted: smart, educated, morally un-suspect.

But hiding my past also meant shutting out the working classes and suppressing a part of myself, and that is something I regret, particularly as I had also been shutting out a valuable part of who my dad was.

He put a screwdriver into my hands so early it never occurred to me to be afraid of tools. He taught me to wire a plug, and how to do it safely by learning what the wires and fuse actually do. Because I wasn't afraid of screwdrivers, I wasn't afraid of screws. If something was broken and wasn't plugged in, then off the back would come so I could see what was inside and maybe even fix it. Soldering, too. Yes, these things can be dangerous, which is precisely why they need to be taught. He knew exactly where the limit was, where I should be encouraged to do something myself and when I needed a guiding hand. Mike wanted a son, that's a fact, but he passed on his knowledge to his daughters anyway, at a time when fathers didn't always do that. These are the skills of someone who couldn't afford and didn't want to hire someone to fix things, but took pleasure in doing it himself.

I keep in touch with him by fixing my own things, taking pleasure in electronics and woodwork. But I also read the same books he did, which is a type of time travel. It's the closest I can get to him in real time. Len Deighton, whom he loved because of his time in the RAF and West Germany. Douglas Adams, Ian Fleming, Anthony Burgess. Mike died when he was forty-four and I was twelve, so reading the books he loved is a way of getting to know him adult to adult, a way of thinking in his headspace.

Opening up that part of myself has been an incredible gift. Exploring my hybrid social class has been revealing.

In researching this book, I reconnected with people from my old estate and, in doing so, learned more about myself than I ever expected. It's not that I'd become a snob, exactly, it's just that I hadn't credited my council-estate upbringing with anything positive. I learned many times that I was wrong about that.

So, this book is sometimes unbelievable in its plot, but all true, and fact-checked to the best of my ability (with necessary changes to preserve anonymities). I have no doubt that out there on other council estates or in hostels or care facilities there are equally unbelievable, equally true stories that deserve to be written, and I hope will be one day, despite the struggle of trying to be heard and the dilemmas in even wanting to be.

If I'm a writer, it's because of Jackie King, who urged me to write from the day I could hold a pen. She taught me to read as soon as possible, and when I started school the teacher asked her to slow down the home learning because I was ahead of the class (she was indignant about this and ignored them).

When I was nine, I started writing a novel. I had a title and an idea. I took a beige school notebook and carefully drew the front cover, which as everyone knows is the most important part of a book, *The Chillside Sword*, in the fanciest lettering I could think of. By Tracy King. In the middle I drew a magical-looking sword in purple felt-tip pen. I thought about what a book needed. Chapters, obviously. On the first page in pencil I wrote the name of the novel again, and under it, a list of chapter names complete with page numbers.

Books, I had noticed, often had a dedication before the

story started. 'To my son James', or whoever. 'To my darling husband.' I flashed forward to the future, when the book was finished and everyone had a copy. Who was I writing it for?

'To my family and friends', I wrote on the inside front cover. On the back cover I wrote 'first published' and the date. There, a proper book. *The Chillside Sword*. Now I just needed to actually write it.

I made up the plot as I went along, writing in pencil in case I wanted to change anything, and drew illustrations every few pages in coloured pencil, with a quote from the text underneath like I'd seen in other books.

I got as far as introducing four characters, including a very shady uncle, a family-heirloom ceramic cat with emeralds for eyes called Emerald Eyes, a rhyming clue that leads to a secret room, and a lengthy description of the dinner menu. I had a vague notion that all this would eventually lead to the discovery of the titular sword, with possibly a murder along the way. But I was nine, so I got bored after writing three chapters.

I kept *The Chillside Sword*, though, because I always planned to finish it. Three years later, a few months after Mike's death, I picked it up again. Taking a red ballpoint pen and my few extra years of literary wisdom, I went through and ruthlessly edited the text. I corrected misspellings, crossed out entire paragraphs, and at one point wrote in the margin, 'Stupid!' My edits are as comical as the original, which I know because I have it in front of me now. On the inside front cover, where I had written the dedication, the twelve-year-old me had added a comma and a new line. It now read:

To my family and friends,
Especially Dad.

I remember adding it in the back of Bernice's car on my way to stay with my grandparents. I remember thinking I should finish the book for my dad, that it was something he would want for me, that he would be proud of. I still haven't finished *The Chillside Sword*, but I did finish this book. It wouldn't exist without his death (or the plot would be something else entirely), and I don't believe he lives on anywhere to be proud from beyond, but I did get half of my genes from him. So in a slightly romantic-science way, I can say that the best way of making him proud of me – the only way – is by being proud of myself. I hope I've done the King family justice, and I'm very proud to have represented us and our story. I'm grateful to my mom and sister for letting me talk about their lives in a book, and grateful to anyone who took the time to read it. I hope you, too, find your candle in the dark.

Cheerio!

Tracy King
August 2023

Acknowledgements

This book contains the love and wisdom of a great many people. Thank you firstly to my partner, who defies description, and to my family for their contributions, time, unwavering support and gallows humour, without which I would be lost. My mother and sister and my aunts and cousins, who prove that family love can conquer all. My extraordinary friends and colleagues, who believed in my story before I'd written a word, and Tim, without whom this book simply wouldn't exist.

To those who agreed to talk to me for this book, many of whom need to remain anonymous, I am grateful from the bottom of my heart for their bravery, generosity and kindness. In particular the 'boys', for whom I have the deepest respect.

And very special thanks to my agent Will Francis, my editor Susanna Wadeson, Larry Finlay and everyone at Transworld, for the opportunity, and for their patience, care and trust. I hope I have done their faith justice. My teachers and mentors, my friends at Jade, and librarians everywhere: I would not have got anywhere without them. It doesn't just take a village to raise a book, it takes a library (and a lot of coffee). To the volunteers of The Samaritans, who were there for me in a tight corner, and to Marion,

James and Karl, for listening and helping me learn. And finally, thank you to the late Carl Sagan, whose book *The Demon-Haunted World: Science as a Candle in the Dark* was in precisely the right place at the right time to change the course of my life.

Credits

Marketing and Publicity
Hannah Winter
Eloise Austin
Milly Reid

Sales
Tom Chicken
Emily Harvey
Bronwen Davies
Phoebe Llanwarne
Louise Blakemore
Neil Green and all the PRH field sales team

Janklow & Nesbit
Will Francis
Corissa Hollenbec
Kirsty Gordon
Michael Steger

USA

Editorial
Gina Iaquinta

Janklow & Nesbit
Melissa Flashman

Additional research and advice
Ian Waites
Stella Sims
Sashy Nathan

Kate Stephenson
DC Turner
Marion Bates
James Theard
Karl Harter

Administrative and transcription support

Carly-May Kavanagh
Kate Demol

Tracy King is a writer, producer and science communicator based in England. She has contributed to media on subjects ranging from science and technology to politics and video games, for the BBC and in the *Guardian*, *Telegraph*, the *New Statesman*, *Stylist* and the *New European*, amongst others. She was a columnist for *Custom PC* magazine for over ten years. Her science and critical-thinking animations include a collaboration with Tim Minchin, *Storm*, which has five million views on YouTube and was adapted into a bestselling graphic novel. Her television and radio credits include *Sky News*, *Newsnight*, *Good Morning Britain* and BBC Sounds.